Project Coldfeet

Project COLDFEET

Secret Mission to a
Soviet Ice Station

William M. Leary and **Leonard A. LeSchack**

NAVAL INSTITUTE PRESS • ANNAPOLIS, MARYLAND

Naval Institute Press
291 Wood Road
Annapolis, MD 21402

First Naval Institute Press paperback edition published in 2018.
ISBN: 978-1-68247-348-1 (paperback)
ISBN: 978-1-55750-514-9 (hardcover)

♾ Print editions meet the requirements of ANSI/NISO z39.48-1992
(Permanence of Paper).
Printed in the United States of America.

26 25 24 23 22 21 20 19 18   9 8 7 6 5 4 3 2 1
First printing

To Margaret MacGregor Leary and Pamela Vipond LeSchack
Wives, partners, friends, and proud Canadians

Contents

9
Conclusion / 148

Preface

Author William Leary first heard about an unusual Arctic intelligence operation while doing research for a study of the aviation businesses (proprietaries) that were secretly owned by the Central Intelligence Agency (CIA) in Asia. His curiosity led to a meeting with Robert E. Fulton, Jr., a former director of one of those proprietaries and inventor of the aerial retrieval system that was used to pluck two intrepid investigators off the ice of a Soviet drifting station that had been hastily abandoned near the North Pole. Leary published the preliminary results of his research in 1994 in the CIA's *Studies in Intelligence* ("Robert Fulton's Skyhook and Operation Coldfeet").

As it had become clear that Project COLDFEET deserved more extended historical treatment, Leary tried to contact other individuals who had taken part in the adventure. After some difficulty, he finally managed to reach author Leonard LeSchack, the central participant in COLDFEET, who was living in western Canada. About the same time, Leary also discovered that James F. Smith, the other investigator of the Soviet drifting station, was residing in Spokane, Washington. Leary arranged to meet with both men in Calgary, Alberta. It marked the first time that LeSchack and Smith had seen one another in more than thirty years.

LeSchack, it turned out, had hoped to write his own account of COLDFEET. He had saved a good deal of material connected with the operation and had written down some of his recollection of events. Leary and LeSchack quickly agreed to cooperate in putting together the story of COLDFEET.

Over the next few months, Leary and LeSchack located most of the participants in the operation and arranged for a first-ever reunion in Las Vegas in January 1995, during which they conducted a number of interviews. The high point of the weekend came when it was discovered that the B-17 employed in COLDFEET and in the first operational use of Fulton's invention was in town in connection with a helicopter convention. Its current owner, Evergreen Aviation, graciously invited the reunion participants to take a ride in the aircraft. Leary, LeSchack, and Smith flew over the desert outside Las Vegas during one of these hops—the first time the two former investigators had been in the B-17 since it had carried them back to Barrow, Alaska, after having lifted them off the Soviet ice station in June 1962.

What follows is a collaborative effort not only by Leary and LeSchack but also by the many individuals who were involved in COLDFEET and who shared their memories and historical material with the two authors. The authors hope that they have done justice to one of the most daring and successful intelligence operations of the Cold War in the far north, and to the courageous men who made it possible.

William Leary wishes to acknowledge the generous support he received for his research through a Senior Faculty Research Grant from the University of Georgia.

Project Coldfeet

Introduction

Project COLDFEET is the story of a highly successful U.S. intelligence-gathering mission conducted against the Soviet Union at the height of the Cold War. The target of the operation was North Pole 8 (NP8), a Soviet scientific drifting station in the high Arctic. Abandoned in haste after a pressure ridge destroyed its ice runway, NP8 lay beyond the range of helicopters. It seemed likely that the Soviets had been able to remove from the station only personnel and the most easily transportable equipment. Because there was no real expectation that anyone would ever visit the base again before it completely disintegrated in the grinding and ever-changing ice pack, no significant attempt would have been made to destroy evidence of data-gathering activities during the many months of successful occupation.

In an effort to penetrate the curtain of secrecy that masked Soviet operations in the Arctic, two American military officers undertook a daring mission to investigate the abandoned drifting station. James F. Smith, an Air Force major in intelligence and a Russian linguist, and Leonard A. LeSchack, a Navy lieutenant (j.g.) and scientist, both of whom had extensive experience in the Arctic, parachuted onto NP8 on May 28, 1962. According to their plan, they would remain on the ice station for three days, collecting artifacts and sifting through data that the Soviets had left behind. At the end of this time, a World War II B-17, secretly owned by the CIA and equipped with the newly designed Fulton Skyhook Aeroretriever System, would appear overhead

1

and pluck them from the ice. As it turned out, execution of the plan would prove a dangerous challenge for the men of COLDFEET.

❋

As the tensions of the Cold War begin to fade, it seems appropriate to recall the state of superpower geopolitics after World War II that set the stage for COLDFEET. With growing hostility between the United States and the Soviet Union, many Air Force officers came to view the polar regions as an area of potential threat. Addressing the graduating class of the U.S. Military Academy in 1946, Gen. Henry H. ("Hap") Arnold, wartime commander of the Army Air Forces, announced that the nation's first line of defense now lay to the north. If the United States were attacked, the enemy "will surely come from over the Pole." To meet this attack, and to launch a counterstrike against the enemy's "homeland military vitals," he told the cadets, "the American people must look to airpower—airpower over the North Pole, the strategic center of our world today."

General Arnold's polar view, shared by most advocates and practitioners of air power, found its most cogent expression with the publication in 1950 of Alexander P. de Seversky's *Air Power: Key to Survival*. De Seversky set forth a geopolitical strategy based on the realities of the new air age. All one had to do, de Seversky argued, was look at the world from the perspective of a North Pole-centered Stereographic Projection map, instead of the more commonly used Transverse Mercator Projection map. The polar view revealed with stark clarity that the two superpowers faced one another not across broad oceans and continents, but, like Rome and Carthage, across a frozen Mediterranean sea—the Arctic Ocean.

Military planners in Washington, D.C. (and Moscow), appreciated the strategic potential of the Arctic area. During the 1950s, billions of dollars were spent on erecting a series of defensive lines in the north to warn against a surprise airborne attack across the Pole. The Distant Early Warning (DEW) Line consisted of a three thousand-mile long chain of radar stations strung latitudinally across the northern continental edge of North America and Greenland between 68° and 70° N. Paralleling this line, some 700 miles to the south, lay the Mid-Canada Line. Still further south in Canada, at about 50° N, stood the Pine Tree Line.

The U.S. Air Force also took steps to establish its own Arctic capability, sending an increasing number of weather-reporting and reconnaissance flights over the Arctic portion of the North American land mass and the international waters of the Arctic Ocean. Recognizing the likelihood that eventually accidents would happen, the Air Force enhanced its search-and-rescue capability in the far north. Also, Air Force planners entertained the possibility of establishing bases on the frozen polar sea.

Much needed to be learned about the Arctic Ocean before it could be exploited for military purposes.[1] The world's fourth-largest ocean, one-sixth the size of the Atlantic, the Arctic measures 2,400 miles from the Bering Strait to Spitzbergen and 1,600 miles from the Canadian Archipelago to the shore of Siberia. A broken and ridged layer of sea ice covers some 75 percent of the ocean (60 percent in summer). Averaging ten feet thick, the ice pack is in constant motion. Ice floes, pushed by wind and currents, jam together to form pressure ridges ten- to fifteen-feet high, with some reaching over fifty feet. Strips of open water, or leads, also appear amid the ice pack. Temperatures that plummet to 40° to 50° below zero[2] in winter, with winds in excess of forty miles per hour, create a hostile environment that effectively protected the polar basin against human intrusion until the 20th century.

The Air Force turned to the establishment of Arctic drifting stations—short-term bases on the floating sea ice that could be used for scientific and, perhaps, operational purposes—as a central part of their program to discover more about the nature of the polar region. Their first attempt to set up an ice station, however, proved a failure. Occupied for a brief period in 1950, it had to be abandoned when a pressure ridge threatened its ice runway. Two years later, Lt. Col. Joseph A. Fletcher established a more permanent station on a massive piece of glacial ice, or "ice island," that had broken off the Ellsemere Ice Shelf in the Canadian Archipelago. Air Force personnel and civilian scientists occupied this ice island, known as T-3, for over two years, marking the real beginning of the U.S. drifting station program in the Arctic.

Although the Air Force took the lead in sponsoring Arctic scientific work, the advent of long-range ballistic missiles at the end of the 1950s caused airmen to lose interest in the surface environment of the far north. Just as the role of manned bombers declined, however, the appearance of the nuclear-powered under-ice submarine added a new dimension to the strategic chess game in the north. The successful transpolar cruise of USS *Nautilus* (SSN 571) in 1958, followed shortly thereafter by similar voyages by USS *Sargo* (SSN 583) and USS *Seadragon* (SSN 584), no doubt caught the attention of the Soviet Union. Certainly, the success of the first submarine-launched Polaris missile in 1960 shook the walls of the Kremlin. Unlike land-based missile launchers or aircraft-delivered weapons, which could be neutralized by enemy countermeasures, the submerged nuclear-powered submarines, detectable only by acoustical means, seemed invulnerable.

The early 1960s saw the United States and the Soviet Union rapidly improving their submarine forces and developing means to detect and acoustically monitor each other's undersea fleet. While improvements in acoustical detection systems eventually might threaten missile-launching submarines in the open ocean, the problems for antisubmarine forces would be compounded if their prey lay under the Arctic sea ice. Pinpointing a submarine with air-dropped sonobuoys and then killing it with air-dropped depth bombs or torpedoes, a standard practice in the open ocean, would be impossible when the ocean is covered with ice ten to twenty feet thick. The only possible defense against a nuclear-powered submarine submerged beneath the Arctic ice pack would be another nuclear-powered submarine. In such a confrontation, victory likely would depend on superior acoustical systems.

American activity in the Arctic paled in comparison to Soviet efforts in the far north. The Soviets, for example, maintained a vigorous drifting station program in the Arctic Ocean during the Cold War, establishing far more bases than the United States. Not only could these stations be used to gather meteorological and oceanographic data, both of which had military as well as scientific value, but drifting stations also provided excellent platforms for gathering the under-ice acoustical data needed for tracking submarines. (COLDFEET investigator LeSchack certainly was well aware of this capability, as he had assisted in the installation of an acoustic data-gathering array while stationed on T-3 in 1959–60.)

The U.S. intelligence community in the early 1960s knew little about what the Soviets were doing on their drifting stations beyond basic scientific work. Did the Soviets have advanced acoustical systems to detect U.S. under-ice submarines? Were they developing Arctic antisubmarine warfare measures? An inspection of a Soviet drifting station, if possible, no doubt would provide the answer to these questions.

❊

One of the most unusual intelligence-gathering operations of the Cold War, *Project COLDFEET* is a tale of high adventure in the far north that rivals the derring-do of the popular fictional secret agent of that time, James Bond. Indeed, the line between fact and fiction often became blurred in the 1960s. As it happened, the same CIA-owned B-17 with Fulton Skyhook gear that retrieved the COLDFEET team from the ice of NP8 in 1962 also appeared in the 1965 James Bond movie *Thunderball*, lifting both James Bond and his leading lady (in fact, dummies substituted for the movie stars) to safety. The circumstances of the COLDFEET pickup, however, went far beyond the imagination of the moviemakers.

1

Arctic Drifting Stations

The idea for an Arctic drifting station[1]—a platform from which scientists could record data as they moved through the polar basin atop the ice pack—was born out of tragedy. In July 1879 Lt. George Washington DeLong left San Francisco in the barque-rigged steam yacht *Jeannette* and headed northward through the Bering Strait toward Wrangel Island. He planned to follow the coastline of the island, which he believed—incorrectly—to be a sizable land mass, to a point close to the North Pole, then proceed by sled to the top of the world. Unfortunately, the *Jeannette* became caught in the ice pack near Herald Island, far short of DeLong's goal. The ship drifted over the shallow waters of the continental shelf for nearly two years before breaking up off the New Siberian Islands. The *Jeannette*'s company of thirty-two men attempted to reach land, but most perished, including DeLong.[2]

Three years later, Fridtjof Nansen happened to read an article in the Norwegian newspaper *Morgenblad* about the discovery of items from the *Jeannette* on the southwest coast of Greenland. The only way the items could have reached this location, he realized, was by drifting on an ice floe across the Arctic Ocean. Nansen, who had been thinking about leading an expedition to the far north, decided to capitalize on the information. "It immediately occurred to me," he wrote, "that here lay the route ready to hand. If a floe could drift right across the unknown region, that drift might be enlisted in the service of exploration—and my plan was laid."[3]

7

It took nine years for Nansen's plans to mature. In June 1893 he left Christiania, Norway, aboard the Scottish-built *Fram,* which had been specially designed to withstand the pressure of the pack ice. The ship became frozen in the ice near Bennett Island on September 25. Nansen and his twelve associates then settled in for what he expected to be a drift lasting perhaps as long as five years. A variety of scientific information would be gathered during this time. The position of the vessel would be recorded every other day. Also, meteorological data, magnetic observations, and measurements of ocean depth and temperature would be made.

The *Fram* handled the pressure of the polar ice pack without difficulty. After nearly two years of drift, however, Nansen grew bored. In March 1895 he and Frederik Johansen left the safety of the *Fram* and set out on foot for the North Pole. After twenty-six days of travel over worsening ice conditions, the two men reached 86°13′ N, the farthest north ever achieved to that time. But they could go no further. Ahead, Nansen observed, lay "a veritable chaos of ice-blocks, stretching as far as the horizon."[4]

It took Nansen and Johansen over a year to reach safety. In June 1896, a month after this epic struggle for survival ended, the *Fram* finally managed to break free of the ice pack north of Spitsbergen. It brought back a wealth of scientific data, which later was published in six folio volumes. As one historian of Arctic exploration wrote, "The drift of the *Fram* across polar regions stands as one of the most important contributions to oceanography."[5]

The use of ships as drifting stations for polar research had been demonstrated by the *Fram.* Two other notable instances of this technique took place in subsequent years. In 1922 Roald Amundsen's *Maud* embarked upon an intentional two-year drift in the same area the tragic *Jeannette* had covered earlier. Fifteen years later, in 1937, the Soviet icebreaker *Sedov,* which had become trapped in the ice of the Laptev Sea, served as a research platform during a three-year period as it drifted along a path similar to the one taken by the *Fram.*

Another type of drifting station was pioneered by Storker T. Storkerson in 1918. Instead of choosing the relative comfort of a ship, Storkerson placed his camp atop the ice itself. Although the scientific results of his expedition would prove disappointing, the technique would gain favor as the preferable way to gather data in the far north.

Storkerson was part of Vilhjalmur Stefansson's great Canadian Arctic Expedition of 1913–18. A seaman and trapper, he had been engaged by Stefansson as "the best 'all around' man it was possible for the expedition to get." Stefansson valued Storkerson's energy and judgment. Also, Stefansson observed, "There was enough of the poet about Storkerson so that he could see as well the romantic side of the search for undiscovered lands, and of such forays into the unknown."[6]

During the winter of 1917–18, Storkerson was on Barter Island, some one hundred miles east of Prudhoe Bay off Alaska's north shore, when he received word that Stefansson had fallen ill. In January 1918 he traveled to Herschel Island, where he found Stefansson recovering from typhoid fever. While discussing plans for the spring, Stefansson proposed a novel idea. He intended to proceed from Cross Island to 74° N or 75° N, then take a small party farther north and camp on the ice for a year. As the floe drifted through the polar basin, Stefansson intended to make meteorological and oceanographic observations. Storkerson agreed to join the traverse and returned to Barter Island to make the necessary preparations.[7]

Stefansson's slow recovery from his illness, however, soon made clear that he would be unable to lead the planned venture. Disappointed, he sent word to Storkerson to proceed without him. The first group of men and supplies left Barter Island on February 24, 1918. By March 11, the expedition had assembled on Cross Island. When Storkerson explained to his men the plan to drift on an ice floe for a year, he was met with opposition. While they admitted that the scheme had great scientific value, Storkerson reported, "none of them were willing to undertake a trip of this kind." Nonetheless, he decided to proceed with the first phase of the program.

On March 15, 1918, Storkerson started northward with twelve men, fifty-six dogs, eight sleds, and eight thousand pounds of provisions and equipment. On April 3 he reached 72° N, 147° W, 105 miles north of Cross Island. At this point he sent three men back to Barter and continued onward with nine men and thirty-six dogs. Two days later Storkerson came across a huge block of ice that later would be labeled an "ice island." Located at 73°30′ N, 148°32′ W, it measured seven miles wide by at least fifteen miles long, with an estimated average thickness of twenty feet. In some locations the ice was fifty to sixty feet thick. This large piece of freshwater ice likely had broken off the Ellesmere Ice Shelf, northwest of Greenland. Although rarely seen amid the pack ice, these stable ice islands provided ideal locations for research stations. (See Appendix A for a discussion of geographical coordinates.)

Storkerson again called for volunteers to remain with him on the ice for a year. Five individuals responded. Storkerson selected four: second officer August Masik and seamen Adelbert Grumaer, L. Lorne Knight, and Martin Kilian. Sending the other men south, Storkerson settled down for the long stay. The occupying party, which included sixteen dogs, had full rations for 101 days and 1,000 rounds of ammunition.

Storkerson, like Stefansson, believed that it was possible to survive on the ice by killing polar bears and catching seals. His men spent most of their time hunting—and with considerable success. By mid-June they had killed forty-two seals and four polar bears. Storkerson, meanwhile, had been engaged in scientific work. A trained navigator, he took astronomical observations and kept track of the drift. He also made depth soundings, recording a level of fifteen thousand feet at one point. Under his supervision, Kilian maintained a weather log.

All went well until late August 1918, when Storkerson developed asthma. "During September," he reported, "I was very sick and wheezed my way through many sleepless nights." With his health deteriorating, Storkerson decided to cut short the planned drift and return to the mainland before the onset of winter. He started out from 73°09′ N on October 9, an unfavorable time of year for traveling over ice. After a two hundred-mile journey that Stefansson considered "the most difficult and dangerous ever attempted in the Arctic," he reached land on November 8.

Storkerson had remained on the ice for 184 days, drifting 400 miles (70 miles straight line). He concluded that no permanent ocean current existed between 72° N and 74° N; all drifts were controlled by the wind. Stefansson, however, considered this judgment "too emphatic." Further study, he suggested, might show that ice movement was not entirely controlled by local winds.[8]

Storkerson's drift proved that Keenan Land, which appeared on the 1912 map produced by the National Geographic Society, did not exist. The drift also demonstrated, Storkerson argued, that men could live on the ice by hunting. Later studies, however, would show that polar bears suffered from the parasitic disease trichinosis, raising questions about the health risks involved with this survival technique. Indeed, many of the scientific results of the expedition have not stood the test of time; nonetheless, Storkerson's six-month drift pointed the way toward future scientific explorations of the far north.

❅

Throughout most of the twentieth century, the Soviet Union led the world in Arctic research. Russian interest in the far north stemmed in large part from a desire to develop a northern sea route that would link the Atlantic and Pacific Oceans. In 1929 Moscow organized the Soviet Arctic Air Service to survey ice conditions in the far north. Three years later, Soviet leaders formed the Chief Administration of the Northern Sea Route to oversee Stalin's goal of opening a maritime connection between Murmansk and Vladivostok.[9]

Ivan Dmitrievich Papanin, a Soviet scientist and later commander of the Northern Sea Route, became captivated by the Arctic following a voyage on an icebreaker to Franz Josef Land. In 1932 he created a model polar observatory on Hooker Island in the Franz Josef Archipelago. Within a short time, Papanin began to develop plans for establishing a scientific station on an ice floe that would be carried to inaccessible polar regions by ocean currents.[10]

Late in 1933, while Papanin was formulating his plans on Hooker Island, the passenger ship *Chelyushkin* became trapped in the pack ice while en route from Vladivostok to Murmansk. On February 13, 1934, the movement of the ice finally crushed the hull of the ship, sending it to the bottom of the Kara Sea. The 103 crew and passengers of *Chelyushkin* camped on nearby ice floes as the Soviet Arctic Air Service mounted the first-ever airlift from the polar pack ice. Over the next two months, Russian aircraft managed to evacuate the *Chelyushkin*'s passengers and crew to safety. Stalin was so pleased with the efforts of the aviators that he created a new medal for them—the gold star of the "Hero of the Soviet Union"—which would remain the highest Soviet award for heroism.[11]

When Papanin submitted his scheme for a drifting station, it received the enthusiastic support of Otto Schmidt, head of the Northern Sea Route Commission. In the wake of the *Chelyushkin* episode, Schmidt had seen the possibilities of using aircraft to establish and support scientific drifting stations and had formulated his own plans for an aerial expedition to the North Pole. "We wanted to settle at the Pole," Schmidt emphasized, "to study the Central Arctic Basin thoroughly, to render it habitable and to use the information obtained in order to add the Arctic to the general economic and cultural wealth of our country and of all humanity." The most immediate value of such a station, he noted, would be to assist the proposed transpolar flights that were scheduled to take place in 1937.[12]

On February 13, 1936, Schmidt and several prominent airmen attended a conference in the Kremlin with Stalin and members of the Soviet leadership. During the meeting, Schmidt outlined plans for an aerial expedition to the North Pole. Stalin gave his approval to the scheme and authorized Schmidt to use the full resources of the Northern Sea Route Commission in carrying out the task.

Over the next year, Schmidt put together the men and equipment necessary to establish a scientific station near the North Pole. As a *Pravda* journalist who accompanied the expedition, L. Brontman, observed, Papanin—"known for his inexhaustible energy, splendid administrative abilities, unbending determination and cheerfulness"— was the natural choice to command the station. Joining him on the ice floe would be radio engineer Ernest Krenkel ("the father of wireless in the Arctic"), hydrobiologist Peter Shirshov, and geophysicist Eugene Fedorov.[13]

Michael Vodopyanov, a renowned Arctic aviator who had participated in the *Chelyushkin* rescue, had the challenging task of preparing the operational plan for depositing Papanin's team on the ice near the North Pole. He intended to use four ANT-6s for the mission. The four-engine aircraft, weighing 22 tons at takeoff and cruising at a speed of 112 miles per hour, was the pride of the Soviet Air Force. They would stage from Rudolf Island, the northernmost island in the Franz Josef Archipelago and one thousand miles from the North Pole. The ANT-6s were specially modified to carry 1,980 gallons of fuel for the eighteen-hour round trip to the Pole.

The Schmidt/Papanin expedition reached Rudolf Island in mid-April 1937. On May 5, after waiting for the weather to clear, a twin-engine ANT-7, flown by Pavel Golovin, set off on a survey flight to locate an ice floe suitable for use as a drifting station. Golovin flew over the Pole, the first Soviet airman to reach the top of the world, but a thick cloud cover prevented him from inspecting the pack ice.

Following further weather delays, on May 21 Vodopyanov decided to proceed toward the Pole in ANT-6 N-170 carrying Schmidt, Papanin's party, and essential equipment and supplies. After ten hours in the air he found a promising floe 35 miles from the North Pole—2.5 miles by 1.2 miles in size—at 89°25′ N, 78°40′ W and landed safely at 11:35 A.M. Moscow time. The three other ANT-6s of the expedition flew to the station during the next two weeks, delivering the balance of the 10.5 tons of supplies needed for a lengthy stay on the ice. The four ANT-6s departed en masse from the station on June 6, leaving the four-man station party to conduct their scientific research in splendid isolation.

Papanin and his companions spent 274 days on the ice floe as it drifted slowly southward toward the east coast of Greenland. During the 1,273 miles of drift (1,086 miles straight line), the scientists studied currents, probed the depths of the ocean, took magnetic measurements, made meteorological observations, and performed other scientific tasks. On February 19, 1938, they left what would be identified later as drifting station North Pole 1 (NP1; in Russian *Sevorny Polyus,* or SP1) off the east coast of Greenland at 70°40′ N, 19°16′ W.

In 1941 the Arctic Research Institute pioneered a new technique to conduct scientific investigations in the far north. Termed the Flying Laboratory Method, it used aircraft to place teams of researchers on the pack ice for short periods of time. During the year, small parties of scientists occupied three stations for a few days of research. Although the scientific results of the program were meager, a precedent had been set for more extensive use of this technique in the years ahead.[14]

Following a wartime hiatus, Soviet Arctic research began again in 1948. Over the next three years, the High Latitude Aerial Expeditions of the Northern Sea Route Commission placed scientific detachments at eighty-seven points on the pack ice. Researchers were able to carry out short-term observations that led to significant advances in Arctic oceanography, meteorology, terrestrial magnetism, and gravimetry. The most important finding to come out of this period of intense activity was the identification of a vast underwater chain of mountains in the polar basin named the Lomonosov Range.[15]

Although the Flying Laboratory Method had advantages, it functioned only during the spring, when flying weather was good. This limitation led to plans for a drifting station that would permit longer periods of scientific work. Late in 1949, A. A. Kuznetsov, head of the Northern Sea Route Commission, authorized the establishment of a drifting station in the little-studied area north of the Laptev Sea. Its task would be to carry on the work of the High Latitude Aerial Expeditions in the fields of oceanography, geophysics, and meteorology. Also, the station would provide regular weather reports to the Weather and Ice Service of the Northern Sea Route Commission.[16]

Preparations for NP2 began in November 1949. Camp equipment would be modeled on the type used by the High Latitude Aerial

Expeditions. The expanded scientific program, however, required a series of special instruments, a portable chemical laboratory, and hydrobiological research equipment. The station, under the command of M. M. Somov, an oceanographer from the Arctic Institute of Leningrad, would support sixteen people. The scientific complement included three additional oceanographers, two specialists in ice research, four meteorologists, and two geophysicists. In addition, the station would house two radio operators, an aviation mechanic, and a motion-picture operator.

Men and supplies gathered at Tiksi, 650 miles north of Yakutsk on the Buor-Khaya Bay, in March 1950. A series of flights over the ice pack led to the identification of a suitable floe for the station at 76°03′ N, 166°36′ W. On April 1 a four-engine aircraft piloted by V. N. Zadkov placed Somov, five companions, and four tons of equipment on the polar ice.

With the sun shining brightly and a temperature of -38°, the initial occupation party set up a large tent and assembled their radio equipment. Within twenty-four hours, NP2 was sending weather data to the base at Tiksi. On April 2 M. A. Titlov landed at the station with the remainder of the scientific party and 1.5 tons of supplies. This marked the beginning of a continuous flow of material over the next two weeks, with aircraft delivering more than sixty tons of freight to the drifting station.

Somov laid out the camp in compact fashion, with personnel and scientific equipment housed in seven small tents. Three large tents also were set up, with one used as a mess hall that could seat all sixteen station personnel at one time. A generator supplied 24-volt electric power for lighting. Propane-butane gas, supplemented by kerosene-burning stoves, afforded heating for the camp, with gas stoves employed for cooking.

As the High Latitude Aerial Expeditions had demonstrated, the period from March to May brought the most favorable conditions for living and working on the ice. With constant daylight and clear, frosty weather, the scientists could collect data without difficulty. Temperatures averaged –30 to –40° in March, rising to –10° in May.

Conditions deteriorated with the onset of warmer weather, with melting snow and ice causing serious problems by the end of June. Small puddles grew into large ponds, as water seeped into living and working quarters. The untanned reindeer skins used as floor covering became soaked and gave off a heavy, rank odor. Accurate observations were more difficult to obtain as many of the instruments, especially those used by the geophysicists, needed a firm mounting that could not be gotten in the slush. Radio masts fell, interrupting communications. Inflatable rubber boats eventually had to be used to reach the ice runway, which became separated from the camp by a broad, open lead. Keeping the runway open posed a constant challenge.

The warm weather also brought the first appearance of polar bears. On July 7 a hungry bear wandered into the camp during a blizzard and threatened two scientists before being shot. As station chief Somov pointed out, polar bears often are considered inoffensive—"even amusing"—animals, but the truth is far different. "The polar bear," he noted, "especially a hungry one, is very dangerous, a powerful and agile predator." The camp maintained a constant watch for the animals. The bears would appear eight times in all. Most were chased off, but three had to be killed.

Disaster struck the station on July 12 when a kerosene-burning stove exploded in the radio tent. As Somov later admitted, the danger of fire had been downplayed. "It was thought that a fire in a tent was not a particular threat," he noted, "except that the tent might be damaged, or in extreme cases, lost." This notion was proved wrong. The explosion of the kerosene stove was followed by a fire so intense that it fused the duraluminum tubes forming the tent's framework and completely destroyed the radio equipment inside. Fortunately, no one had been in the tent at the time of the explosion. Had someone been dozing in a sleeping bag, Somov emphasized, "he would not have escaped the flames."

Loss of the radio equipment posed a problem for the camp. Not only did it interrupt vital communications with the outside world, but it also ended essential radio direction finding for aircraft. "The airplanes could find the drifting camp among the boundless ice expanses," Somov reported, "only with the aid of radio compasses beamed in on the radio signals from the floe."

The camp had an emergency transmitter among the stored equipment, but all attempts to establish radio contact with the mainland failed. Radio operator K. M. Kurko worked for forty-eight hours without sleep to assemble a transceiver from spare parts. The jury-rigged set worked, and radio contact was reestablished. The next month a new radio station was parachuted into the camp.

On August 12 Northern Sea Route commander Kuznetsov proposed to Somov that the station remain in operation for an additional six months. And since the idea of continuing their scientific work through the Arctic winter appealed to the station's personnel, they readily consented to the extension.

On October 25 the first two aircraft landed on the station's ice runway, which had been unusable during the summer months due to melting. This marked the first landing in the central Arctic during polar night. A crack in the ice, however, soon put the runway out of action, leading to an unfortunate airdrop. A large, four-engine aircraft was en route to NP2 when the damage to the runway made landing impossible. Rather than return his cargo to the mainland, the pilot decided to free-fall the load into the camp. For over an hour the crew tossed out food, soap, cigarettes, and other supplies. It was clear from the outset that the free-fall procedure was not working, but attempts to contact the aircraft failed, since the radio operator was busy dropping freight. "As a result of this barbaric dropping without parachute," Somov reported, "all supplies without exception were lost."

Following repairs to the runway, landing resumed on October 31. Over the next few weeks aircraft delivered twenty tons of freight to the camp, as Somov prepared for the long polar night. The Arctic Institute scheduled a limited scientific program for the months ahead and ordered station personnel reduced to eleven.

Camp life became more difficult in the constant darkness. Temperatures fell, reaching $-50°$ in January. Low temperatures often were accompanied by a sharp wind; working in the open air meant risking frostbite. Rime and hoarfrost covered everything left in the open. The radio masts suffered most under the weight of the hoarfrost, constantly breaking and falling to the ice.

The grinding of the pack ice became a source of constant worry. As the ice pushed together and formed pressure ridges, the floe on which the camp stood experienced a series of shocks. On February 4, 1951, a number of intense shocks and sharp cracking sounds shook the camp. Two large cracks, reaching a width of six to eight feet in places, split the camp. One crack cut the ice runway in half, while the other toppled the radio masts and windmill generator. "Thus," Somov reported, "the drifting station was deprived of its lone airfield in the course of a few minutes and for a time it lost radio contact with the mainland."

The cracking of the breaking ice continued throughout the day. On February 5 Somov inspected the floe and found that it had been intersected by a network of cracks radiating in all directions.

Over the next week, Somov wrote, "the crash and crunch of

hummocking could be heard continuously." On the night of February 13 an especially loud crash of breaking ice resounded to the east of the camp. A large pressure ridge appeared some one hundred yards to the southeast. "It rose literally before one's eyes," he reported, "and moved in the direction of the camp." As the ridge reached a height of six to seven feet, it came to a halt. Two other pressure ridges quickly formed, one coming within forty yards of the mess tent.

NP2's floe had been reduced to an area of forty by seventy yards. It was surrounded by cracks. "The time was critical," Somov observed. If a fourth pressure ridge formed, it likely would pass directly through the camp. "All the equipment and supplies," he pointed out, "would be literally chopped to pieces, as in a gigantic meat grinder."

It was clear that the floe had to be evacuated as soon as possible. Search parties were dispatched to locate a more stable piece of ice for the camp. Their efforts, however, were thwarted by a heavy snow-storm that began on February 14. When the storm ended, the searchers fanned out in all directions. Traveling in the Arctic darkness, they made slow progress through the jumbled mass of ice and broken leads that now surrounded the station.

On February 17 the searchers discovered a suitable floe about a half mile west of the camp site. In order to move heavy equipment to the new location, Somov ordered the assembly of a jeep that had arrived in pieces the previous fall. The task was made difficult when it was discovered that several parts were missing. While the jeep was being put together, work began on carving out a road to the new location. It was a race against time as the men hacked through pressure ridges and smoothed the ice as best they could.

The evacuation began on the morning of February 19. By this time the camp's floe had been reduced to an area of thirty by forty yards. The jeep was loaded with gas cylinders, flour sacks, and other bulky items. It pulled behind it a train of six sleds containing other camp equipment.

Moving the large tents posed an especially difficult problem. They were frozen solid and impossible to disassemble. Even when chipped free of ice, they were too heavy to be lifted by the station's entire complement of eleven men. Furthermore, the tents had a greater diameter than the jeep.

M. K. Komarov, the camp's mechanic who had worked wonders in assembling the jeep, again came to the rescue. He placed a platform of boards and ropes on the top of the vehicle to support the tents.

"Naturally," Somov observed, "only such a virtuoso as the inventor of the platform could drive the automobile under a hat such as that formed by the tent, with forward visibility zero."

By the evening of February 19 the relocation had been completed. Conditions at the new site were far less comfortable than the winterized camp that they had left behind. As Somov observed, however, the accommodations were not much different than the spartan quarters of the High Latitude Aerial Expeditions. He quickly reestablished the scientific routine. "During the transfer of the station," he reported with pardonable pride, "only one regular meteorological observation was missed."

On April 11, 1951, the personnel of NP2 closed down the station and departed by air for Wrangel Island. They had drifted northward through the pack ice for 376 days, reaching a position of 81°44′ N, 163°48′ W. The scientific results of their year-long stay in the polar basin justified the effort. Somov's scientists made 285 depth measurements of the Arctic Ocean, their data leading to the drawing of a new bathymetric chart of the area. They had taken thirty-one samples of sediment from the ocean bottom and studied the currents and temperature of the ocean at various depths. Also, meteorologists had taken eight surface observations daily and launched radiosonde balloons to obtain information on upper air temperatures and winds. These systematic observations afforded the first picture of year-round climate in the central portion of the Arctic basin.

In addition to studying oceanography and meteorology, scientists made advances in cryology (ice studies), geomagnetism, and gravity. As Somov emphasized, publication in 1956 of the data secured during the year-long drift of NP2 "strengthens the hold of the Soviet Union on first place in the study of the nature of the central Arctic."

❋

The Soviet Union, of course, was not the only nation interested in learning more about the far north. In an era of Cold War between the world's two great superpowers, the Arctic region became an area of crucial geopolitical significance. "Study your globe," observed Gen. Henry H. ("Hap") Arnold, retired chief of the Army Air Forces in 1946, "and you will see the most direct routes [between the United States and the Soviet Union] are not across the Atlantic or Pacific, but through the Arctic." If a third world war breaks out, he warned, "its strategic center will be the North Pole."[17]

In June 1946 the newly formed Strategic Air Command (SAC) ordered the 46th Very Long Range (VLR) Reconnaissance Squadron to Ladd Field, Fairbanks, Alaska, to conduct secret survey missions of the polar basin. The primary task of Project NANOOK was to assess the Soviet threat in the far north. In addition, SAC headquarters expected the squadron to develop an accurate system of polar navigation, survey and map the Arctic, conduct weather and magnetic studies, and test the ability of men and equipment to operate under the harsh environmental conditions of the region.[18]

The 46th Reconnaissance Squadron launched its first mission on August 2, 1946. Flying an F-13, the photographic reconnaissance version of the B-29, Capt. Richmond McIntyre passed over Point Barrow, then headed out over the pack ice. McIntyre maintained radio silence as he turned onto a straight-line course midway between the coast of Siberia and the North Pole. After flying along this track for several hours, he reversed course and retraced his path back to Point Barrow and Ladd Field. Air Force officials judged this mission sufficiently hazardous to justify the awarding of Distinguished Flying Crosses to the crew.[19]

In March 1947 the 375th Reconnaissance Squadron (VLR) Weather—later redesignated the 58th Strategic Squadron (Medium) Weather—joined the 46th Reconnaissance Squadron in Alaska. Brig. Gen. D. N. Yates, chief of the Air Weather Service, personally commanded the first weather reconnaissance flight from Ladd Field to the central polar basin, covering a 3,200-mile route in 16 hours and 30 minutes. By the summer, Ptarmigan weather missions, as the reconnaissance flights were known, were being conducted every few days.[20]

The activities of the 46th and 375th Reconnaissance Squadrons created a demand for enhanced search-and-rescue (SAR) capabilities in the far north. The 10th Air Rescue Squadron, activated in March 1946, lacked the training and equipment for long-range SAR work. As a result of an investigation conducted by SAC during the winter of 1946–47, the 10th Rescue Squadron was reorganized and reequipped. By early 1948 the squadron had three detachments: "A" at Anchorage's Elmendorf Air Force Base (AFB), "B" at Ladd Field, and "C" at Adak in the Aleutians. New equipment for long-range rescue work included four-engine B-17s and C-54s. In addition, Alaskan Air Command established an Arctic Indoctrination School at Marks AFB, Nome.[21]

Despite the efforts to meet the deficiencies of the 10th Rescue Squadron, progress came slowly until Col. Bernt M. Balchen took command of the unit in 1948. A pioneering Arctic and Antarctic aviator, the Norwegian-born Balchen proved the ideal choice for the assignment. His energy and experience soon transformed the squadron into an organization that was capable of operating in the most inaccessible Arctic locations.[22]

As part of the training for the squadron, Balchen experimented with landing aircraft on the polar ice pack. The unit's ski-wheeled C-47s first ventured out onto the ice pack in the spring of 1949. The next year brought a more ambitious program. On March 21, 1950, Lt. Col. Eugene O. Strouse, flying a C-47, accompanied a C-54 with a glider in tow to an area fifty miles north of Barter Island, where Balchen had established a temporary base. The C-54 released the glider, which landed on the ice, testing its strength. Satisfied that the ice was thick enough to support the heavy C-47, Strouse then landed on the floe. He remained on the ice for thirty-five minutes as his crew readied the glider for a successful pickup by the circling C-54. Strouse repeated the exercise the following day, this time landing on an 1,800-foot clear area amid pressure ridges some 100 miles north of Barter Island.[23]

While primarily concerned with the use of ice floes for rescue purposes, Balchen also believed they could serve as bases for scientific research. In April 1950 a C-47 Douglas transport from the 10th Rescue Squadron carried scientists John F. Holmes and L. V. Worthington of the Woods Hole Oceanographic Institute to a floe 135 miles north of Barter Island. Unfortunately, the aircraft damaged its landing gear as it set down on the ice. Scientific equipment had to be off-loaded to lighten the Douglas transport, which then immediately departed. The equipment was retrieved two weeks later, but no further landings were attempted.[24]

Despite the failure of the scientific project, Balchen remained characteristically enthusiastic about the year's progress. "We are having a terrifically interesting time up north with this work of ours!" he wrote to Adm. Richard E. Byrd, his boss on the first flight over the South Pole in 1929. Even greater progress, he told Byrd, could be expected in the future.[25]

Although Balchen left Alaska in January 1951 to become project officer for the construction of a giant air base at Thule on the northwest coast of Greenland, the work that he had initiated continued. Balchen had wanted to test the ability of men to remain on an ice floe for extended periods of time. On February 20, 1951, in accordance with plans that he had drawn up prior to his departure, a party of eight men from the 10th Rescue Squadron was deposited on an ice floe located 115 miles north of Barter Island. Under the direction of Capt. Marion E. Brinegar, they set up four Jamesway huts—semicylindrical, Quonset-like structures with wooden frames covered by insulated mats—and settled down for a long stay on the ice.

All went well until a strong gale blew up on March 9. At 4:00 A.M. the next morning a two hundred-foot crack developed in the floe one hundred feet from the camp. It soon became evident that the base was doomed, and a call for help went out. Rescue planes arrived at noon, by which time the floe had split in two. Brinegar and his men walked over a mile to a nearby floe, where the planes could land. They were evacuated safely but had to leave their equipment behind. Subsequent search flights could find no trace of the camp; apparently all huts had been destroyed.[26]

The 10th Rescue Squadron also continued to support the scientific program that had gotten off to an unsuccessful start the previous year. On April 10, 17, 20, 22, and 23 a C-47 flown by Capt. J. R. Whitmer of Detachment B landed with a team of scientists from the Air Force Cambridge Research Center on the ice pack north of Barter Island between latitudes 73° N and 76° N. Albert P. Crary, Robert D. Cotell, and Jack Oliver remained on the ice for four to six hours each time, taking acoustical soundings, making gravity observations, and studying ice movement. Operating in an area that Storkerson had covered in 1918, they registered ocean depths of 11,000 to 12,500 feet. They concluded that Storkerson's measurement of 15,400 feet in the area was likely erroneous.[27]

Although Balchen and his successors were unaware of the Soviet High Latitude Aerial Expeditions that had been taking place in secret since 1948, the successful landing of the Cambridge Research Center scientists on the ice in 1951 mirrored the Russian work.

While the 10th Rescue Squadron was conducting operations on the ice pack from its forward base on Barter Island, Lt. Col. Joseph O. Fletcher, who took command of the 58th Weather Squadron in 1950, was developing more ambitious plans for the establishment of a drifting station on one of the massive pieces of glacial ice that had earlier been discovered amid the polar floes.

Since the beginning of reconnaissance flights in 1946, the Air Force had identified three huge "ice islands" drifting in the Arctic ice pack. On August 14, 1946, an F-13 from the 375th Reconnaissance Squadron spotted an enormous heart-shaped mass of ice, more than two hundred square miles in size, located less than three hundred miles north of Point Barrow. Later designated T-1, this ice island, larger than Guam, was often seen on radar or visually over the next three years as it drifted northward.[28]

In May 1950 Fletcher, who had arrived in Alaska from an assignment as head of the Geophysics Research Directorate at the Cambridge Research Center, organized a search for other ice islands by the RB-29s of his 58th Weather Squadron. On July 20 Maj. Lawrence S. Koenig took a radar photograph of a large ice formation located two hundred miles from the North Pole. Named T-2, the ice island had been seen by another RB-29 crew two days earlier but had not been recognized. A third ice island, T-3, showed up on Koenig's radar on July 29. This 4.5-by-9-mile kidney-shaped piece of ice, smaller than the other two, was located at 75°24′ N, 173°00′ W. (It was discovered later that T-3 had been photographed by Royal Canadian Air Force [RCAF] Squadron Leader Keith R. Greenaway three years earlier in 1947.)[29]

Fletcher soon began to promote the idea that one of the ice islands should be used as a base for a U.S. scientific drifting station. This notion, it should be emphasized, was developed independently and not as a result of the Soviet Arctic program. "The Soviet post-war activity was unknown to the West," Fletcher later pointed out. The existence of NP2, in fact, would not be announced by Moscow until 1952. Had Washington been aware of the scale of Soviet activity in the Arctic, Fletcher continued, "it would not have been so difficult to get authorization and support for [U.S.] Arctic Basin investigation."[30]

As it was, Fletcher had to fight a year-long battle for his project. The sudden breakup of the 10th Rescue Squadron's ice floe camp in March 1951 made senior officers in Alaskan Air Command skeptical about the possibility of maintaining a station on the ice for long periods of time. Fletcher's efforts to distinguish between ice floes and ice islands all too often fell on deaf ears.

In his campaign to win support for the project, Fletcher first won the approval of his superior, Col. Marcellus Duffy, commander of the 2107th Air Weather Group at Elmendorf AFB. Fletcher next convinced Maj. Gen. William O. Senter, chief of the Air Weather Service, of the potential benefits—and practicality—of a surface meteorological station near the North Pole. Senter, Fletcher emphasized, "stood almost alone among Washington officialdom with the foresight to see the worth of the project and the moral courage to back it without reservation."[31]

With Senter's backing, Fletcher finally managed to persuade Maj. Gen. William D. Old, head of Alaskan Air Command, to accept operational responsibility for the scheme. Old's decision, Fletcher later wrote, came in the midst of "dire predictions from above and below" that the plan was certain to fail. In January 1952 Old gave Fletcher the approval to go ahead with Project ICICLE.[32]

Fletcher immediately began work to establish a base on one of the ice islands. He first enlisted the assistance of Kaare Rodahl, a physician at the Arctic Aeromedical Laboratory at Ladd AFB who had been conducting physiological studies involving members of the 58th Weather Squadron. Rodahl earlier had spent over a year on the isolated northeast coast of Greenland and knew how to survive in the Arctic. "The success of any arctic expedition," Rodahl emphasized, "depends first and foremost on the thoroughness of the preparations."[33]

Lt. Robert R. Danner from the 2107th Air Weather Group was another key addition to the ICICLE team. Over the next few weeks, Danner made the logistical arrangements for the expedition. As Fletcher noted, this was no simple task. Danner had to overcome countless obstacles, which he managed to do "with immense skill and energy."[34]

As a trial run, Fletcher set up a camp on the frozen Chena River near Ladd AFB, where every essential piece of equipment was unpacked and tested. Several items were found to be faulty and had to be replaced. Finally, on February 27 Fletcher and several project personnel, together with 27,000 pounds of equipment, flew from Ladd AFB to the newly opened U.S. Air Force base at Thule in northern Greenland, which was to serve as the launching point for the expedition. The remaining personnel and 68,000 pounds of additional supplies followed in early March 1952.[35]

Owing to its favorable location near the North Pole, the smallest ice island, T-3, seemed the best site for the camp. On March 8 and 12, Ptarmigan weather reconnaissance flights looked for T-3 while en route to the Pole but failed to locate it. After discussions with Maj. Gordon F. Bradburn of the 10th Rescue Squadron, who was in charge of the aerial phase of ICICLE, Fletcher decided to use Bradburn's radar-equipped C-54 to search for the ice island.

On March 14 the C-54 lifted off the long runway at Thule carrying four pilots, five navigators, and the initial ICICLE landing party of Fletcher, Rodahl, and Major Brinegar of the 10th Rescue Squadron, who had commanded the earlier experiment to set up a camp on an ice floe.

The aircraft had sufficient fuel to remain in the air for sixteen hours. The weather was clear and the sometimes quirky radar was working perfectly as the C-54 droned over the ice pack. "Nevertheless," Rodahl recalled, "there was a noticeable feeling of tension among us, for the future of the project depended greatly on the results of this mission."

Some thirty minutes after the team reached the North Pole, Bradburn's radar operator detected a large object on the surface. It was T-3, located at 88°17′ N, 166°30′ W, or 103 miles from the Pole and 850 miles from Thule. Bradburn descended to one hundred feet to enable Fletcher, Rodahl, Brinegar, and Capt. Lewis Erhard, pilot of the C-47 scheduled to land on the island, to get a good look at the target. "What we saw," Rodahl noted, "was exactly what the photographs had led us to expect: a vast white flat field surrounded by tight pack ice with only narrow fissures and frozen leads between the floes. It was approximately five by nine miles in size, judging by the time it took to fly across it at a known speed; in shape, it was oblong with rounded corners, and slightly elevated at the center." Erhart believed that a ski landing would pose little difficulty. "It's a cinch," he told Rodahl.

Erhart's C-47 lacked the range for the 1,700-mile round-trip between Thule and T-3, even with a 400-gallon tank in the fuselage. On March 17 he deposited six drums of gasoline on a frozen lead between Greenland and Ellesmere Island. He planned to refuel en route to T-3, provided that his navigator, Capt. Edward F. Curley, could find his way back to the gasoline cache!

Bradburn's plans called for the C-47 to be accompanied by two C-54s. Capt. Edmund G. Smith would fly ahead with the radar-equipped aircraft to locate T-3, while Bradburn would rendezvous with the C-47 following its refueling stop and accompany it to the target. As the three aircraft were being loaded on March 18, General Old showed up in a C-54 with six thousand pounds of additional equipment. His aircraft would be added to the growing aerial armada, while Old himself would join Erhart on the C-47 as copilot.

Project ICICLE launched from Thule on March 19. Erhart took off at 8:10 A.M., carrying the expedition's personnel and essential supplies. Shortly before noon, Erhart spotted six tiny black dots on the ice ahead. Navigator Curley had done a superb job. The C-47 touched down at 11:50 A.M. After Old and Fletcher rolled the drums across the ice to the aircraft, flight engineer Howard Clohesey pumped the gasoline into the fuselage tank. The C-47 took off without difficulty at 12:20 P.M. "Thank God that's over with," General Old commented.

Although the planned rendezvous with the C-54 failed to take place, Erhart was unconcerned as he proceeded northward in excellent weather. By the time he arrived in the search area at 4:00 P.M., however, conditions had deteriorated. The sun now was low on the horizon, and haze covered the ice below. Erhart saw no sign of T-3. Establishing radio contact with the C-54s, he learned that Smith had been searching for thirty minutes but had been unable to pick up the island on his radar. Within minutes, however, Smith reported that he had located the target. Erhart took a bearing on Smith's radio signal and headed for the area. He arrived at T-3 to find the three C-54s stacked over the island at one thousand-foot intervals.

Erhart made several low passes over the island, looking for a place to land. The surface, which had appeared smooth when inspected from the air on the earlier reconnaissance flight, now seemed hazardous, as a strong wind had blown the snow cover off a series of ridges. To Rodahl, the ice below looked "rough and ragged." Erhart touched down gently on his skis at several points on the island only to discover that the snow cover between the ridges was soft and deep. Finally, he selected a promising spot for a landing. After three trials, he placed the full weight of the aircraft on the skis and settled into the snow.

General Old was not impressed with T-3. It was extremely cold, at least fifty degrees below zero. Although marginally suitable for landings by ski-equipped C-47s, it could not be used for wheeled landings by C-54s without extensive preparations. Old was ready to call off the operation. Only Fletcher's persuasive talents gained Old's reluctant consent to continue.

The men unloaded the C-47, then marked a drop zone with fluorescent flags. The C-54s parachuted three thousand pounds of equipment and supplies, including four drums of fuel for the C-47. Old and the crew of the Douglas transport helped Fletcher and his two companions erect a large double-walled mountain tent that would serve as their initial shelter, moved the air-dropped supplies to the site, then took their leave. After four hours and twenty minutes on the island, the C-47 made a jet-assisted (JATO) takeoff and headed back to Thule. "As the three of us stood there alone on the ice and watched the plane disappear," Rodahl remembered, "we were probably as isolated as anyone can be in this world. . . ."

Over the next few days, Fletcher and his companions explored the ice island and improved the camp. They erected another tent, which became a kitchen, and built two twelve-foot square huts of snow, covered by tarpaulins. They used one hut for storage and the other for emergency shelter. Erhart returned to T-3 on April 1, carrying Albert Crary of the Air Force Cambridge Research Center and Capt. Paul L. Green, a radio specialist. Erhart also brought a large sign, which he nailed to a pole in the snow: "Fletcher's Ice Island." After unloading Green's radio equipment and other supplies, Erhart left for Thule, carrying Rodahl with him.

The C-47 returned several times during April. Lieutenant Danner, the logistical magician of the 2107th Air Weather Group, flew in to replace Brinegar, and Dr. Cotell of the Cambridge Research Center arrived to assist Crary. On one flight the C-47 delivered a weasel, a small tracked vehicle used to begin work on carving out a runway that could accommodate C-54s. As Crary noted in a letter to his parents, "General Old insisted on the runway for our ICICLE project."[36]

Gradually, the camp took on a more permanent appearance. Three insulated huts, sixteen feet square, arrived in sections. One became sleeping quarters, another served as the mess, and the third was used as the radio and weather station. Most of the work on the island centered on meteorology, with Green transmitting weather reports to Thule every six hours. Crary set up his hydrographic equipment on the nearby sea ice. As T-3 drifted in the polar basin, he took seismic soundings of the ocean depths and measured the temperature and salinity of the water at various levels.[37]

On May 3 Fletcher, Crary, and Cotell embarked on a special mission that was sponsored by Air Force headquarters and was aimed more at generating favorable publicity than acquiring scientific data. Together with two public information specialists, the group left T-3 on a C-47 piloted by Lt. Col. William P. Benedict. After a one-hour flight, Benedict landed on a floe at the North Pole. The group posed for a number of photographs, then Crary and Cotell took a gravity reading and a depth sounding. "We got 14,150'," Crary reported, "which checks pretty good with the Russian Schmidt in 1932 who had 14,070." (Actually, it was Papanin who took a reading of 14,075 feet on June 7, 1937.)[38]

The C-47 returned to T-3. After a few hours of sleep, Benedict took off again with Crary and Cotell to search for T-1, which was grounded about forty miles north of Ellesmere Island. Locating the target, he landed close to one edge of the large mass of ice. Crary and Cotell surveyed the contours of the island and took two ice samples. After four hours on the ice the C-47 proceeded to the Ellesmere Ice Shelf of Ward Hunt Island, where Benedict again set down so the two scientists could take cores of the shelf ice to compare with the ice on T-1 and T-3. He then headed for the Canadian weather station at Alert on Ellesmere to refuel and rest before returning to T-3.

En route to Alert, Benedict spotted some sort of marker on the ice below. Upon landing to investigate, he discovered a signpost that had been left by Robert E. Peary in 1909. Nearby was a cairn from which a sled runner projected; it had been built in 1919 by Admiral Godfred Hansen, a Danish explorer.

In late June Fletcher, Cotell, and Green left T-3. Their replacements, a nine-member scientific team that included an oceanographer, marine biologist, and two geophysicists, took up residence on the island for a lengthy stay that would last through the winter. The drifting station remained in continuous operation for over two years. On May 14, 1954, the island approached the weather station at Alert, on the northern tip of Ellesmere Island, and lost its geographical advantages. It was abandoned. It had drifted a straight-line distance of 351 miles to the south, while covering a total of 1,691 miles. The station was reoccupied on April 25, 1955, then abandoned again five months later.

✳

The Arctic remained an area of vital concern to the Air Force, as witnessed by the beginning of construction in 1954 of the DEW Line. Over the next three years some half billion dollars were spent building a three thousand-mile long chain of radar stations along the 69th parallel, stretching from Greenland to the Aleutian Islands. At the same time, however, Air Force interest in drifting stations waned. Investigation of the polar basin held a low priority, as the information obtained from scientific studies of the area seemed increasingly irrelevant in an age of intercontinental ballistic missiles.

The diminished concern of the United States with Arctic research came at a time when the Soviet Union was greatly expanding its scientific programs in the far north. The Russians established two drifting stations, NP3 and NP4, in April 1954. NP5 appeared in April 1955, followed by NP6 in April 1956. High Latitude Aerial Expeditions also took place with increased frequency. During the 1956 season alone, 35 aircraft placed small parties of Soviet scientists on the ice at 150 locations for up to five hours (see Figure 1).[39]

Even the information on the extent of Soviet work in the Arctic that finally began to appear in the mid-1950s failed to provoke an American response. It took the demands of the International Geophysical Year of 1957 to renew U.S. interest in venturing out onto the polar ice pack once more.

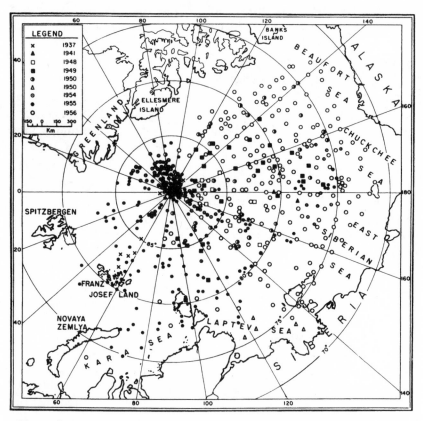

Figure 1
Soviet aircraft landings on Arctic pack ice.

2

Bravo and Alpha

The concept of an International Geophysical Year (IGY), a cooperative effort by scientists throughout the world to learn more about the nature of Earth, took shape in the midst of an expanding Cold War. In April 1950, two months before North Korea attacked its neighbor to the south, a group of American scientists spent an evening with Professor Sidney Chapman of Queens College, Oxford, who was considered by many to be the greatest living geophysicist. One of the participants, Dr. Lloyd V. Berkner, suggested that the time had come for a new Polar Year. Twice before, in 1882 and 1932, the international scientific community had come together to investigate the polar regions. Berkner, in fact, had taken part in the Second Polar Year in 1932.[1]

In July 1950, as fighting raged on the Korean peninsula, Berkner and Chapman presented their proposal at a meeting of the Mixed Commission on the Ionosphere in Brussels. The commission endorsed the idea and sent it to the International Council of Scientific Unions for action. In 1951 the council created a special committee to formulate plans for a Third Polar Year. Chapman suggested that the focus for the event be broadened and that the name be changed to the International Geophysical Year. The council's general assembly approved the designation of the IGY in October 1952. At the same time, it established a special committee for the IGY, with Chapman as president and Berkner as vice president.

With the IGY scheduled to begin on July 1, 1957, and extend through December 31, 1958, a period that would coincide with the expected peak of sunspot activity, invitations went out to nations throughout the world to participate in what was expected to be the premier scientific event of the century. At a time when the world seemed to be moving ever closer to the brink of nuclear holocaust, scientists and diplomats looked at the IGY as a way to defuse international hostilities. "Many saw it as the great hope for mankind," one observer noted, "setting a pattern of cooperation that could lead to permanent peace."[2]

Initial responses to the committee's request were mixed. On the one hand, the Soviet Union seemed eager to join the scientific adventure. Moscow announced that not only would it participate in the IGY, but it also would give governmental priority to a broad spectrum of research projects. The United States, on the other hand, only slowly warmed to the idea of committing resources to the worldwide scientific endeavor.

When plans for research activities in the Arctic were discussed in Brussels at the third plenary session of the IGY's Special Committee, the U.S. National Committee had few projects to offer. The Soviet Union, in contrast, presented proposals for a wide variety of projects. Washington was chagrined. Spurred by a sense of competition and national pride, American policy makers set out to remedy the defects in the U.S. effort. At a meeting of the Special Arctic Budget Committee in October 1955, a number of ideas were discussed, including a suggestion from Charles Bates of the Navy Hydrographic Office to establish scientific drifting stations in the far north.

Two months later the full Arctic Committee endorsed Bates's idea and recommended that provisions for two drifting stations, located approximately at 78° N, 160° W and 85° N, 100° W, be included in the U.S. IGY program. While IGY funds would be used to support most of the scientific research work on the two stations, the committee called upon the Department of Defense to establish and maintain the facilities.[3]

The Department of Defense accepted the charge and ordered the U.S. Air Force to conduct the operation. The Air Force, in turn, divided what it called Project ICE SKATE into two parts. Northeast Air Command would be responsible for the easternmost location, designated Station Bravo and located on T-3, while Alaskan Air Command had the more difficult assignment of setting up Station Alpha near the North Pole.

Col. Harvey P. Huglin assumed overall command of Project ICE SKATE-Bravo in October 1956, with Col. Robert W. Gates in charge of airlift support. On March 7, 1957, a construction team from Thule AFB landed on T-3, now located 120 miles off the north coast of Ellesmere Island, and quickly prepared a 5,000-foot runway. In April, as giant C-124 transports began landing on the ice island with supplies and equipment, responsibility for the project passed to SAC after Northeast Air Command was deactivated. The change of command had no effect on the preparations underway on T-3, and Station Bravo opened on schedule.

Alaskan Air Command selected Colonel Fletcher of earlier T-3 fame for the more challenging task of directing efforts to establish a polar drifting station. He hoped to locate an ice island similar to T-3 for Station Alpha. If one could not be found, however, an ice floe would have to be used. In March 1957, as WB-50s from the 58th Weather Squadron began to search the polar ice pack for a suitable location, the occupation party assembled at Barrow. Maj. Richard E. Freeman would command Station Alpha. Accompanying him on the initial survey would be Fletcher; Fr. Thomas Cunningham of Barrow, Alaska, a Roman Catholic priest, Air Force Reserve chaplain, longtime resident of the far north, and expert on the behavior of pack ice; T/Sgt. Pat Garrett from Alaskan Air Command's Survival School; Inuit construction workers Louis Reich and Arthur Fields from the village of Kotzebue; and Mike Schiercz, a "sourdough" carpenter from Fairbanks.[4]

Initial reconnaissance flights failed to locate an ice island, although several potential floes were spotted. Plans called for two ski-equipped C-47s, carrying the occupation party and essential supplies, to rendezvous with a WB-50 and SA-16 air rescue aircraft over a suitable floe. Toward the end of March one of the search aircraft radioed Barrow that it had found a likely candidate at 79°20′ N, 148° W. The two C-47s immediately took off and proceeded toward the location, some five hundred miles off the Alaskan coast. Reaching the area, they observed the WB-50 circling an egg-shaped floe approximately five miles long by three miles wide.

Capt. Burton P. Jenkins carefully inspected the floe, then landed his C-47 to take an ice core sample. It revealed a thickness of seven and a half feet. While marginal for large aircraft, the floe could be used as a temporary base to extend the search area of the short-range C-47s. Jenkins mounted a radar reflector atop several empty gasoline drums so that he could more easily locate the floe, then returned to Barrow.

Unfortunately, when Jenkins flew over the ice pack the next day, he could not find the floe, even with the aid of the radar reflector. This forced Freeman to change his plans. When a search aircraft again discovered a suitable floe for inspection, Freeman intended to land and establish a temporary base. He would set up a radio beacon, enabling aircraft to home in on the isolated location. If the ice proved thick enough to support large aircraft, the floe would be used as Station Alpha; otherwise, it would serve as a base to continue the search.

In the early morning hours of April 5, 1957, a WB-50 informed Barrow that it had located an area of large floes at 79°20′ N, 168° W. The two C-47s, SA-16, and an Air Rescue C-54 departed at 6:00 A.M. Four hours later, they established radio contact with the WB-50 and were directed to the site. Jenkins selected a floe, three miles long and a half-mile wide, that looked like it could support a C-47. After several low passes, he landed without incident. He kept the engines running while Freeman and his companions took a few hurried ice core samples. As the floe seemed unusually thick—eleven feet—Freeman ordered the second C-47 to land. Both aircraft were quickly unloaded, then departed. The Air Rescue C-54 air-dropped additional emergency equipment. Finally, a C-124 appeared and parachuted drums of fuel to the seven men on the floe.

Freeman and his companions first set up a ten-man tent for temporary housing. Next they unpacked the radio beacon, which went on the air at 5:00 P.M. Freeman then divided his party into three two-man teams. Fletcher and Cunningham explored the floe and took ice core samples while Reich and Fields retrieved the fuel drums and looked after the power units. Schiercz and Garrett maintained the radio and set up the emergency gear.

Search missions continued over the next few days as Freeman still hoped to locate an ice island or a larger floe as the site for Station Alpha. The WB-50s, however, were unable to find a more promising area. Freeman, after consulting with Fletcher and Cunningham, finally concluded that the temporary camp should be made permanent. On April 10 he recommended to Alaskan Air Command that his current location be designated Station Alpha. Two days later, Freeman's superiors accepted his choice.

Work soon started on setting up camp facilities and constructing a runway for large aircraft. On April 15 C-47s brought in three communications specialists, three heavy equipment operators, two cooks, a medic, and a Jamesway hut. Two days later, a C-124 Globemaster air-dropped a D-4 Caterpillar tractor, which floated down on four one hundred-foot parachutes, and an M-29 weasel.

The Jamesway hut was quickly assembled; it would serve at first as the headquarters, barracks, and mess hall. Next, the men built a three-sided latrine, using snow blocks. Fritz Awe, a noted Arctic construction expert, then set to work on leveling the ice for a runway. His crew used dynamite to break up the largest hummocks that studded the floe, while an ice ripper attachment on the bulldozer dealt with smaller ones. The bulldozer then pushed fresh snow onto the leveled surface, which was compacted. Awe soon had an ice runway that could accommodate C-124s. The giant transports began landing at three-hour intervals by the end of the month, bringing in twenty Jamesway huts and other supplies.

On May 21 Gen. James H. Davies landed to inspect Alpha and drop off the first scientific party. Pleased at the progress of the camp, Davies declared Alpha officially open. Although the IGY would not begin until July 1, 1957, the scientific team was anxious to set up their instruments and record observations. Davies wished them well, then departed.

The Lamont Geological Observatory of Columbia University, under contract from the Air Force Cambridge Research Center, had responsibility for the geophysical research program on Alpha. Included on their agenda were studies in gravity, seismology, geomagnetism, and oceanography. In addition, the Office of Naval Research (ONR) funded an extensive meteorological research effort. The initial scientific party on Alpha included Maurice J. Davidson of Lamont, the leader of the group; Kenneth L. Hunkins, an oceanographer from Lamont; Norbert Untersteiner of the University of Washington, an expert on thermal budget; meteorologist Arnold M. Hanson of the University of Washington; and Lt. Thomas S. English, a marine biologist with the Air Force Arctic Medical Laboratory at Fairbanks.[5]

Although preliminary scientific work got underway at the end of May, the official start came on July 1 with the launching of the first large balloon to record upper air winds and temperatures. To the delight of the observers, it was possible to track the balloon to 80,000 feet. Balloons were sent aloft daily thereafter, with one reaching an altitude of 157,000 feet.

Meanwhile, oceanographers used seismographic techniques to measure the depth of the ocean as Alpha drifted across the Arctic basin, three hundred miles from the North Pole. The first echo-sounding shot, using a half stick of dynamite, took place on July 6. Daily shooting began the next week, followed by twice daily shots beginning on July 21. Bottom depths were consistent at 10,000 to 12,000 feet until August 6. The depth then decreased abruptly to 6,000 feet. On August

13 the seismic system recorded a depth of 4,683 feet. The bottom then dropped to 8,048 feet three days later. The undersea range detected by the scientists later was named the Alpha Cordillera.

July and August brought temperatures ranging from the low 20s to the high 30s. Considerable melting took place on the floe, rendering the ice runway unusable. Frequent airdrops, however, kept the camp amply supplied. On August 27 a C-54 managed to land and evacuate Freeman, who had incurred a hernia while wrestling with heavy diesel fuel drums. Lt. Col. Helmuth E. Stromquist replaced him.

The sun dipped below the horizon for the first time on October 7. The temperatures began to fall as the Arctic winter approached. After November, the thermometer seldom registered above 0°. In the last two weeks of December it averaged –51°. The colder weather made it possible to smooth out a landing strip measuring five thousand by two hundred feet. A string of lights was placed along the ice, enabling C-124s to land in the darkness of the Arctic night.

The first anniversary of Alpha's occupation brought problems for the station. In April 1958 a part of the floe broke off. Then a newly formed pressure ridge advanced into the camp area and forced the evacuation of half the station's twenty personnel. On May 2 the decision was made to move the camp to an adjacent floe, one mile distant. This meant jacking up the station's twenty-one buildings, placing runners beneath them, and moving them to the new location. Power cables had to be dug out of the ice, and a new runway had to be built. The difficult task had no sooner been completed when two leads formed across the new runway, rendering it unusable. Still another landing area had to be carved out of the ice. When the warmer weather of Arctic summer caused melting problems, the runway had to be drained through holes drilled with ice augers.

On June 22 a C-54 landed at Alpha, the first aircraft to arrive in two months. The relief of the camp's personnel, however, proved short-lived. The aircraft had no sooner departed when a crack formed across the runway and it had to be closed. Alpha had to rely on air-drops until late September, when colder weather permitted the reopening of the runway.

✳

As Alpha prepared for its second winter, Alaskan Air Command selected Capt. James F. Smith to take over command of the station. Destined to play a key role in Project COLDFEET, Smith brought a rich and varied background to what would prove to be a brief but challenging tour on the drifting station.

A master parachutist, experienced Arctic survival instructor, Russian linguist, and trained intelligence officer, Smith was born in Fort Worth, Texas, on July 15, 1923. His father, Jay Fiske Smith, was a prosperous businessman in Texarkana; he died when Smith was four years old. The family fell on hard times with the onset of the Great Depression, and Smith's mother took her four children to live with her mother in Lawton, Oklahoma. Life during the 1930s, Smith recalled with understatement, was "difficult" for the family.[6]

Smith dropped out of high school during his senior year and joined the Army as a $21-a-month "grunt" in July 1941. "I thought I was too smart," he reflected; it was a decision made by "a typical dumb-ass kid." While at boot camp at Jefferson Barracks, Missouri, Smith scored well enough on intelligence/aptitude tests to qualify for the Army Air Corps. He was attending aircraft armament school at Lowry Field, Colorado, when the Japanese attacked Pearl Harbor in December 1941. Lowry Field became a flurry of activity at the outbreak of the war, with everyone putting in twelve- to fourteen-hour days to arm the aircraft that came through the base.

Early in 1942 the newly designated Army Air Forces sent Smith to Shaw Field, South Carolina, where he trained as a weather observer. In June he was assigned to the remote station of Sondre Stromfjord, code named Bluie West 8, on the west coast of Greenland, just above the Arctic Circle.

Bluie West 8 was part of a chain of airfields forming the infrastructure for a northern ferry route that enabled single- and twin-engine aircraft to fly from the United States and Canada to England via Newfoundland (or Labrador), Greenland, Iceland, and Scotland. In the fall of 1941 Gen. H. H. Arnold, chief of the Air Corps, had called Bernt Balchen into military service to direct the construction of a field at Sondre Stromfjord. Balchen, who had piloted the aircraft carrying Richard E. Byrd on the first flight over the South Pole in November 1928, tackled the assignment with characteristic energy. His extensive polar experience was combined with an enthusiastic "can do" temperament to accomplish the most difficult of tasks.[7]

Task Force 8—three ships carrying 1,500 men and 50,000 tons of supplies—left the United States in late September 1941. After stopping at Godthaab, a Danish settlement south of Sondre Stromfjord, to pick up a coastal pilot, Balchen's ship, *Munargo,* proceeded to the mouth of the fjord leading to Sondre Stromfjord.

"The fjord," Balchen observed, "is a mile wide at its mouth, almost blocked at its entrance by a small island called in Eskimo Simiutak, which means 'cork stopper,' and runs inland northeast over a hundred miles." The vessel steamed up the fjord, initially between mountains that rose straight up out of the water on both sides to an elevation of five thousand feet. As the *Munargo* got deeper into the fjord, the steep mountains gave way to rounded granite and glaciated hills, with patches of heather and willows in bright autumn colors.[8]

Arriving at Sondre Stromfjord on October 9, Balchen faced the difficult problem—the first of many—of unloading his supplies across a half-mile mud flat. He welded together two barges, which he used to lighter the supplies toward the beach at high tide. From the point where the barges ran aground he built a tramway to the firmer terrain beyond. The process was time consuming, but the weather remained clear and dry, permitting the men to put in long workdays. By the end of November a camp had been built, along with a temporary runway.

The news of Pearl Harbor lent added incentive to the labors of Balchen's men. Despite worsening weather, work on a permanent runway continued. On March 14, 1942, a British Royal Air Force Hudson bomber became the first of thousands of aircraft to land at Bluie West 8.

When Smith landed at Sondre Stromfjord in June 1942, he thought that he had reached the ends of the earth. He was in for a rude shock. Instead of the relative comforts on the main base, he would be going to the tiny island of Simiutak at the mouth of the fjord, part of a twenty-two-man detachment that included Air Force weather observers and communicators and five Coast Guardsmen operating a navigational beacon for ships. The assignment to Bluie West 8, Smith recalled, was "pure misery." The cold would settle off the ice cap in the interior of Greenland, then funnel into the fjord. Icy gales of 60 to 70 miles per hour were commonplace. Even worse than the weather was the boredom. With little else to do in his spare time, Smith learned Morse code and the fundamentals of radio communications procedures. After ten miserable months on "the rock," he had to spend another three months at the main base of Sondre Stromfjord before he was able to put Greenland behind him.

Smith happily returned to the United States in September 1943. Assigned to a weather reconnaissance squadron at Presque Isle, Maine, he flew first as a weather observer, then as a radio operator, on the unit's B-25s. His duties involved lengthy missions over the North Atlantic ferry route, mainly flying between Labrador and the southern tip of Greenland. He recalled hours upon hours of boredom as the aircraft droned over the empty ocean, punctuated by moments of excitement when ice built up on the wings and caused the aircraft to sink toward the surface of the ocean before warmer air enabled the pilot to regain control of the B-25.

Smith's routine changed early in 1944. Between February and June he made numerous flights from the Azores to collect weather data for what turned out to be the D-Day invasion of Europe. In July he transferred to a B-17 weather reconnaissance squadron that was based at Manchester, New Hampshire, where he remained until the end of the war.

Discharged as a staff sergeant in September 1945, Smith returned to Oklahoma and for a time took classes at a junior college in Altus. Deciding to make the service a career, he rejoined the Army Air Forces—soon to become the United States Air Force—in February 1947. Shortly after reenlisting he took advantage of an opportunity that allowed senior enlisted personnel to apply for a commission. After gaining his second lieutenant's bars in September 1948, Smith was posted to Shepard AFB, Texas, as a squadron adjutant.

Smith served in a series of administrative positions over the next three years. In the fall of 1951 he abandoned his desk job and volunteered to become an instructor at the Air Force's survival school at Stead AFB, Nevada. Smith spent five years at Stead, conducting classes in survival and escape-and-evasion. In 1954 he completed a parachute training course at the Army's jump school at Fort Benning, Georgia, followed by six weeks of Special Forces training at Fort Bragg, North Carolina, in 1955.

Smith's military career took another turn in 1956 when he was accepted for Russian-language training. He spent one year at Syracuse University in intensive language studies, an experience he thoroughly enjoyed. Following completion of the course in April 1957, he was sent to Ladd AFB in Fairbanks, Alaska, as a staff intelligence officer with the Eleventh Air Division.

✳

Largely because of his survival school experience, Smith was selected to take over the command of Station Alpha as it prepared for its second Arctic winter. He arrived on September 23, 1958. The main camp, he found, was located on the western end of an oval-shaped floe of sea ice, approximately 3,000 by 4,000 feet in size. The runway, 3,800 by 150 feet, was on a separate section of the original Alpha floe. Distance between the camp and runway was approximately one-half mile in a straight line, or three-quarters of a mile by a foot path that crossed two closed leads. "Both floes," Smith reported on September 28, "though not as large as would be desirable, are fairly well shaped to withstand movement and pressures." There were twenty people in the camp, including Smith—half scientists and half Air Force support personnel.[9]

Smith also reported to the commander of the 11th Air Division on "the mission and value" of the station. He believed that Alpha served a number of useful purposes. Results of the meteorological research being done on the ice floe, he argued, would affect the entire Air Force, both offensively and defensively, as the Arctic represents "the shortest route" between the United States and the Soviet Union. Furthermore, investigations in the field of magnetism and signal propagation would have an impact on the early warning capability of the United States in the far north. Smith rejected the idea that the Air Force should "unload" the research station on the Navy, a proposal based on the notion that the scientific results obtained from drifting stations had greater implications for submarine-launched cruise missiles than for Air Force weapons. "As systems progress," he pointed out, "it may well develop that air-launched IRBMs [Intermediate Range Ballistic Missiles] will enter Air Force inventory. Arctic geodesy will become a matter of prime concern in such an instance."

Finally, Smith argued, attention should be paid to the fact that the Soviets were keenly interested in the Arctic. "They have been active in the area constantly, and show no inclination to withdraw," he observed. "It may be a dangerous mistake to assume that we can accrue in a short time the knowledge they have generated over a period of years."

Smith had no sooner completed his initial assessment on the condition and value of Alpha when the first of what proved to be a series of severe storms punished the isolated outpost. On October 12 a crack opened through the middle of the camp as strong winds and currents caused stress on the sea ice. It took Smith and his men twenty-four hours to move all essential structures, equipment, and supplies to the main portion of the floe. Two structures came apart during the move and were lost.[10]

A second storm the following week caused 30 percent of the main floe to break off. A short time later, the two pieces rejoined, forming a pressure ridge along the northern perimeter of the camp, with fractures extending toward the base. A third storm—"with particularly vicious winds"—caused the distance between the camp and the runway floe to widen to one and a half miles. The runway itself was unusable due to waist-high drifts of hard-packed snow. Smith reported that movement between the two areas, now separated by a half mile of shatter ice and small floes, had become "progressively more difficult and dangerous." Nonetheless, the runway had to be reopened. Thanks to the efforts of S/Sgt. Thomas A. Boger, A/1C Ronald N. Beaupre, and A/2C William A. Sprague, who kept the station's small bulldozer and grader operating for 48 hours, a 4,000-by-150-foot landing strip was cleared.

Smith recommended that half of the station's personnel be evacuated until the situation on Alpha became stable. As soon as the runway was ready, a C-54 left Ladd AFB to accomplish the task. Severe icing over the Brooks Range in northern Alaska, however, caused the aircraft to turn back. Before a second flight could be attempted, Smith informed Ladd AFB that a falling barometer and wind shift indicated that another storm was approaching.

The fourth storm battered Alpha on November 1, 1958, causing cracks that resulted in the loss of 40 percent of the main floe, with new fractures extending into the camp area. The next day, as the weather cleared, Smith set out to inspect the runway. He was accompanied by Father Cunningham, the Roman Catholic priest from Barrow who had served as an Arctic adviser to the Alaskan Air Command, and Arnold Hanson, the meteorologist from the University of Washington.

The three men first had to negotiate the hazardous 1.5 miles of jumbled and broken sea ice that separated the camp and runway. They proceeded slowly, probing ahead to test the ice for each step. "An unwary step on the thin ice hidden under drifted snow," Smith knew, "could mean a frigid, shocking bath in freezing sea water." Reaching the end of the runway, they started down the snow-covered strip, walking abreast, fifty feet apart in the November darkness. Hanson's probing flashlight soon picked out a thin black line slanting across the white surface. When they reached the area, they discovered that the runway had been severed. As they shone their flashlights down the seven-foot ice walls to the seawater below, Father Cunningham quipped, "Ten feet wide and 10,000 feet deep."

Fortunately, the runway had split into two unequal pieces. Smith, Cunningham, and Hanson separately paced off the larger portion, then averaged the three counts to give a distance of just over 2,200 feet. The runway was too short for the C-54s that usually landed at Alpha, but it might accommodate a C-123 twin-engine transport.

When Smith returned to camp he informed Dr. George Cvijanovich, the lead scientist, that he was going to recommend the base be abandoned. He then sent a radio message to Brig. Gen. Gordon A. Austin, commander of the Eleventh Air Division, explaining the situation and requesting immediate evacuation. Austin, in turn, alerted Air Force headquarters in Washington, SAC in Omaha, and the Alaskan Air Command at Elmendorf AFB. Within hours of Smith's request, the Air Force had set in motion a complex scheme to retrieve the twenty men on Alpha.

SAC planned to use two ski-equipped C-123s at Harmon AFB in Newfoundland for the evacuation. They would fly to Sondre Stromfjord, then on to the new base at Thule on the tip of northern Greenland. Alpha, now 250 miles from the North Pole, lay 600 miles from Thule, well within the range of the C-123s. While awaiting the arrival of the C-123s, General Austin ordered continuous air coverage of Alpha. A weather reconnaissance RB-50 from Ladd AFB arrived first over the station. Six hours later it was replaced by a C-54 that had refueled at Barrow, some nine hundred miles from Alpha. This aircraft orbited the station for six hours, then departed for Thule. A variety of aircraft circled Alpha over the next few days, including a KC-97 aerial tanker that remained overhead for fourteen hours before returning to Thule and completing a thirty-hour mission.

The atmosphere on Alpha was optimistic, at least at first. "Conversations became free," Smith recalled, "and there was a show of enthusiasm as packing and other details were worked out." He ordered that all choice cuts of meats be taken out of the station's six-month supply of food. "If nothing else," Smith figured, "we would eat well."

After the evening meal on November 2, Smith sat in the small hut he shared with Father Cunningham. The two men reviewed the situation. Smith believed that it would take about two days for the C-123s to arrive, assuming no mechanical or weather delays. Just to be conservative, Smith decided to inform the station's personnel that they could expect to be evacuated in four to six days. In the midst of the conversation, Smith and Cunningham felt a lurching motion. They went to the door of the hut and turned on their flashlights. A black scar now passed within 15 feet of their hut. Further inspection revealed a new four-inch crack that ran halfway across the camp floe before disappearing in a series of hair-line fractures.

The evening hours of November 3 brought the return of heavy ice movement between the camp and runway floes. "Standing at the edge of the camp floe," Smith noted, "one could hear the soft rumbling and feel vibrations, occasionally punctuated by sharp cracks, grinding and crashes as large pieces were forced up, broke and tumbled." The next morning Smith again made the hazardous trip to the runway floe to inspect for damage. The shorter portion of the strip had broken into four pieces. The longer section, however, remained intact. "Luck was with us," Smith sighed.

The C-123s, as Smith had feared, were delayed in Greenland by weather and mechanical problems. As the ice movement continued, the apprehension on Alpha increased. Small pieces of ice broke away from the camp floe on November 5. The next morning the barometer took a downward turn. As the day wore on (day being a figurative term, as the station was in continual darkness), the wind switched from south to north-northwest. This was a familiar pattern: A major storm could be expected within twenty-four hours.

Just as the station's personnel were finishing their evening meal, a welcome message arrived. A C-123 had left Thule and would arrive at Alpha within three hours. It would be able to carry out personnel only. "The sense of relief that flowed through the group," Smith observed, "was a tangible thing."

The men promptly began to make their way to the runway floe, carrying only the scientific data that had been accumulated over the past month. They had no sooner completed the difficult and time-consuming trip when Smith spotted the red and green navigational lights of the C-123 and an accompanying C-54. As he made contact with the aircraft on his hand-held emergency radio, Sergeant Boger deployed a flare-lighting team along each side of the runway. Smith knew that Boger had flares for only twenty minutes of illumination. Once the flares were lit, the aircraft would have to land within that time frame.

Smith advised Capt. Joe B. Sullivan, pilot of the C-123, that he should make his approach over the lights of the camp (which had been left on), then land on his wheels rather than his skis. The three inches of snow covering the short runway should not be a problem, and he would be able to use his brakes in addition to reversing his propellers.

Sullivan called for the flares to be lit as he made his initial approach. As the red magnesium lights sputtered to life on each side of the runway, Sullivan lined up on the strip and turned on his landing lights. He came in, touched down, then applied full power and lifted off. Satisfied that the surface of the ice floe would support the aircraft, Sullivan came around for his landing approach.

"Once more we watched in silent fascination as the great white eyes settled toward the flares," Smith reported. "Crunch! The landing lights remained on! The engines roared, but this time the propellers were in reverse pitch to slow the plane. It stopped short of the end of the runway, completely hidden in a cloud of snow thrown up by the reversed propellers." Sullivan had made his first landing on ice in total darkness. It had been "sort of hairy," he noted.

The C-123 taxied to the end of the runway and turned around. Smith counted "nineteen dark forms" as they hastened aboard, "carrying small bundles and packages of treasured data." Smith then entered the aircraft and called the roll. He accounted for each person by sight—"Later would not be the time to discover that someone was absent"—then gave Sullivan a thumbs up.

"The big piston engines and the small jet engines in the wing-tip pods screamed at full power," Smith noted. "The plane lurched heavily as the brakes were released. We were rolling! The cargo deck canted— the nose went up—we were in the air!" Sullivan later received the Distinguished Flying Cross for his superb airmanship.

✳

The abandonment of Alpha created a major problem for ONR. Anxious to expand its Arctic research activities to drifting stations, ONR had arranged to take over responsibility for the scientific programs on Alpha at the end of the IGY on December 31, 1958. Whether or not the Department of Defense would agree to provide emergency funds to establish a new drifting station remained to be seen. Nonetheless, the dramatic voyage of the nuclear-powered submarine USS *Nautilus* (SSN 571) to the North Pole on August 31, 1958, gave new impetus to the Navy's growing interest in the far north as a strategic area for undersea operations.

The Schmidt Polar Expedition in front of ANT-6 N-170 en route to Rudolf Island, March 25, 1937: pilot Mikhail Vodopyanov, Dr. Otto Schmidt, copilot M. S. Babushkin. *(Boris Vdovienko / R. E. G. Davies)*

A. Volkov (navigator), K. Kekushev (mechanic), Pavel Golovin (pilot), and V. Terentiev (mechanic) in front of the ANT-7 twin-engine reconnaissance aircraft that flew over the North Pole on May 5, 1937, the first such flight by a Soviet aircraft. *(Boris Vdovienko / R. E. G. Davies)*

An ANT-7 of the Soviet Arctic Air Service, c. 1937. *(Boris Vdovienko / R. E. G. Davies)*

Project ICICLE's first landing on T-3, March 19, 1952. T-3, a large ice island near the North Pole, became the first U.S. ice station to be maintained and occupied for any length of time. *(U.S. Air Force)*

The headquarters hut at T-3, April 1952. *(U.S. Air Force)*

Clearing snow for take-off of C-54 on T-3, 1952. *(U.S. Air Force)*

Members of Project ICICLE pose for a photograph at the North Pole, May 3, 1952: (standing) A/1C Robert L. Wishard, M/Sgt Edison T. Blair, Fritz Ahl, Albert Crary, Lt. Col. Benedict, S/Sgt Harold Turner; (kneeling) Robert Cotell, 1/Lt. Herbert Thompson, Lt. Col. Fletcher (in sweater). *(U.S. Air Force)*

Inventor Robert E. Fulton, Jr., demonstrates the principle of the anchoring method used by his Skyhook, a mechanical device that, when attached to the front of an airplane, can be used to retrieve objects and personnel from the ground via a nylon line held aloft by a balloon. *(John D. Wall)*

Fulton's Stinson, on which he first tested the Skyhook, and a P2V during extensive Skyhook tests at El Centro, California, in October 1954. *(Robert E. Fulton, Jr.)*

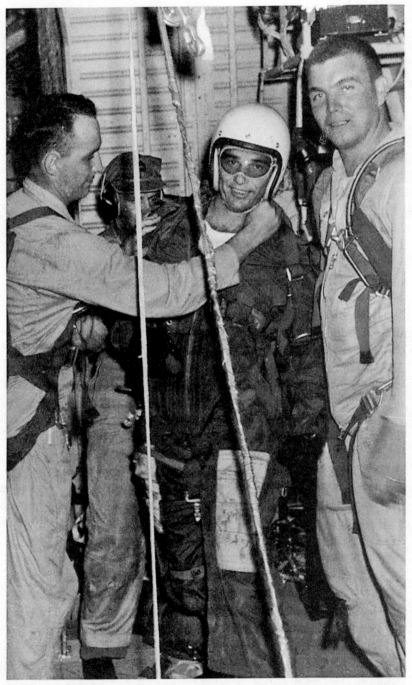

Sgt. Levi Woods (in helmet) on P2V after first human Skyhook pickup, August 12, 1958. *(Robert E. Fulton, Jr.)*

The IGY Byrd Station Traverse Party upon returning to Byrd Station, Antarctica, February 1958: William Long, Lt. (jg) Leonard LeSchack, Dr. Charles Bentley (seated), Vernon Anderson, Jack Long, and Ned Ostenso. The party traveled 1,200 miles in ninety-six days while taking seismographic readings and conducting ice studies as part of an ongoing project to determine the nature of the Antarctic land mass.

(BELOW) LeSchack poses in front of Tucker Sno-Cat. (Note Rensselaer Polytechnic Institute banner.) Byrd Station, 1958.

Dr. Waldo K. Lyon (left), a pioneer of undersea Arctic exploration, and Cdr. William R. Anderson on board the USS *Nautilus* (SSN 571) during the submarine's historic submerged trip to the North Pole, August 1958.

The USS *Skate* (SSN 578) at the North Pole on March 17, 1959. The *Skate* was the first submarine to surface at the Pole. *(U.S. Navy)*

Capt. James F. Smith (USAF) and Max C. Brewer unfurl the U.S. flag after landing on the ice floe that would support Drifting Station Charlie from April 13, 1959, until January 15, 1960, when it was abandoned following a series of destructive storms. Charlie represented the most ambitious attempt by the U.S. to establish a durable drifting station for the purpose of conducting research in micrometeorology, oceanography, sea-ice structure, navigation, and geophysics. *(James F. Smith)*

C-123 lands at Drifting Station Charlie, April 25, 1959. *(James F. Smith)*

Assembling Jamesway huts on Drifting Station Charlie, April 1959. (*James F. Smith*)

C-124 unloads road grader at Drifting Station Charlie, May 1959. (*James F. Smith*)

Soviet Ilyushin Il-14D unloading supplies at Soviet drifting station North Pole 9 (NP9), April 1960. *(Boris Vdovienko / R. E. G. Davies)*

LeSchack being brought on board P2V following his first Skyhook pickup, October 13, 1961. *(U.S. Navy)*

3

ONR in the Arctic

World War II marked the growth of an extraordinarily fruitful partnership between the academic community and the military services. Working together, scientists and military personnel produced technologically sophisticated weapons that made a significant contribution to the Allied victory. In May 1945, as the fighting in the Pacific reached a crescendo of violence, Secretary of the Navy James Forestal took steps to ensure that this relationship would continue in the postwar years. By executive order, Forestal established the Office of Research and Inventions under Vice Adm. Harold G. Bowen. A dynamic leader and savvy bureaucrat, Bowen recognized the need for a more permanent foundation for the office. As he put it, "In Washington, one cannot accomplish anything without a statute in front of him and an appropriation behind him." Thanks in large part to Bowen's lobbying efforts, Congress in August 1946 enacted legislation that created the Office of Naval Research.[1]

In the years immediately following World War II, as one historian of the Office has pointed out, ONR became "the principal federal agency supporting scientific research."[2] From the beginning, ONR demonstrated an interest in the Arctic, with Lt. Comdr. M. C. Shelesnyak taking the lead in advocating the development of research programs in the far north. In February 1947 Shelesnyak flew to Barrow, Alaska, to investigate the possibility of setting up a research laboratory within the main supply camp of the Navy's Petroleum

Reserve Number Four. His recommendation led, in August 1947, to the formation of the Arctic Research Laboratory (ARL).[3]

The mission of ARL, as defined by ONR, was "to conduct fundamental research related to Arctic phenomena." The laboratory served as the home for civilian scientists under contract to ONR who developed a broad range of programs to learn more about the nature of the far north. Initially, research centered on earth sciences and biological sciences. In 1949, however, ARL's Committee on Oceanography recommended that an "airborne arctic expedition" be organized to study "the area from Point Barrow to the North Pole."[4]

In spring 1949 John F. Holmes and L. V. Worthington of the Woods Hole Oceanographic Institute, acting in conjunction with the U.S. Navy Hydrographic Office, visited ARL to explore the possibility of conducting oceanographic research on the pack ice north of Point Barrow. The following year, as noted in Chapter 1, they attempted to establish a research station on an ice floe 135 miles north of Barter Island with the assistance of the 10th Rescue Squadron but had to abandon the project when the C-47 carrying the scientific party damaged its landing gear.

Although the operation in 1950 had been a failure from a scientific point of view, Rear Adm. T. A. Solberg, Chief of Naval Research, was encouraged about the possibility of using aircraft for Arctic research. In September 1950 he sent a request to the Chief of Naval Operations, asking that a suitably modified R4D (the Navy's designation for the C-47) be assigned to ONR's oceanographic program in the Arctic. "There is a distinct possibility," he pointed out, "that within the next few years the Navy may have a requirement for operating submarines or surface ships in the Arctic Ocean. At the present time there is almost no information known about the Arctic Basin. Even such simple things as the depth of the ocean, composition of the ice cover, and the general current pattern are unknown." Solberg's request met a sympathetic response, and ONR secured the aircraft.[5]

In February and March 1951 ONR conducted Project SKIJUMP I. The R4D, fitted with skis and modified for cold weather operations, made twelve landings on the pack ice between one hundred and four hundred miles off the north coast of Alaska. Scientists Holmes and Worthington, now under contract to ONR, spent brief periods on the ice, collecting information on the depth, temperature, salinity, and density of the Arctic Ocean.[6]

Lt. Comdr. Edward M. Ward, pilot of the R4D, judged the operation to be an unqualified success. "Arctic ice," he reported to his superiors, "forms a carrier deck from Point Barrow to the North Pole." He recommended that ONR establish a chain of oceanographic stations on the ice, stretching from the Alaskan coast to the interior of the polar basin.[7]

SKIJUMP I had gone so well that ONR planned an even more elaborate SKIJUMP II for 1952. The Navy added two P2V patrol aircraft to the project in order to extend the range of the research activities. Five hydrographic stations were established on the ice during March. On March 26 the R4D and a P2V landed on an ice floe at 82°22′ N, 145°20′ W—the farthest north attained during the operation. The P2V, as planned, refueled the R4D and returned to Barrow. The oceanographers set up their equipment and went to work. The next morning, while attempting to take off, the port landing gear of the R4D collapsed. The aircraft had to be abandoned, and the scientists were removed from the floe by a P2V.[8]

Although the oceanographers had secured valuable data on the nature of the Arctic Ocean, ONR's interest in hydrographic stations soon waned. Over the next three years, while the Soviets were greatly expanding their research activities in the far north, the Air Force drifting station on T-3 became the sole American research facility in the polar basin. Before the end of the 1950s, however, the advent of nuclear-powered submarines would prompt renewed naval concern with the Arctic.

While the Air Force viewed the polar region as a vital theater for aerial operations in the event of a conflict with the Soviet Union, the interest of the Navy in the area was less clear. During World War II the Arctic Ocean had seen a limited number of submarine operations as German U-boats attempted to disrupt the Soviet's Northern Sea Route. At the height of the German submarine campaign in 1944, U-boats operating in the Kara Sea sank two steamers, a destroyer, and four smaller vessels. Although the Germans remained primarily in the open seas, Soviet counteraction occasionally drove the U-boats under the pack ice for brief periods.[9]

It was largely through the efforts of Dr. Waldo K. Lyon of the Navy Electronics Laboratory (NEL) at San Diego that the United States held Arctic submarine trials in 1947 and 1948. Lyon had worked with a Canadian oceanographic group during World War II, conducting experiments in cold-water acoustics in the Pacific Northwest. When a large-scale operation in the Antarctic, known as HIGH JUMP, took place in 1946–47, Lyon headed the NEL contingent on board the submarine *Sennet* (SS 408). Until that point, he later recalled, "I'd never seen a piece of ice on the sea." Lyon saw a great deal of ice during the five months that he spent on *Sennet*. The submarine, which remained on the surface while in the ice pack, demonstrated that it could tolerate the battering of broken ice. No effort was made, however, to go under the ice.[10]

Lyon returned to NEL intrigued with the problem of operating submarines beneath the ice pack. He knew that USS *Atule* (SS 403) had attempted to go under the ice in Baffin Bay in the summer of 1946 but had come out after striking its periscope on a submerged pinnacle of ice. Believing that the problem should be approached through the combined efforts and equipment of scientists and the submarine operators, he approached Capt. Rawson Bennett, head of NEL, with a plan to use a submarine for under-ice experiments. Bennett gave the proposal his enthusiastic support. Fortunately, Vice Adm. A. R. McCann, commander of submarines in the Pacific (ComSubPac), had a long-standing interest in the Arctic and agreed to assign USS *Boarfish* (SS 327) to the project.

In August 1947 *Boarfish*, with Lyon on board, headed for the pack ice of the Chukchi Sea. Lyon had equipped *Boarfish* with QLA scanning sonar, developed during World War II to enable submarines to penetrate minefields. The QLA displayed objects in the submarine's path as bright spots on a screen, similar to the display on a radar scope. *Boarfish* also carried an upward-looking echo sounder to register the distance to the underside of the ice cover.

With Lyon interpreting the readings of the upward-looking echo sounder from his position in the forward torpedo room, and his colleague, Art Roshon, in the conning tower doing the same with the QLA sonar, *Boarfish* cautiously crept under the ice. The submarine penetrated some five miles inside the ice pack, then returned to open water. Two additional dives took *Boarfish* further under the ice, with the longest test covering about twelve miles.

Encouraged by the results, and with Admiral McCann still in ComSubPac, Lyon scheduled a second trial for September 1948. USS *Carp* (SS 338), operating in the same area as *Boarfish*, traveled under the ice for a distance of fifty-four miles. It also surfaced inside the ice field in open water areas, known as polynyas, to recharge its batteries.

In his final report on the trials, Lyon concluded: "The reality of a polar submarine that could navigate the *entire* Arctic Ocean is not only admissible but may be an immediate practicality." The official Navy position, however, was not as sanguine. The *Navy Arctic Operations Handbook,* published in 1949, noted the experiments with *Boarfish* and *Carp* and observed that extended under-ice navigation was practical with an efficient echo sounder and scanning sonar. Nonetheless, it reached a different conclusion than had Lyon. "Development of the trans-Arctic submarine," the *Handbook* announced, "remains in the realm of fantasy."[11]

Lyon took the *Handbook*'s conclusion as a personal challenge. He recognized the obstacles that had to be overcome before extended submarine operations could become a reality. For example, little was known about the bottom of the Arctic Ocean beyond the Chukchi Sea; submarines did not dare go east of Point Barrow. Also, there was much to learn about the nature of the ice cover. "We had to know its properties," he pointed out, "its chemistry, and particularly acoustically, which no one had done—what sort of reflector it was, how did it scatter sound, how did it change with temperature and pressure when it is underwater in the sea, and so forth." Despite the enormity of the task that lay ahead, Lyon was confident that a partnership between scientists and naval officers ultimately would bring success.[12]

With the support of his superiors at NEL, Lyon put together a small group of scientists who spent the next six years collecting information about the Arctic. Working mainly with icebreakers that operated in the far north each summer and cooperating with Canadian scientists, Lyon's team accumulated large quantities of data that would be helpful for under-ice operations. A major problem, however, was the lack of a military requirement for pushing the project. "This was just people interested in doing these things," he noted, "because there was no thought at the time of military operations in Arctic areas."[13]

Funding for the project, always a problem, nearly ended in 1956 when the Bureau of Ships directed NEL to stop its Arctic work. Lyon's superiors at NEL disagreed with the decision and "lost" the order for six months. By the time the order had been "found," the prospects for Arctic operations by the new nuclear-powered submarines had rendered it moot.[14]

Until 1957 endurance and navigation were the two greatest limitations for submarines operating under the polar ice. The diesel-electric submarine could remain submerged on battery power for only thirty hours at a speed of three knots. Also, the accuracy of even the best gyroscopic compass deteriorated over time. Nuclear propulsion solved the first problem; inertial navigation systems resolved the second.

The two technological innovations came together with the voyage of USS *Nautilus* in 1958. During the previous year the first nuclear-powered submarine had penetrated within 180 miles of the North Pole, navigating under the ice with a Sperry MK19 gyrocompass. When the gyrocompass lost power, however, *Nautilus* was forced to turn around. In preparation for a second under-ice voyage, the Autonetics Division of the North American Aviation Corporation installed in *Nautilus* their N6A inertial navigation system, a modified version of a system being used by the Air Force. At the same time, Lyon supervised the placement of new and more sensitive sonar instruments on the submarine.[15]

On August 1, 1958, *Nautilus* dived beneath the ice pack north of Point Franklin, Alaska. Sixty-three hours and over one thousand miles later, on August 3 at 11:15 P.M., the submarine—with Lyon on board—reached the North Pole. As historian Michael T. Isenberg has observed: "*Nautilus* had done more than prove her technology; she was changing the world."[16]

Nine days later, USS *Skate* (SSN 578), the lead boat of the first nuclear submarine class, also reached the North Pole. With a hardened sail, inertial navigation system, forward scanning sonar, and downward- and upward-looking precision sonars, *Skate* developed techniques for surfacing in the ice pack.[17]

The years 1958–60, Lyon recalled, represented a "golden age" for Arctic submarines. In March 1959 *Skate* returned to the Arctic and demonstrated that submarines could operate in the polar basin in winter as well as summer. During this voyage, on March 17, *Skate* became the first ship in history to surface at the geographic North Pole. The following February USS *Sargo* (SSN 583) conducted extensive tests in the far north, employing a new forward-looking, narrow-beam sonar system, somewhat similar to the wartime QLA. The voyage of USS *Seadragon* (SSN 584) in August and September 1960, traveling from Portsmouth, New Hampshire, to Pearl Harbor under the ice via the Northwest Passage, marked the end of an era of experimentation. By this time submarines had operated under the ice in shallow water, learned how to detect and avoid icebergs and the deep-draft keels of pressure ridges, could identify polynyas and break through ice cover, and had collected extensive bathymetric data on the entire Arctic basin.[18]

The trans-Arctic submarine had been transformed from fantasy to reality, thanks in large measure to Lyon's persistence. In August 1962, while Lyon was on board *Skate*, President John F. Kennedy announced that the determined scientist had been awarded the prestigious Presidential Medal for his pioneering development of the knowledge, techniques, and instruments that had made possible submarine operations under the ice pack.[19]

❋

As it happened, the Navy's renewed interest in gathering scientific data about the polar basin with the advent of the nuclear-powered submarine in the mid-1950s coincided with the appearance of two scientists at ONR and ARL who also wanted to expand naval research activities in the far north. Dr. Maxwell E. Britton, a plant ecologist at Northwestern University who had worked at ARL under an ONR contract in the early 1950s, joined ONR in 1955. Recruited by Dr. Louis O. Quam, head of the Geography Branch of the Earth Sciences Division, Britton initially served as scientific officer for Arctic research. When Quam moved up to head the Earth Sciences Division, he named Britton as director of Arctic research.[20]

Ever since he arrived at ONR, Britton had lobbied Quam to appoint a new full-time director for ARL. When Quam agreed, Britton proposed Max C. Brewer for the position. Britton believed that Brewer, who had been at Barrow in charge of the Geological Survey's Arctic Ice and Permafrost project, would be ideal for the post. A talented scientist-administrator, Brewer accepted the job in September 1956. As noted in the official history of ARL, Brewer's appointment marked the beginning of "a new era" for the laboratory.[21]

Both Britton and Brewer were anxious to expand ONR's Arctic research program into the polar basin after the end of the IGY in 1958. They agreed that the maintenance of elaborate drifting stations, with permanent airstrips that could accommodate large aircraft, was both too expensive and unnecessary. Instead, they advocated the use of more spartan stations that could be established and resupplied by light aircraft landing on unprepared strips, similar to what had been done during Project SKIJUMP in 1951–52. The loss of Station Alpha in November 1958 gave Britton and Brewer an opportunity to promote their idea for a new drifting station.[22]

As the abandonment of Alpha threatened to curtail severely the Navy's research program on the ice pack, Dr. Quam sought emergency funds to establish a new drifting station. In early January 1959, following extensive negotiations between the Navy and the Air Force, Assistant Secretary of the Navy Garrison Norton asked the Department of Defense for $750,000 to continue the research program in the Arctic. Britton then attempted to convince Quam "to keep the funds within the arctic program and try a new and less expensive approach to establishing research stations." Quam, Britton recalled, "appreciated the merit of my arguments but felt it would be offensive to a sister military department to go it alone at this point."[23]

Quam flew to Alaska late in February to discuss support for the proposed ice station with the Alaskan Air Command. Maj. H. M. Brittenham, who was placed in charge of the project, had developed a logistical plan that would cost $933,000. Quam was appalled! As $250,000 of the emergency funds would be needed to replace the scientific instruments and equipment lost on Alpha, only $500,000 would be available for logistical support. Brittenham went back to the drawing board and came up with a scaled-down version of his original plan that fell within ONR's fiscal guidelines.[24]

Capt. James Smith, who had served less than two months of his scheduled six-month tour on Alpha, volunteered to command the new station. In late March, P2V patrol aircraft from Kodiak Naval Air Station searched for suitable floes on which to establish Drifting Station Charlie (initially called Alpha Two). Based on their information, Smith and Brewer decided to inspect a floe at 75°02′ N, 158°30′ W. On April 13, 1959, they left Barrow on two Cessna 180s, single-engine light planes that were assigned to the ARL. Piloted by Robert Fischer and Robert Main, the aircraft landed on a recently frozen lead about one mile from the selected floe. Smith and Brewer determined that the lead was thick enough to support the landing of a C-47. After an accompanying C-47 dropped gasoline for the Cessnas, the group refueled and returned to Point Barrow.[25]

The following day the two Cessnas and a C-47 landed on the frozen lead at noon and dropped off Smith and a construction party of fourteen men. An hour and a half later, two C-124 Globemasters from the 62nd Troop Carrier Wing at Larson AFB, Washington, air-dropped supplies and equipment, including two M-29 weasels. By the end of the first day, despite the cold and wind, Smith's men had set up a sixteen-by-sixteen-foot shelter, started a generator, and established radio contact with the Eleventh Air Division.

High winds and blowing snow prevented the scheduled airdrops on April 15. Smith, after scouting the five-by-seven-mile floe, decided to move the camp nearer to the center of the floe, closer to the proposed runway. Two C-124s arrived overhead the next day and dropped additional construction equipment, including a D-4 Caterpillar tractor. Still not satisfied with the location of the runway, Smith again moved the camp to a new site.

Airdrops continued during the next four days. By April 21, thanks to fourteen- and sixteen-hour days, the construction crew had managed to erect three Jamesway huts and carve out a 2,500-by-100-foot runway. Four days later, a C-123 became the first aircraft to land on Charlie, as this new station was named.

On April 29, with the runway now extended to four thousand feet, a C-54 landed with Maj. Gen. Conrad F. Necrason, commander of the Alaskan Air Command. Necrason spent an hour and forty-five minutes inspecting the floe. He told Smith that he was satisfied with the progress to date, then conducted a brief ceremony officially establishing the station. "The General's visit," Smith wrote in the station log, "did a great deal for troop morale."[26]

By mid-May Smith's men had enlarged the runway to 5,400 by 200 feet. The huge C-124s could now land on the floe, bringing in supplies, scientific equipment, and the researchers who would work at Charlie over the summer. As the temperatures rose, the runway began to deteriorate. Early June brought days of above-freezing temperatures and constant problems for the men who were trying to maintain the runway. On June 16, with the runway reported "wet and soggy," a C-123 landed and took off under increasingly hazardous conditions. Smith had no choice but to close the runway. "Guess at 60 days for the next aircraft to land," he wrote in the station log on June 22, when the temperature reached 37°. His prediction would prove overly optimistic.

Now dependent upon airdrops for mail and supplies, the station settled into a summer routine as the scientists began their work. One research program, conducted by personnel from the U.S. Weather Bureau, involved the operation of a standard weather observing station, including radiosonde for winds aloft data. The University of Washington was responsible for a second program of ONR-funded research, with scientists working in micrometeorology, oceanography, sea-ice structure, and navigation. In addition, scientists from Columbia University's Lamont Geological Laboratory conducted research in geophysics under the program funded jointly by ONR and the Air Force Geophysical Research Directorate, while the U.S. Navy Hydrographic Office carried out studies on the local movement and changes in the pack ice.[27]

The U.S. Navy Underwater Sound Laboratory brought seventeen tons of equipment to Charlie for their research. Scientists Edward G. Democh and Elton P. Kelley established a station some one thousand feet south of the main camp site, away from the normal noises of the base, where they worked with researchers on Bravo/T-3 on problems of underwater sound. They also employed aircraft that dropped depth charges at various locations from Charlie, enabling them to study sound propagation paths of varying lengths in both shallow and deep waters.[28]

While the scientists did their research, Smith saw to the efficient operation of the base. His main problem involved moving structures from their pedestals of ice, a condition created when the exposed areas around the buildings melted in the sun while the ice directly under the huts remained frozen. On July 31 Smith made a lengthy entry in the station log that well described the activity on Charlie during the summer months.

> Normal operations. Levelling structures. Relocation of remaining structures will be accomplished at rate of one or two per day until completed. Work schedule throughout this month held to eight hour day, six days per week, with odds-and-ends type activities Sundays and holidays. Usually have pizza-pie and whatever anyone has to contribute for drinks on Saturday evenings following movie. Barbecued ribs and chicken outside twice. 'Normal operations' repeated so frequently [in log] includes 16 hours per day for food service, 24-hour power production, communications. Otherwise, servicing equipment, continual levelling or movement of structures, guying antennas, stacking and restacking outside storage, water procurement, fueling shelters, repainting runway markers, trash disposal, etc. Vehicle operation has been restricted to the immediate camp area. Movement any distance is exceedingly difficult and somewhat dangerous due to melt ponds. Movement on foot is far easier. Only trash disposal runs are being made away from camp. To date, some relatively minor personal frictions have manifested themselves. Nothing of particular note. Essentially an unusually well adjusted group of 28, mature and tolerant. Exceptions exist, both civilian and military.

The men on Charlie experienced their first sunset on August 23, as the sun dipped briefly below the horizon. Smith had hoped that the runway would return to operation by the end of the month, but continuing warm temperatures left the landing strip unusable. A botched airdrop five days later contributed to the plunging morale of the station's personnel. Parachutes on two of six bundles dropped by a C-124 failed to deploy due to faulty rigging. One bundle contained the men's Post Exchange orders. "Wound up as powdered cigars, cigarettes, pipe tobacco, soaked in aftershave lotions," Smith lamented. "Disappointing, since quite a few personnel are now out of tobacco."

By early September Smith was noting that the shortage of "creature comforts" was causing "'bitching,' irritability, etc., with some personnel." News of the death of Father Cunningham, victim of a heart attack on September 3, came as "a shock to most of us who knew him well. He'll be missed." Smith ordered the station's flag to be flown at half-mast for Cunningham's funeral.

"Morale of individuals is fluctuating somewhat from day to day, and from hour to hour, in some instances," Smith wrote on September 8. "This applies to military and civilian alike. Apparently hinges on emergency runway capability, along with tobacco and other shortages, plus the fact that a number of the civilian members have commitments for teaching, etc, which they will not be able to meet on time."

Work on the runway continued to frustrate Smith. The temperature remained above freezing, with melt ponds on the runway that were too large to fill in by hand and could not support heavy equipment. Adding to his problems was an infestation of polar bears. Dangerous animals with no fear of humans, the impressive creatures had to be shot to ensure the safety of the station's personnel. On September 12 a polar bear over six feet tall and weighing in excess of three hundred pounds was killed close to the camp. A second and larger bear had to be destroyed the following day. Two more bears were shot near the Undersea Sound Laboratory hut on September 16.

As the days grew shorter, the temperature began to drop at long last. On September 20 Smith reported that the sun was now below the horizon for ten hours each day and the temperature had reached 10°. Work on the runway accelerated. By September 30 a usable strip measuring six thousand by two hundred feet had been prepared. Two days later, on October 2, a C-54 landed on Charlie, the first aircraft to touch down in 109 days. To the relief of everyone, personnel could now rotate in and out of the station.

Smith remained on Charlie until October 21, 1959, when he was replaced by Capt. Arthur H. Schroeder. Smith returned to Ladd AFB and took over Schroeder's responsibility as logistics officer for Charlie and Bravo/T-3.

Scientific work resumed on Charlie as the periods of daylight grew shorter. By the end of October there remained only brief periods of twilight in the early afternoon as the sun remained below the horizon. Temperatures plunged in the growing darkness, reaching –45° in December. Frostbite was now a constant danger. Diesel equipment was hard to start as engine oil assumed "the consistency of chewing gum."[29]

In mid-December the first of two violent storms swept over Charlie, now located four hundred miles northwest of Point Barrow. On January 6, 1960, following the second storm, Schroeder and chief scientist Kenneth O. Bennington surveyed the damage caused by the weather. A vast pressure ridge had formed about one mile north of the camp. Shatter ice lay to the east, with deep cracks and faults. There were new leads to the south and west. The floe had been reduced to one-quarter of its original size. Ominously for the camp's future, a three-inch crack had appeared across the runway.

Given the extent of the damage to the floe, Schroeder informed the Eleventh Air Division, the loss of another piece of ice could make the difference between the withdrawal of all personnel and equipment and the emergency evacuation of personnel only.

Schroeder's message caused consternation at Ladd AFB. "Not only was there real danger that the whole effort of drifting station research would be scrubbed, because of the short duration of both ALPHA and CHARLIE," observed Dr. Quam of ONR, "but also the Navy had planned an extensive and significant research exercise to be conducted between the drifting station CHARLIE and the nuclear submarine SARGO, scheduled for Arctic maneuvers in February 1960."[30]

Dr. Britton, who had rushed to Alaska in an effort to prevent the station from being abandoned, argued strongly against complete withdrawal. Smith even volunteered to return to the station with a small staff and keep the generators and navigational aids in operation so that Charlie could be reoccupied for the underwater sound experiments with *Sargo*. The Alaskan Air Command agreed to this proposal, but only if the Navy would take responsibility for evacuating personnel by submarine if further breakups took place. The Navy hesitated: *Sargo* might not be able to transit the Bering Strait. In the end the Navy told the Alaskan Air Command to proceed with the evacuation

of Charlie. (*Sargo* did reach the North Pole in February and conducted experiments with Bravo/T-3, a less satisfactory exercise due to
T-3's location in shallow water near the Alaskan shoreline.)[31]

On January 8, 1960, two C-130s landed at Charlie to begin the
removal of all supplies, equipment, and personnel. Two days later
another crack developed in the runway, reducing its usable length to
3,500 feet. The C-130s still had sufficient runway for their operations,
but not by much. "The planned withdrawal of equipment continues
in an orderly and efficient manner," Schroeder noted in the station
log. "All material of value will be saved."

The end came on January 15, when Capt. William A. Culling
brought out Schroeder, Smith (who had flown out to the station to
take a last look around), S/Sgt. Theodore Narasaki, and A/1C Gary
Stanfill. Before departing, the four men and the crew of the C-130
stood at attention as the wind-tattered station flag was lowered for the
last time. (It was presented to General Austin at the Eleventh Air
Division.) There remained on Charlie only two Jamesway huts, left
behind for use in emergency, and the barren flagpole.[32]

✳

Shortly after Charlie was abandoned, Britton and Brewer sat in a
restaurant in Fairbanks and mulled over the possibilities of setting up
a replacement station. They were convinced, Brewer recalled, that a
new station would have to be "austere and temporary." On the back
of a table place mat, they drew up a design for a drifting station that
would not be tied to prepared runways and large aircraft. Capable of
supporting eight scientists and four support personnel, it would con-
sist of eight 12-by-16-by-8-foot prefabricated buildings, each heated
by a 30,000-BTU oil stove. The buildings, they estimated, would cost
approximately $1,500 each and would weigh two thousand pounds.
The pieces, which could be manufactured at ARL, could be trans-
ported to the campsite by a twin-engine aircraft that was capable of
landing on unprepared strips.[33]

Britton returned to Washington, D.C., and began a campaign to
sell the idea to his superiors. Dr. Quam immediately endorsed it, but
Rear Adm. Rawson Bennett, Chief of Naval Research, was less enthusiastic. Bennett wanted assurance on three items: First, the station
should not require additional funding. Second, the operation had to
be safe; it should not embarrass the Navy or place a burden on

search-and-rescue forces in the Arctic. Finally, Bennett did not want a negative reaction from Alaskan Air Command, which had taken the lead in establishing and operating drifting stations. After Britton satisfied his concerns, Bennett agreed to the plan.

"Administrative approval is one thing," Britton noted, "how to do the job another." He had been arguing for some time that ARL needed twin-engine aircraft to support their programs in the Arctic, but without success. Now, the use of a twin-engine aircraft was essential for the new drifting station. At Brewer's suggestion, they telephoned Sigurd Wien of Wien Alaska Airlines for assistance. Wien said that he would check with his chief pilot and call back. A half hour later, Wien responded: "Nothing to it."

Preparations for the establishment of what later was designated Arctic Research Laboratory Ice Station I (ARLIS I) took place at Barrow from February through April 1960. In early May one of ARL's Cessna 180s made a reconnaissance flight, searching for a suitable floe. Problems soon arose, however, that threatened to end the project. At the last minute, Wien informed Brewer that he was running into insurance difficulties for the twin-engine aircraft. After a series of delays, the insurance company came up with a figure that both he and Brewer considered exorbitant. By mutual consent, the charter was terminated.

Although disappointed, Britton soon hit upon an alternative. Instead of using an aircraft to establish ARLIS I, he secured approval to employ the icebreaker USS *Burton Island* (AGB 1), which could accomplish the task as part of its normal duties. Although this would mean that the station would be farther south than planned, Britton had no choice in the matter.

On September 3, 1960, *Burton Island* departed Barrow with sixty-five tons of prefabricated buildings, fuel, generators, a weasel, supplies, and station personnel. Capt. Griffith C. Evans found the pack ice unusually heavy to the north. After calling in a P2V from the patrol squadron at Kodiak Naval Air Station to fly a reconnaissance mission, he proceeded eastward along the Alaska coast toward Barter Island. About eighty miles west of Banks Island he turned north, then penetrated the ice pack westward from McClure Strait. On September 10, after traveling 210 miles into the pack, he stopped at 75°10′ N, 136° W. With the assistance of the ship's crew, the camp for ARLIS I was set up in forty hours.[34]

Brewer planned to use ARL's Cessnas to support the camp through-out the winter. Before this operation began, however, ARL obtained a large aircraft. The University of Alaska had been given a twin-engine Lockheed Lodestar, a wartime patrol bomber that had been refurbished, as an executive aircraft. ONR paid for the extensive overhaul of the Lodestar, in return for its full use. Although the aircraft was not capable of landing on the ice, it could be employed for airdrops. On November 21 the Lodestar dropped 3,200 pounds of supplies on ARLIS I. Two additional drops were made before the end of the month.

The Cessna operation also began in late November. For the first time, single-engine aircraft made night landings on ice floes. As chief pilot Robert J. Fischer pointed out, the two aircraft that flew between Barrow and ARLIS I played "a vital role" in supporting the station. Over the next four months, the Cessnas made 26 landings on the ice, bringing in 15,600 pounds of cargo. This amounted to 85 percent of all supplies received by ARLIS I.[35]

The scientific team on ARLIS I, headed by Dr. Kenneth Bennington, began their studies on September 15. The researchers worked through the Arctic winter, gathering their data for studies in meteorology, geo-physics, oceanography, marine biology, and ice physics.

As the station drifted in a westerly direction, Brewer recognized that its scientific value was becoming limited. In March 1961 he decided to evacuate ARLIS I. Two Cessnas arrived on March 18 and began to shuttle supplies from the main camp to a frozen lead 1.5 miles distant. Over the next four days the light aircraft made 82 flights, moving 24,000 pounds of material. Brewer then employed a newly acquired R4D, assigned by the Navy to the University of Alaska for use by ARL, to move the men and material from the frozen lead to Barrow. It took six flights to accomplish the task. On March 25 the R4D and two Cessnas left ARLIS I for the last time.

Brewer was pleased with the results of the experiment. "A consid-erable number of good scientific data were accumulated," he noted, "and new applications of old concepts of drifting station operations tried in an attempt to develop methods of operating that would enable a continuation of Arctic drifting stations under the existing environment for United States research in the Arctic."[36]

Britton agreed. ARLIS I had been paid for out of ARL's normal budget with the exception of $10,000 to purchase generators. The total logistics cost to operate the station for nearly seven months had been only $75,000. "It is sufficient to say," Britton reported, "that from an administrative point of view it was demonstrated that drifting stations could be operated on a modest scale. . . ." He believed that "there was real hope for future stations and for improvements."[37]

Britton and Brewer promptly secured approval to establish a replacement station for ARLIS I. With the R4D, they now had the means to implement their original scheme. On May 8, 1961, Brewer briefed ARL's pilots on likely locations to search for suitable ice floes to support the new station. The Lockheed Lodestar and R4D took off the next day to investigate the area north of Point Barrow. Fog and poor visibility, however, hampered their efforts. The bad weather halted the search until May 22, when some promising floes were located in the area of 76°30′ N, 158°45′ W. Brewer decided to use one of these floes for the new station, ARLIS II.[38]

On May 23 a small ARL air armada departed from Barrow. Chief pilot Fischer, with Brewer on board, led the way in one Cessna, while pilot Robert Main and equipment foreman Kenneth Toovak, a Barrow native, flew in the other. Lloyd Zimmerman and Richard Burt piloted the R4D, which carried station leader John Beck, radio operator Otha Whitsett, sections for one prefabricated building, two stoves, two generators, and fuel.

About one hour north of Point Barrow, Fischer and Brewer noticed a discoloration in the ice pack and descended to take a closer look. After several passes over the area, it was clear that they had come across an ice island. Although the location—73°01′ N, 156°05′ W—was farther south than Brewer would have liked, he decided that the permanence and stability of an ice island far outweighed the problem of location. On the spot, he decided to establish ARLIS II on the ice island below.

After testing the surface with touch-and-go landings, Fischer set the Cessna down on the ice. A quick inspection confirmed that it would be suitable for the station. The second Cessna and R4D then came in. Over the next two weeks the R4D made 28 flights between Barrow and ARLIS II, delivering 156,300 pounds of supplies. The first prefabricated hut went up by the evening of May 24. In less than a week a six-man construction crew completed the remaining twelve buildings for the camp. The first scientific measurement took place on June 1, 1961.

Air operations continued until June 16, when melting made landings impossible. Over the next two months ARL's Lockheed Lodestar made four airdrops, bringing in additional supplies. The icebreaker

USS *Staten Island* (AGB 5) reached ARLIS II on August 18, delivering a D-4 tractor, two M-29 weasels, and 125 tons of material for the twelve scientists and four support staff on the ice island. The icebreaker returned on September 5 with an additional one hundred tons of supplies. Two weeks later, with the onset of colder temperatures, the R4D was able to land on the refrozen surface. By this time ARLIS II was located at 76°06′ N, 173° W and drifting northward.

✳

While the U.S. drifting station program continued after the end of the IGY due to the efforts of ONR, the Soviets had been conducting even more extensive research activities in the polar basin. Station NP6, established on an ice island in April 1956, recorded a record drift of 5,371 miles in 1,245 days before it was abandoned. NP7 did nearly as well, lasting from April 1957 to April 1959. The Soviets occupied NP8 in April 1959, followed by NP9 in April 1960. In addition, the High Latitude Aerial Expeditions continued, with greater reliance on placing automatic telemetry stations on the ice.[39]

Dr. J. W. Horton, technical director of the Navy Underwater Sound Laboratory, pointed out in 1959 that the Soviet Union had taken the leading role in Arctic research. "The Russians," he said at an antisubmarine warfare conference in August, "know a great deal about the vast and mysterious sea beneath the Polar ice. We know very little. It is one of the most important water areas of the world for submarine operations."[40]

With the advent of nuclear-powered submarines, Dr. Britton noted, ONR's Arctic research had become more "mission oriented." There was much greater emphasis, for example, on acoustics.[41] ONR assumed that Soviet research also reflected the realities of this new phase of the Cold War in the polar regions. Soviet submarines, equipped with cruise missiles, were operating in the Arctic Ocean. Also, there seemed little doubt that the Soviets were working on countermeasures to U.S. submarines. The extent of Soviet work, however, especially in acoustics, remained unknown. It was this lack of knowledge that attracted the attention of a young officer at ONR and would lead to Project COLDFEET.

4

LeSchack at ONR

Project COLDFEET, a bold and innovative scheme to investigate a hastily abandoned Soviet drifting station, sprang from the mind of Leonard A. LeSchack, a lieutenant (j.g.) in ONR during the summer of 1961. To a large extent, COLDFEET reflected LeSchack's personality and background. Indeed, it seems doubtful that the operation would have been attempted, much less have succeeded, without his particular combination of personal qualities and experience.

LeSchack was born in New York City on March 6, 1935. His father, David B. LeSchack, had emigrated from the Ukraine as a child and practiced law in Manhattan; his mother, Selma K. LeSchack, taught history in a public high school. LeSchack's father had wanted him to become a concert violinist. When he was five years old, his father presented him with a small violin that his uncle had made. Eight years of violin lessons followed. "Leonard," his father would say, "you will never become the life of the party if you do not learn to play the violin!" At age thirteen he gave up violin lessons, to his father's great regret. While he had never enjoyed the hours of practice, the experience left him with a lifelong love of violin music.

LeSchack spent his formative years growing up on Long Island, spending summers at the family cottage in Connecticut. As early as he could remember, the bedtime stories that his parents read to him included not only the usual children's literature but also tales from the *Book of Knowledge*. He especially enjoyed the stories of great scientists, inventors, and explorers. Not surprisingly, he became an inveterate daydreamer and fantasizer, imagining himself as the hero in all manner of adventures of derring-do.

In 1948 LeSchack entered Forest Hills High School in Queens, then one of the more prestigious secondary schools in the New York City system. He maintained a "B" average in his studies, enjoying the sciences more than the humanities. He developed a special interest in chemistry, especially explosives. And while his mother taught at a different high school, she made sure that his grades in history remained respectable by tutoring him from a common curriculum.

LeSchack's great love was amateur radio. His father studied radio theory, operation, and repair during the war years, and LeSchack became fascinated with all aspects of the marvelous technology. By the age of ten he had built his first shortwave set. He received his federal license at age fifteen after passing a difficult test (on his fifth try) that required mastery of Morse code. He went on the air as W2FBW and talked to people all over the world, an enjoyable exercise that built his self-confidence. The only problem came with the advent of television in his neighborhood. LeSchack's transmitter interfered with local TV signals, leading to numerous complaints.

It was a comfortable family environment, which later included two younger brothers (born in 1940 and 1946). Current events were often the subject of dinner table conversations. His mother, an Eleanor Roosevelt Democrat, had strong liberal views. Active in the League of Women Voters, she later gained prominence as an advocate for women's rights at the United Nations. LeSchack's father tended to share his wife's political sentiments, although he was inclined toward fiscal conservatism. Neither parent attempted to influence LeSchack in any particular direction, at least after his father became reconciled to his lack of interest in the violin.

Although he did not particularly enjoy high school, LeSchack always assumed that he would go on to college. He wanted to attend the Massachusetts Institute of Technology but was turned down for admission. Disappointed, he entered Rensselaer Polytechnic Institute (RPI) in Troy, New York, in September 1952. LeSchack started out as an electrical engineering major, a natural extension from his interest in amateur radio. He also joined the Air Force Reserve Officers Training Corps (ROTC).

LeSchack's first two years at RPI proved frustrating. He disliked rote learning and soon lost interest in electrical engineering. Air Force

ROTC fared no better. In fact, at the end of his sophomore year the Air Force terminated LeSchack as unlikely officer material. After he switched his major to geology, a discipline offering the opportunity to work outdoors, LeSchack's attitude—and grades—improved.

In his senior year, LeSchack became interested in the plans for the IGY, which would begin on July 1, 1957. A classmate had received a letter from Albert Crary—the experienced polar scientist who earlier had worked on T-3—rejecting his application for the then-forming IGY Antarctica expedition because he had not yet graduated. LeSchack, who had become intrigued with the polar regions after viewing a movie at the RPI Geology Club on glaciological research on the Greenland ice cap, initiated a correspondence with Crary, who had been selected as chief scientist for the U.S. IGY program in Antarctica and leader of the scientific party at the Little America V station.

As nothing had come of the correspondence with Crary at the time LeSchack graduated from RPI in January 1957 (he lost a semester when he switched majors), he took a job with Shell Oil Company in Houston, Texas. There was a demand for geophysicists for Gulf exploration, and Shell had a special relationship with RPI. Over the next eight months LeSchack participated in Shell's excellent training program in seismology, magnetics, and gravity. His career in oil exploration, however, had hardly begun when a letter arrived from Crary's office offering him the position of assistant seismologist with the U.S. Antarctic contingent. After Shell agreed to release him (with the oil business in a cyclical downturn, there was less need for geophysicists), LeSchack happily signed on with Crary. The decision to go to the Antarctic, he recalled, was based on "pure romance."

LeSchack shared the enthusiasm of scientists throughout the world for the IGY. Termed by Hugh Odishaw, responsible for organizing the American effort, as "the single most significant peaceful activity of mankind since the Renaissance and Copernican Revolution," the IGY involved sixty thousand scientists from sixty-six nations. The world had never before seen such a widespread cooperative scientific endeavor. It would be, President Dwight D. Eisenhower proclaimed, "one of the great scientific adventures of our time."[1]

Following orientation at the Davisville, Rhode Island, Navy base, LeSchack flew to New Zealand, then to Antarctica, arriving on November 13, 1957. Originally slated to be Crary's assistant on the Little America V exploration traverse, he was reassigned at the last minute to Byrd Station, located in the interior of Marie Byrd Land at 80° S, 120° W.

The project to investigate the Antarctic represented one of the most ambitious goals of the IGY. A great sheet of ice covered 98 percent of the continent at the bottom of the world, representing an area larger than the United States and Mexico. What was the nature of the land below? Could Antarctica be two land masses, separated by a trough linking the Ross and Weddell seas? Perhaps Antarctica was a string of islands? Scientists set out an extensive agenda to determine the nature of the little-explored region.

Byrd Station, LeSchack learned, had been built under extremely difficult conditions. In November 1956 a reconnaissance party had set out from the main research base at Little America V (there was a third station at the South Pole) on a 650-mile trek to the proposed site of the station. It had taken five weeks for the party to negotiate the difficult terrain. At one point the tractor train had encountered a series of nearly impassable crevasses that threatened to bring the entire project to an end. Construction of the station had proved equally challenging, with cold temperatures and constant windblown ice making work difficult. Finally, in the early months of 1957, sufficient structures had been erected to house the twelve scientists, their equipment, and ten support personnel.[2]

LeSchack reached Byrd Station just in time to embark on a three-month trek to explore the interior of Marie Byrd Land. Led by seismologist Dr. Charles R. Bentley and glaciologist Vernon H. Anderson, the six-man expedition got underway on November 19, 1957. The party traveled in three Tucker Model 743 Sno-Cats, vehicles that featured four tracks rotating around four pontoons, with heated cabs for living and working quarters. Each Sno-Cat could haul up to 2,300 pounds of cargo and passengers. Three cargo sleds, towed behind the Sno-Cats, each contained another 5,000 pounds of equipment and supplies. The column moved at five to seven miles per hour and had a range of three hundred miles. Deliveries of fuel by Navy and Marine Corps R4Ds would extend the range.[3]

LeSchack's party proceeded in a northeasterly direction toward a group of unnamed mountains near the coast, then turned right and headed for the Sentinel Mountains. The party usually traveled thirty to fifty miles a day, pausing every three miles to take readings of gravity, magnetism, and elevation. The group would stop on alternate days and make camp. The seismologists would work in the surrounding area, setting off explosions for echo sounding to determine the thickness of the ice, while glaciologists would dig pits for their ice studies. During the month of December alone the scientists made 110 gravity and magnetic readings, 13 short refraction profiles, 55 intermediate-depth ramsonde measurements, and 12 glaciological pit studies.

The group spent six days exploring the isolated Sentinel Mountains, which only twice before had been sighted, and only from the air at a great distance. The peaks, Bentley reported, spread "as far as the eye could reach." They counted fifty mountaintops and estimated the range was five hundred miles long, comparable in size to the Rockies. Rock samples indicated that the Sentinels were similar to the Andean formation of the Palmer (or Antarctic) peninsula, adjacent to South America.

After paralleling the mountains for a short distance, the party turned back to Byrd Station. About one hundred miles short of their destination seismic shots showed a depth of fourteen thousand feet—the deepest ice sounding ever recorded. The traverse ended on February 23, 1958. The six men had covered some 1,200 miles during their 96-day trek. They took satisfaction in the knowledge that they had accomplished their objective of determining the general nature of the ice sheet and mountains in eastern Marie Byrd Land.

During the long Antarctic winter LeSchack and his companions worked on the scientific data they had accumulated during their trek. In his spare time LeSchack also learned the fundamentals of celestial navigation. There were twenty-four men—twelve scientists and twelve U.S. Navy support personnel—who spent the winter in the remote camp, some six hundred miles from the South Pole. There was ample time, LeSchack recalled, to "reflect on our young lives."

On November 1, 1958, with the onset of Antarctic summer, Bentley, LeSchack, and four other scientists left Byrd Station on a second exploratory trek, this time heading south toward the Horlick Mountains, another range that previously had been seen only from the air.[4] By late November, when they were joined by Philip Benjamin, a reporter from the *New York Times*, the group had traveled 320 miles and were within sight of the mountains. After a night's sleep in the Sno-Cat, Benjamin accompanied Bentley and LeSchack on what for the two scientists was a typical day of work.[5]

It began with a "tooth-rattling" trip over a ridged ice field on board the seismology Sno-Cat—"with high explosives bouncing around inside"—to a site ten miles from the camp. LeSchack used an auger to bore a hole in the ice some 13 feet deep and 4 inches across while Bentley paid out 1,110 feet of wire, attaching 12 geophones at intervals. LeSchack placed a pound of explosives into the deep blue hole, then ran a wire to the detonator. Meanwhile, Bentley prepared the seismograph inside the Sno-Cat to record the blast.

When all was ready LeSchack detonated the dynamite. It went off with a thump. The sound sped downward through the ice, hit bedrock, then bounced back. Bentley recorded the interval between the explosion and the echo, which he converted to the thickness of the ice. In this case the ice sheet was 4,900 feet deep.

Bentley and LeSchack repeated the procedures a dozen times during a ten-mile stretch. Bentley also took frequent readings on a sensitive gravimeter that was capable of detecting a change of one three-millionth in gravitational pull. "It was long, hard work in bitter wind and cold," reporter Benjamin observed. At the end of the twelve-hour day the Sno-Cat returned to the camp, and the tired crew had a meal of hot stew.

On November 28, 1958, after a day's delay due to bad weather, the party continued its trek toward the Horlicks. The three orange-colored Sno-Cats, each pulling a cargo sled, traveled single file with the lead vehicle three miles ahead of the other two to record elevation changes barometrically (observers in the lead and second vehicle would each read simultaneously sensitive altimeters and the elevation difference over the three-mile segment was used to create an elevation profile). The lead Sno-Cat was also equipped to detect crevasses that could swallow the vehicles. Four large metal bowls, fixed on wooden beams protruding from the lead Sno-Cat, set up an electrical field that would be disturbed by a crevasse, thus giving, at least in theory, sufficient warning to stop the vehicle. In fact, it rarely worked properly.

The terrain became more difficult as the scientists neared the mountains and encountered frequent crevasses. Fifteen miles short of their goal, they had to give up. The party returned to camp for a Thanksgiving dinner of chicken and cranberry sauce.

The next day nearly brought disaster. The party had pushed fourteen miles to the east in hopes of finding a route to the mountains. Without warning, the right front pontoon of the lead Sno-Cat opened up a crack in the ice. Before the vehicle could be stopped, the right front runner of its trailing sled dropped two feet into the crevasse. Although the Sno-Cat managed to extract the heavy sled before it disappeared into the ice, it broke the fifth wheel, the horizontal plate on which the pontoons turned. The expedition had to stop and await the arrival of a replacement part.

On December 1 a Navy ski plane from Little America V flew out a fifth wheel and a portable arc welder. After Jack B. Long, a mechanic and member of the expedition, made the necessary repairs, the traverse resumed.

It took another week to reach the Horlicks. On December 8 Bentley and three companions (LeSchack had opted to remain behind because he wanted relief from the forced intimacy) climbed 4,000 feet to the top of the ice-covered range, which stood 10,006 feet above sea level. They spent nineteen hours in the mountains, the first to set foot on this remote area of the world, noting the petrified trees, leaf fossils, and seashells. The Horlicks, they discovered, were rich in coal, containing what appeared to be one of the world's most extensive fields of the fossil fuel.

Bentley and his fellow scientists proceeded parallel to the Horlicks for several days, then turned back toward Byrd Station to complete a counterclockwise loop. They reached their base on January 20, 1959, having accumulated a wealth of scientific data.

LeSchack matured during his time in Antarctica. While Bentley had been a difficult taskmaster and LeSchack had developed a hearty personal dislike of him, he nonetheless respected the older man. Bentley taught LeSchack how to conduct research and how scientific data should be recorded, giving him "a real understanding of how research was done." Bentley also showed him "how to be careful and safe in a polar environment." Problems usually arose from poor planning, Bentley stressed. With proper care, it was possible to accomplish a great deal with safety under difficult climatic conditions. LeSchack learned these lessons well.

LeSchack left Byrd Station in March 1959. After a pleasant three-week vacation in New Zealand, followed by another three weeks in Australia, he boarded USS *Arneb* (AKA 56) in Sydney for the voyage home. He no sooner had set foot in New York when his local draft board made a determined effort to induct him into the Army. LeSchack responded by applying for Naval Officers' Candidate School (OCS). He managed to stall the draft board while the Navy's administrative machinery slowly processed his request. Finally, in July 1959, shortly after receiving his "final" draft notice, he was able to enlist in the Navy.

LeSchack spent four months at OCS (class 45) at Newport, Rhode Island. At age twenty-four he was one of the older officer candidates, as most of his classmates were recent college graduates. Shortly after his arrival in Newport, LeSchack was taken under the wing of his section chief, BMC Edwin H. Todd, who had served on an icebreaker with Task Force 43 in the Antarctic. It was just as well that LeSchack had someone looking after him. Although conversant with naval customs and procedures from his tour in Antarctica, the outspoken student soon ran afoul of a junior training officer. The friendly chief saved him from what could have turned into an unpleasant situation.

LeSchack requested staff duty in New Zealand as his first choice of assignment, with duty on an icebreaker in Antarctica as his second. Not surprisingly the Navy opted for the icebreaker. Shortly before his graduation, however, LeSchack received a telegram from the Arctic Institute of North America offering him a position as civilian geophysicist on the U.S. Air Force Drifting Station Bravo/T-3. LeSchack replied that he would like to accept; however, he now was in the Navy. Would it be possible to go as a naval scientist? The Arctic Institute, which was a prime contractor for ONR's Arctic programs, said that they would look into the matter.

LeSchack's request ended up on the desk of Dr. Britton, head of ONR's Arctic Program. As Britton thought it would be a good idea to have a naval presence on the Air Force drifting station, he approved the request and sent it up the chain of command. With ONR's recommendation, the Bureau of Personnel was prepared to act—but not quickly.

The day after LeSchack graduated from OCS, his classmates decided to go into Newport to the Hotel Viking and celebrate. LeSchack, depressed at hearing nothing about his request to work on T-3, preferred to remain in his barracks and sulk. In mid-afternoon, however, a yeoman came into the room and informed him that his orders to the icebreaker had been changed. LeSchack was going to T-3!

❋

LeSchack reached T-3 on December 18, 1959, the only naval officer on the Air Force station. He was not impressed with Bravo's commander, Lt. Col. Marshall G. Hassenmiller, a pilot from SAC who seemed to view his assignment to the ice island as a punishment. Hassenmiller spent most of his time either reading western novels or lengthening the runway, apparently in an effort to accommodate his beloved B-52s. The rest of the twenty-one-man station party was composed of Air Force enlisted personnel and civilian scientists.

Living conditions on Bravo seemed lavish to LeSchack, compared to the primitive facilities at Byrd Station. The Air Force had flown in fourteen stainless-steel trailers, and there was ample room for living and working. Overall, however, LeSchack judged, Bravo was a poor station from a scientific point of view. There were weather observers, a Japanese graduate student studying sea-ice physics, and biologists from the University of Southern California. They seemed to lack the intensity and enthusiasm of the Antarctic scientists.

LeSchack set up his geophysical program, using a gravity meter and a seismograph similar to the ones he had trained with at Shell Oil and then used in the Antarctic. He also had an opportunity to employ the celestial navigation skills he had acquired in Antarctica and polished at OCS under the tutelage of his navigational instructor, QMC Douglas Dunn. Within a short time after his arrival LeSchack became responsible for plotting the position of T-3 as it drifted slowly westward along the edge of the North American continental shelf, usually remaining about one hundred miles offshore. Due to his navigational talents and previous polar experience, LeSchack, then only an ensign, won the respect of the enlisted men who ran the station.

On January 27, 1960, Lt. Comdr. Beaumont M. Buck of ONR arrived on T-3 with four scientists to conduct a classified project in cooperation with the Navy Underwater Sound Laboratory. Buck's task, LeSchack soon learned, was to establish a listening array to detect and track the nuclear-powered submarine *Sargo*. He called upon LeSchack to survey and orient the multielement sonar hydrophone array that would be used in the exercise. As LeSchack surveyed the holes in the ice at precise locations for placing the hydrophones into the water below, he learned a good deal about the Navy's acoustic program and about submarine activity in the far north.

LeSchack left T-3 on March 26 and went to the Air Force Cambridge Research Center to reduce the data he had gathered on the ice island. Assisted by Crary, who by that time was working at the center, he spent three months preparing his first scientific paper. It appeared in the journal *Arctic* in December 1964 under the title "Long-Period Vertical Oscillation of the Ice Recorded by Continuous Gravimeter Measurements from Drift Station T-3."

After he finished his work in Boston, LeSchack traveled to

Washington, D.C., to speak with his detailer at the Navy's Bureau of Personnel about his next assignment. The detailer offered two options: sea duty or ONR. Sea duty, the detailer advised, would be the best career choice. LeSchack opted for ONR.

❊

LeSchack reported for duty at ONR's Arctic Program in July 1960. Over the next year, with much guidance from Britton and Evelyn Pruitt, head of the Geography Branch, LeSchack learned how to function within the Washington bureaucracy. Much of his time was spent attending conferences on Arctic research and underwater acoustics. He also enrolled in night courses in oceanography at the graduate school of the Department of Agriculture. This two-year program in oceanography, he believed, could help him should he remain in the Navy or be useful if he decided to pursue a civilian scientific career.

During this period LeSchack and Britton frequently lunched together, as often as possible away from the government cafeterias. Bassin's and Duke Zeibert's restaurants were their favorites. They used these lunchtimes to review key happenings at the office and to discuss research projects that the Arctic Program was sponsoring. They also drank many a lunchtime martini, their beverage of choice at the time.

Britton, then aged fifty, and LeSchack, twenty-six, maintained a relationship halfway between father and son (Britton had no children) and professor and graduate student. During one of these lunches LeSchack brought up the possibility of continuing the drifting station oceanographic research that he had begun on T-3. Britton agreed that LeSchack could visit ARL for administrative reasons. If he could confine his research to no longer than two weeks away from the office, he would be given orders to go to ARLIS I, the Navy's drifting station. While ONR would issue the necessary orders, Britton warned, any equipment that he needed had to be scrounged or paid for by someone else.

To this end, LeSchack approached John Schule, Jr., a senior civilian scientist at the Navy Hydrographic Office who taught a course in "Ocean Waves" in the oceanography curriculum in which LeSchack had enrolled. LeSchack proposed the idea of using Hydrographic Office equipment for his research on ocean waves on ARLIS I. Schule, who was familiar with the Arctic, liked the idea and suggested that LeSchack meet him after class for a beer at a bar across the street from the hydrographic office. There, in the dimly lit and beery atmosphere of the tavern, he helped LeSchack write an official request from ONR to the Navy Hydrographic Office for loan of the equipment.

LeSchack had learned by now that official requests from one government agency to another often were co-written by officers of these separate agencies so that the requirements and politics of each agency were taken into account, while maintaining the purpose and intent of the request. In this fashion official requests, which by regulation had to get the approval of senior officials at the originating office, also would receive approval at the top of the chain of command at the receiving office. With the "skids greased," LeSchack obtained the equipment he required to conduct his research project. What he now needed for his research was a new Navy drifting station: While gathering his equipment, ARLIS I had been abandoned!

LeSchack did not have long to wait. Britton, he learned, had secured approval to establish a replacement station, which was scheduled to be occupied in May 1961. LeSchack packed up his gear and headed northward. After convincing a recalcitrant Northwest Airlines crew to carry his delicate instruments in the forward cabin instead of the cargo hold, he reached Anchorage on May 20, then proceeded to Barrow.

Three days after LeSchack's arrival at ARL, Brewer landed on an ice island and ordered the establishment of ARLIS II. While the camp was being set up LeSchack made several flights to the site on ARL's R4D. The R4D pilot, "Zim" Zimmerman, seemed to have walked out of the pages of Milton Caniff's comic strip, "Terry and the Pirates." The colorful aviator had flown in Southeast Asia and was married to a Vietnamese. He had become acquainted with many of the native people on the northern coast of Alaska and was welcome in their villages.

Heading out of ARLIS II on the logistical flights from Barrow, Zimmerman took the R4D up to several hundred feet to clear the ground fog that generally obscured the coastline during the summer. Once clear of the coastal fog, he dove under the overcast and followed the radio beacon to the station. LeSchack found it a strange sensation as the aircraft roared at 200 feet and 120 knots over the vast, unending, ever-changing panorama of pressure ridges and pack ice. At one point Zimmerman startled a seal sunning itself on the pack; with one graceful leap it dove into an open lead and was gone.

As ARLIS II was only a little over a hundred miles from Barrow, it took an hour to reach the site. On a clear day the ice island would loom up ahead quite strikingly, with the mountains of glacial debris contrasting sharply with the brilliant white ice that supported it.

After flying over the pack ice, a remarkably smooth ride due to the uniformity of the air over the ice, Zimmerman came in for a landing on the unprepared strip on ARLIS II. The area looked about the same as any other part of the ice island, except that it had flags along it to delineate the landing strip. Zimmerman approached the far end of the strip and throttled back. The aircraft gently settled over the runway, seeming to hang in the air. Then the R4D hit the ice with a teeth-rattling, jarring bang. To LeSchack it felt more like a controlled crash than a landing.

On May 30, 1961, Fischer and Robert Main flew LeSchack and his equipment to ARLIS II in ARL's two Cessna 180s. With the help of William McComas, a junior scientist from the Navy Hydrographic Office who would continue to take the readings that LeSchack started, he set up the instruments necessary for the oceanographic research project. LeSchack took his first measurement on June 1, marking the beginning of the scientific program on ARLIS II.

LeSchack also volunteered to survey the ice island. A true ice island—that is, a freshwater glacial plate that had broken away from the Ellesmere Ice Shelf—its periphery could be distinguished from the surrounding sea ice. With the assistance of McComas, LeSchack planned to conduct a pacing survey around the island's circumference. McComas would walk ahead, then LeSchack would take a bearing on him with his compass, pace the distance to McComas, and record both readings in his notebook. The broad shape and dimensions of the ice island—3.5 by 1.6 nautical miles—had been provided by ARL pilot Fischer. From this information LeSchack calculated that the survey should take about a half day to complete.

The two scientists set off with a canteen of water, some sandwiches, and an M-1 rifle. A polar bear had been shot the day before LeSchack's arrival, and it was feared that other bears might be in the area. It was a beautiful and exciting walk, with numerous changes of ice forms and weather along the survey route. Because it was now June, there was light for twenty-four hours a day; the intent was to keep walking around the island until the survey was completed. About ten hours after he had started the trek, LeSchack became worried. Although his compass measurements showed that they had rounded the island and were turning back, it seemed that they were following the new course forever. Also, a patch of ice fog drifted in and caused near whiteout conditions, adding to LeSchack's growing apprehension.

Were Brewer and Fischer correct? Was this an island? If so, they would eventually return to their starting point if they kept walking around its circumference. Was LeSchack's compass working properly, since compasses were notoriously unreliable this far north?

LeSchack decided not to communicate his worries to McComas. Although McComas, a strapping West Virginian about LeSchack's age, was having no trouble with the physical effort of the walk, this was his first time on the ice and LeSchack knew that he was relying wholly on his senior partner's judgment. They kept pacing, recording measurements, and taking turns carrying the heavy M-1. Finally, they made a nearly ninety degree turn that buoyed LeSchack's spirits. They kept pacing. Fourteen hours after they started they finally saw the flags that marked the end of the runway. They stopped the survey at this point, planted a marker flag, and followed the runway back to camp. Exhausted, LeSchack and McComas crawled into their bunks and promptly fell asleep. They completed the remaining portion of the survey the following day.

LeSchack returned to Barrow on June 5 and left the following day for Washington, D.C., keeping within the two-week period that Britton had authorized. Before he left Barrow, however, Brewer came over to exchange a few remarks. With a twinkle in his eye he told LeSchack that ARLIS II foreman Ken Toovak had observed that the M-1 had been turned in with a snow-packed barrel. "It's a good thing that you had no need to fire it," Brewer commented, to LeSchack's chagrin.

When he got back to Washington, D.C., LeSchack wrote an article about the establishment of ARLIS II that later was published in the *Naval Research Reviews*. It included the map that he and McComas had surveyed (see Figure 2).[6] He also found, waiting for him on his desk, orders promoting him to lieutenant (j.g.).

Shortly after LeSchack resumed his normal duties at ONR, an item came across his desk that attracted his interest. While he had been on ARLIS II a Navy patrol aircraft conducting an Arctic Ocean aeromagnetic survey had reported sighting an abandoned Soviet drifting station. On April 2 Moscow radio announced that it had been necessary to evacuate a polar research station that was in danger of breaking up. This station, NP9, was the one that had been spotted by the patrol aircraft.

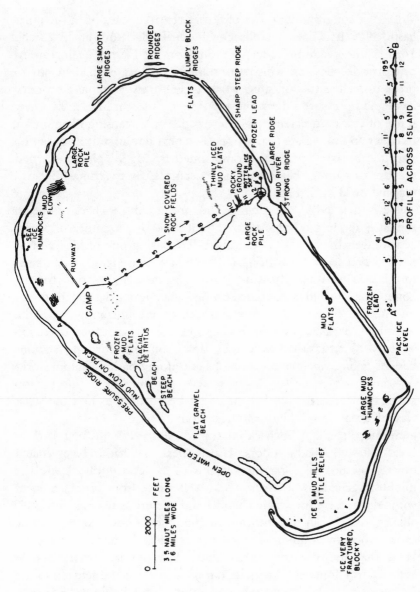

Figure 2
LeSchack's map of ARLIS II.

One of a continuing series of Soviet research stations in the polar basin, NP9 had been established on April 28, 1960, at 77°23′ N, 163° E, under station leader V. A. Shamont'ev. During its northward drift, the ice floe on which the station was located had begun to break up. The situation grew worse in February 1961, as a series of cracks and pressure ridges split the floe in two. On March 27 a new series of cracks threatened to destroy the camp, causing Shamont'ev to order an immediate evacuation. The next day aircraft of the High Latitude Aerial Expedition, commanded by M. M. Nikitin, carried out the task under hazardous circumstances. By this time NP9 had reached 86°30′ N, 176° E.[7]

News that NP9 had been found prompted LeSchack to begin thinking about a way to discover more about the nature of Soviet activities on their drifting stations. While having one of his frequent martini lunches with Britton, he sketched out an idea that had been forming in his mind. It stands to reason, he told Britton, that the Soviet Union would be interested in obtaining tracking data on the growing number of American submarines that were operating under the polar ice pack. Had the Russians begun to deploy acoustical detection systems? What exactly were they doing on their drifting stations besides taking weather observations and doing basic scientific work? Although the secretive Russians were releasing little information about their activities, perhaps it might be possible to find out what was taking place on their drifting station.

Sooner or later, LeSchack continued, all ice floe drifting stations break up as NP9 had just done. Usually, personnel had to be evacuated quickly by aircraft using the remains of an ice runway. These last minute evacuations, as Britton was well aware from his experiences with Alpha, were inevitably chaotic, and there was never space available on the aircraft to return much equipment. Also, there was little time to destroy equipment that must be left behind. Since everyone knew that the longevity of ice stations at this advanced stage of breakup was limited and that aircraft could not use the remains of the ice runway, no one would expect the station ever again to be visited. There was no need, therefore, to hide the evidence of work being done on the station.

LeSchack argued that considerable intelligence could be gathered from investigating an abandoned Soviet drifting station like NP9. Equipment, procedures, notes, areas of specialization and concentration, and other information could be gleaned from a clandestine visit to a drifting station. Above all, it should be possible to assess Soviet progress with acoustical detection systems.

The problem with such a clandestine operation, both men realized, was not placing investigators on the drifting station—this could be done by parachute. No, the major difficulty would be in retrieving them. NP9 was about two hundred miles from the North Pole, far beyond the range of helicopters (which could not be refueled in mid-air during the early 1960s), and aircraft could not land on the remnants of the ice runway. However, LeSchack reminded Britton, there just might be a way of getting the investigators off the ice. ONR had been funding the Fulton Skyhook aerial retrieval system for some time. In fact, it had been successfully tested in the Arctic the previous year. Although intended by the Navy for rescue work, why could it not be used to pluck the investigators from the ice?

Britton was noncommittal. LeSchack's idea, at first glance, seemed to border on the bizarre. Nonetheless, Britton agreed to think about it. He would take a closer look at the progress being made by Fulton and his Skyhook.

5

Fulton's Skyhook

Robert Edison Fulton, Jr., developer of the innovative aerial retrieval system that LeSchack hoped to use in the Arctic, surely had an appropriate name for an inventor. He may even have been a collateral descendant of the steamboat inventor, although he never bothered to check the genealogical connection. Edison had been a family name long before it became associated with the famous inventor. Fulton's own family background was rooted in transportation. His maternal grandfather, Ezra Johnson Travis, had started a stagecoach company in the nineteenth century. By the time of his death in 1919, he had become a millionaire and president of the Pacific Coast Stage Coach Company.[1]

Fulton's father was a pioneer in motor transportation. In the early years of the twentieth century he held the American sales rights for the German-built Mercedes automobile. He later joined the Saurer Motor Company, a truck manufacturer. In 1911 Saurer combined with the Hewitt Motor Company and the Mack Brothers Motor Company to form the Mack Truck Company. Fulton Senior took over as president of the new corporation that dominated the truck manufacturing industry for many years.

Born on April 15, 1909, Fulton grew up in affluent circumstances in New York City. His world was filled with automobiles; his father's manufacturing shops became his playgrounds. He recalls the day that his father came home with an armload of blueprints. "These prints are fading away," he told his son. "When they're gone, we won't know how to build our trucks anymore." He then offered to pay Fulton fifty cents for every blueprint that he copied. The young boy quickly set out to save the company—and to earn the fifty cents per copy. As his father had intended, Fulton's introduction to mechanical drawing was a profitable pleasure.

There were numerous trips abroad, and Fulton's early schooling took place both in New York and Switzerland. He attended Exeter and Choate, then went on to Harvard. Following his graduation in 1931 with a degree in architecture, Fulton spent a year at the University of Vienna, continuing his architectural studies. Fulton was visiting England prior to his return to the United States when he came up with a novel idea for the journey home: Instead of taking an ocean liner, he wanted to ride a motorcycle eastward around the world!

Kenton Redgrave, a motorcycle manufacturer and family friend, provided the necessary machine. After it was fitted with a luggage rack and extra gasoline tank that extended its range to 350 miles, Fulton set out on his great adventure. Over the next seventeen months he traveled some forty thousand miles through thirty-two countries as he made his way across Europe, North Africa, India, the Malay Peninsula, and China. After touring Japan he sailed across the Pacific to San Francisco. His journey ended in Amarillo, Texas, where someone stole his motorcycle.

Fulton filmed the entire trip, marking the start of a lifelong love of photography. He also kept careful notes of his experiences, which formed the basis for a book—*One Man Caravan*—that was published by Harcourt, Brace and Company in 1937.

Following a lecture tour of the United States in 1935, Fulton was hired by Pan American Airways to make a documentary film of the airline's attempts to span the Pacific Ocean. Fulton thus had a unique vantage point to observe one of the great pioneering ventures of commercial aviation. Under the dynamic leadership of Juan T. Trippe, Pan Am built a series of seaplane bases across the central Pacific, from Hawaii to the Philippines via Guam, Midway, and Wake islands. On November 22, 1935, the *China Clipper* lifted off San Francisco Bay and headed across the vast reaches of the Pacific. Seven days later, after fifty-nine hours and forty-eight minutes in the air, the Martin M-130 flying boat reached Manila. Fulton captured on film the months of hard work that had gone into the construction of the infrastructure that made this epic achievement possible.

Flying soon became another of Fulton's passionate interests. His cousin, A.C. ("Chet") Travis, Jr., was working on a machine that would teach primary flying to students in the same way that the Link trainer taught instrument flying. Travis built what he called an Aerostructor. Unlike the Link trainer, which moved on a cushion of air in response to pressure by the student on the stick and rudder, the Aerostructor was stationary. Instead, a picture of the horizon would tilt in response to movement of the controls. But Travis had no suitable picture, so he turned to his photographer cousin.

Fulton went to the top of the Empire State Building and took forty pictures to create a 360-degree panorama of the New York skyline. The results were impressive, presenting the student with a sharply defined horizon. While the device worked, the two men were unable to find a market for it. In 1941, as the United States expanded its pilot training program in the face of a threatening international situation, Fulton attempted to interest the Navy in the Aerostructor. At one point in his tour of the Navy bureaucracy he met a man whose imagination matched his own: Capt. Louis de Florez.[2]

A mechanical engineer, inventor, pilot, and oil millionaire, the dynamic de Florez had been called to active duty as a special assistant to Vice Adm. John Towers, head of the Bureau of Aeronautics. Towers wanted de Florez to come up with ways to shorten and improve training courses for the large number of naval aviators who were joining the service. It was not long before de Florez became interested in the use of what were then known as synthetic devices and which are now termed simulators.

Fulton and de Florez immediately hit it off. In discussions of the Aerostructor, de Florez suggested that the device could be more useful for gunnery instruction than for primary flight training. Could Fulton modify the machine? Could he come up with a proposal? If so, de Florez was prepared to offer him a developmental contract.

Fulton accepted the challenge. After Travis decided to bow out, he hired Theodore N. Polhemus, a talented electrical engineer, to help with the design of the new Gunairstructor. The two men began work in a barn in Greenwich, Connecticut. Fulton learned how to weld, enabling him to put together the entire framework of the device. Motion pictures replaced the static horizon. The work was progressing well, but Fulton was running out of money. At a critical point in the development of the trainer he was approached by a businessman who had learned about the project from carpenters who had done some work on the trainer. The individual, who also had read *One Man Caravan*, offered Fulton a loan of $2,000. The inventor gratefully accepted.

In May 1942, nine months after his initial contract with de Florez, Fulton delivered the Gunairstructor to Washington, D.C., where it was placed in the main lobby of the Navy Building, then on Constitution Avenue. De Florez, who was now head of the Special Devices Division, was delighted with the trainer. Could Fulton deliver fifteen machines in six months? No, de Florez corrected himself, make that fifty machines. Fulton said that he would try.

Unable to locate a subcontractor willing to undertake the work, Fulton had to put together his own manufacturing facilities for what the Navy termed Gunnery Trainer 3A2. The Gunairstructor proved a huge success. The trainee sat in a cockpit on a raised platform that was some twenty feet away from a movie screen. His task was to "shoot down" a Japanese Zero that passed across the screen. When he used the controls, the screen would tilt. "The illusion was perfect," noted one description of the trainer, "the screen is so large, the sound of engines so convincing, and the sky and Zero so realistic that the average student becomes completely absorbed. . . ." The millions of young people who now spend their quarters on video arcade games would be familiar with the operation of the simulator.[3]

Fulton also wrote a training manual that explained the geometry of gunnery, a pamphlet that he considered "probably more important than the machine" in teaching pilots the lead required with various angles and speeds to hit a fast-moving target. These lessons in deflection shooting paid rich dividends for Navy pilots in air battles over the Pacific.

By the end of the war Fulton had produced five hundred trainers at a cost to the government of $6 million. As Fulton's company had been capitalized at only $15,000, much of the profits were returned to the Treasury Department in the form of wartime excess profits taxes. Fulton, however, did have enough money remaining to purchase fifteen acres of land adjacent to the airport at Danbury, Connecticut, where he built a house and workshop.

Fulton became caught up in the postwar enthusiasm for light aircraft. World War II, many observers believed, had ushered in a new air age. Air Force veterans would want to become private pilots. The demand for light aircraft, the Department of Commerce had predicted in 1943, would top twenty thousand per year. The prediction erred on the side of caution: The light-plane industry sold 33,254 aircraft in 1946.

Fulton believed that the future of private aviation lay in the production of an aircraft that also could function as an automobile. Working with chief mechanic Wayne Dasher, he set to work on what he termed an airphibian. In November 1946 the Mark I took to the air at Danbury. As an aircraft the airphibian could carry two passengers and 50 pounds of baggage at a speed of 120 miles per hour over a distance of 400 miles without refueling. With wings and tail detached (a task that could be accomplished without tools in six minutes) it became an automobile with a top speed of forty-five miles per hour.[4]

Months of testing followed the initial flight as Fulton worked to perfect his invention. By mid-1947 the first production model of the airphibian—the Mark II—was ready to begin the lengthy process of certification by the Civil Aeronautics Administration (CAA). The airphibian by this time had received extensive publicity through articles in *Life* magazine, the *Saturday Evening Post*, and other national publications.

Fulton's airphibian became the first flying automobile to receive an Approved Type certificate from the CAA. As CAA administrator Donald W. Nyrop commented, Fulton's invention represented "a real advance in the utility of personal aircraft." Unfortuntely, it also turned into an economic disaster. Fulton had built eight machines—five for tests and three production models—when his financial backers (who owned 51 percent of the company) decided to sell the hard-won CAA certificate and manufacturing rights to the airphibian. Given the precipitous plunge in the postwar light-plane market, their decision made sense. The new air-age balloon had burst. Light-plane sales fell to 15,617 units in 1947 and 3,545 in 1949.

❋

Although disappointed that his hard work on the airphibian had come to naught, Fulton soon had a new project that claimed his time and attention. While flight testing the airphibian he often had wondered what might happen if he had been forced down in rugged terrain beyond the limited range of existing helicopters. There was a need, he had concluded, for a system by which aircraft could pluck people from the ground without landing.

Fulton had seen the All American pickup system demonstrated in London after World War II. This innovative pickup method, reportedly used to extract British agents from behind enemy lines during the war, was based on a mail pickup system invented by Lytle S. Brown during the 1930s and perfected before Pearl Harbor by All American Aviation. It featured two steel poles, set fifty-four feet apart, with a transfer line strung between them. An aircraft approached the ground station in a gentle glide of ninety miles per hour, while a flight mechanic paid out a fifty-foot steel cable. As the aircraft pulled up, a four-finger grapple at the end of the cable engaged the transfer rope, shock absorbers cushioned the impact, and then the flight mechanic winched the mail pouch on board.[5]

In July 1943 the need to rescue airmen from difficult terrain led to tests of this system by the Army Air Forces. Initial results, using instrument containers, had not been promising. The instruments recorded accelerations in excess of seventeen Gs following the pickup, a force far in excess of what the human body could tolerate. Changes in the transfer line and modifications in the parachute harness, however, brought this down to a more acceptable seven Gs. The first live test, with a sheep, failed when the harness twisted and strangled the animal. On subsequent tests, however, the sheep fared better.

Lt. Alex Doster, a paratrooper, volunteered for the first human pickup, made on September 5, 1943. After a Stinson aircraft engaged the transfer rope at 125 miles per hour, Doster was yanked off the ground and then soared off behind the aircraft. It took less than three minutes to retrieve him.

The Air Force continued to improve the system, even developing a package containing telescoping poles, transfer line, and harness that could be dropped by air. The first operational use of the system came in February 1944, when a C-47 snagged a glider in a remote location in Burma and returned it to India. Colonel Balchen employed the system in the early 1950s to pick up gliders from the pack ice as part of the rescue capabilities of his 10th Rescue Squadron.

During the Korean War the CIA became interested in the All American system as a way to retrieve clandestine agents from behind enemy lines. In the spring and summer of 1952 the CIA tried to establish a resistance network in Manchuria. Civil Air Transport (CAT), an ostensibly commercial airline that was in fact owned by the CIA, dropped agents and supplies into Kirin Province as part of a project known to the pilots as Operation Tropic. The All American system seemed to solve the problem of how to bring people out of Manchuria.[6]

In the fall of 1952 CAT pilots in Japan made a number of static pickups, then successfully retrieved CAT mechanic Ronald E. Lewis. On the evening of November 29, 1952, a CAT C-47 with CIA officers John T. Downey and Richard G. Fecteau departed Seoul for Kirin Province, intending to pick up members of a team that had been inserted the previous July. A double agent, however, had betrayed the team. The Chinese shot down the aircraft when it came in for the pickup, killing the pilots and capturing the CIA officers. Fecteau was not released until December 1971; Downey was freed in March 1973.

Even before the All American system had been employed in Korea, Fulton was at work on a superior pickup system. Initial tests began in 1953 on a small grass field adjacent to Fulton's workshop at Newtown, Connecticut. He flew the tests himself, using a three hundred-horse-power gull-wing Stinson Reliant. Fulton mounted a V-shaped yoke on the Stinson's left wing, then placed cameras on the top of the wing and the fuselage. He attached a five-pound sandbag to a three hundred-pound test nylon line, which was raised by a weather balloon. At the top of the line, beneath the balloon, he tied knots at ten-foot intervals. As the aircraft flew into the line, it would slide along the yoke until one of the knots caught in the one-eighth-inch slot at the base of the yoke. Fulton then used an outrigger hook to pull the lift-line to the door of the aircraft, from where he could haul in the load.[7]

As the tests proceeded, Fulton gradually increased the weight of the sandbag until it reached thirty-five pounds. He tried out lift-lines of lengths from 200 to 1,000 feet, with strengths of 80 to 550 pounds. He measured the acceleration forces with a simple device, rigging a recording tensiometer with a pencil secured to a spring scale. When the load came off the ground, the pencil moved with the scale's pointer and recorded the force on a piece of tape.

Tests showed that the load would be lifted off the ground in a nearly vertical trajectory, then make a gradual transition to the horizontal as it streamed behind the aircraft. G-forces varied. The shorter the line, the higher the G-forces; the heavier the load in relation to line strength, the higher the G-forces. Also, the higher the airspeed (Fulton tried speeds ranging from 80 to 150 knots), the higher the G-forces. For example, with 400 feet of line and an airspeed of 150 knots, cargo was subjected to 5 Gs for less than two seconds. When the length of the line was doubled, G-force was reduced by half.

By May 1953 Fulton had made thirty-nine pickups and established the basic parameters for the Skyhook system. "Emphasis throughout the project," he wrote in a draft report, "has been placed on *simplicity*. It is realized that operations will have to be conducted under conditions of poor weather, darkness, high winds and difficult terrain. Furthermore, personnel being picked up will not always be familiar with procedures and details. Under such circumstances, complication of any kind cannot be tolerated."[8]

Following additional safety tests with a larger, Twin-Beechcraft, observing the motion of heavier loads and higher pickup speeds, Fulton approached ONR for a developmental contract. Although de Florez was no longer with ONR, his high opinion of Fulton's ability no doubt contributed to the Navy's decision to fund initial tests of Skyhook.

In October 1954 Fulton flew his gull-wing Stinson to the test facilities of the Joint Air Force–Navy Parachute Unit at El Centro, California. The climate brought a note of realism to the tests. Temperatures in the desert often reached 120°F. It was alternately calm and windy but always dusty. A Lockheed Neptune P2V-2 was equipped for the tests, using a larger yoke and a heavier slotted-type anchor and anchor plate. At first the Navy pilots were reluctant to fly into the pickup line. After Fulton demonstrated the procedure with his Stinson, however, the military pilots decided they could do anything the slightly built civilian could do!

Using sandbags and rubber torso dummies, pickups were made using weights that increased from 25 to 150 pounds. All went well at first. The Navy pilots intercepted the pickup line without difficulty. After the knot secured the line to the slotted anchor, a J-hook was used to retrieve it. The line then was attached to a twenty-eight-volt electrically powered winch, which had been lashed to the floor in the aft cabin, and the load was brought on board.[9]

Problems arose during the fourth test on October 15. This mission called for the P2V to pick up a two hundred-pound weight. The aircraft, flying at 125 knots, intercepted the 1,000-foot line at approximately 750 feet. The load, as usual, lifted vertically off the ground to a height of fifty feet, then began streaming behind the aircraft. At this point the line broke. Fulton believed that the problem likely was due to one of three factors: The intercept angle could have been at fault, as two balloons had not been able to raise the one thousand-foot line to a nearly vertical position. A faulty knot could have caused the problem; or the yoke-eye might have cut the lift line.

Fulton decided to use a stronger knot for the next test. Also, he mounted a camera on the yoke to record the moment the line attached to the slotted anchor. A pickup of one hundred pounds was made without incident on October 21. On the next test, however, the line caught on the camera, then wrapped around the yoke. Although the yoke was severely bent, it held the two hundred-pound weight.

Further tests revealed that the knots on the nylon lift line were melting when rapidly tightened by weights over 125 pounds. Fulton substituted small metal links for the knots. The styrofoam-covered links could bear heavier loads, but they tended to come loose and hit the windscreen of the P2V.

All in all, Fulton believed that the tests had been successful. Instrument readings had shown that acceleration forces were only six Gs for less than a half second when a five hundred-foot line was used. The problem with the metal links remained to be solved, but Fulton did not consider this a major flaw in the system. He recommended to the Navy that Skyhook be subject to further development and testing.

ONR, in response, sought an independent opinion. In March 1955 North American Instruments delivered its report on the "Analytic Investigation of Aerial Pickup Systems." Looking into a variety of possible pickup methods, the report concluded that Skyhook, while at the furthest stage of development, had a number of limitations, especially during conditions of low visibility. Instead of Skyhook, the authors of the report believed that the Long Line Circling System offered "the best ultimate solution" to the problem of aerial pickups.[10]

Fulton, who had done some preliminary work on the Long Line system, was given a contract to make a further study of that technique. The tests were not promising. Trailing a five thousand-foot line, Fulton would circle in an attempt to place a sandbag in a designated location on the ground. In a calm wind the technique worked well. In even moderate winds, however, it proved impossible to lower the sandbag to the ground without severe damage. It was soon clear that Long Line was not the answer, and Fulton again turned his attention to expanding the Skyhook concept into an integrated system.

The first and most important task he faced was to come up with a better way to attach the lift-line to the aircraft. This proved Fulton's most challenging assignment. The way that the lift-line had attached itself to the yoke during the El Centro trials gave him the insight that led to the development of the sky anchor. When the lift-line entered the slot at the base of the yoke, it triggered a powerful spring that caused a steel bar to rotate several turns as the line wound on top of itself. A large ratchet prohibited the line from unwinding and bore the force of the pickup.

The sky anchor became the heart of the Skyhook system. Fulton also had to design and build harnesses, lift-lines, balloons, helium storage bottles, and drop containers. Work had to be done on safety lines to prevent the lift-line from fouling the propellers of the aircraft in the event of a missed pickup. He designed a collapsible yoke that was bolted rather than welded together and could easily be dismounted. Considerable effort went into perfecting an electrical winch that could haul in a three hundred-pound weight at two hundred feet per minute.

By December 1957 Skyhook was ready for operational development tests at the Marine Corps Reservation at Quantico, Virginia. Using a Marine Corps crewed P2V-5, a series of pickups were made with static loads. Tests then were conducted with a two hundred-pound anthropomorphic dummy that was provided by the Navy's Aero-Medical Acceleration Laboratory and permitted the simultaneous recording of vertical, transverse, and lateral Gs. The vertical forces recorded during pickup ranged from 10.5 Gs to 4.5 Gs. Transverse and lateral Gs proved negligible. This compared to a force of over 30 Gs in some parachute jumps.

Fulton next used monkeys and pigs as test loads. The monkeys had their arms and legs taped together and were encased in bags "to prevent their running up the lift-line before the appointed time." While the monkeys caused no problems, the first pig began to spin as it flew through the air at 125 miles per hour. Electrocardiogram telemetry equipment showed almost no pulse change during the pickup, and it arrived on board the aircraft without damage but in a disoriented state. Once the confused animal recovered, it attacked the crew. On subsequent pickups the pigs were hog-tied and given mild sedatives.

The only significant problem that arose during the tests involved the balloons used to raise the lift-line. The thin neoprene circular-shaped balloons had a tendency to "excursion" back and forth across the line of flight in winds over twelve knots. Fulton's answer to the control problem was to substitute a dirigible-shaped balloon, which vaned into the wind and provided the pilot with a stable target in the strongest winds.

By June 1958, following sixty-five successful pickups (nineteen with animals), Fulton believed that the time had come to take the next—and most important—step. "In view of the system's satisfactory performance record and the statistical data set forth above," he reported to ONR, "it is felt that Skyhook is now ready to pick up a human being, and then be channeled into operational air/sea rescue work."[11]

Fulton scheduled himself for the first live pickup, but the Navy demurred. If something went wrong, they informed him, they wanted someone around to blame! Instead, S/Sgt. Levi W. Woods, an experienced U.S. Marine Corps parachutist, volunteered for the assignment.

In the early evening of August 12, 1958, Sergeant Woods sat quietly on the ground at Quantico as a P2V, flown by Capt. Stanley Osserman, U.S. Marine Corps, approached the pickup line at a speed of 125 knots. Osserman engaged the line, and Woods began his historic journey. "I felt like I was being eased into the air," Woods later reported. "There was no jerk or jolt. I sort of sat in a high chair and looked around at the people below me. Then I began to move up faster. It seemed like I went almost straight up."[12]

As Woods began to streamline behind the aircraft, he extended his arms and legs. This prevented the oscillation that had plagued the pig. It took about six minutes to winch him on board. "As far as I'm concerned," he said, "it really was a good ride and I'm ready to do it again as many times as you like" (see Figure 3).

Following the first live pickup, Skyhook underwent a series of operational tests. The Navy was especially interested in using the system for rescue work in the Arctic. As Captain Smith had pointed out to his superiors following the hasty evacuation of Drifting Station Alpha in 1958, a "snatch pickup technique" could be useful in emergency situations. Unaware of the work being done by the Navy on the Fulton system, Smith had in mind the All American pickup method. The Air Force, he believed, had spent over $100,000 in perfecting the equipment in the years following the end of the Korean War. With more and more air traffic passing over the Arctic, there would surely be a need for rescue operations. "The potential of this [All American] system," he recommended, "should be exploited."[13]

In August 1960 Capt. Edward A. Rodgers, commander of the Naval Air Development Unit, flew a Skyhook-equipped P2V to Barrow, Alaska, to conduct a variety of pickups under the direction of Max Brewer. With Fulton on board to monitor the equipment, the P2V began the tests with a demonstration pickup for the scientific personnel at Barrow. Shortly after the aircraft took off, the weather

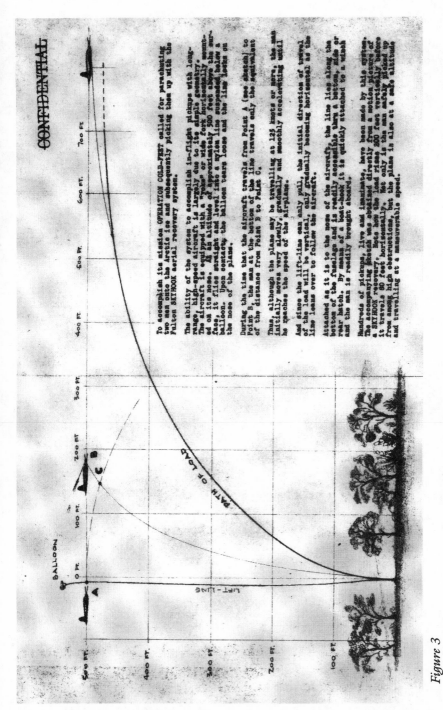

Figure 3
Diagram of the "simple geometry" of the Fulton Skyhook aerial recovery system.

deteriorated as a fog bank rolled in. The balloon, however, rose above the fog, permitting the pilot to engage the line and make the pickup. The people on the ground were impressed when the package slowly ascended into the fog and disappeared.

A series of operational tests brought equally impressive results. Brewer wanted to see how the system would function under a variety of circumstances. Twice, the P2V located Fletcher's Ice Island/T-3 and picked up mail from the drifting station. Next, the aircraft retrieved artifacts, including mastodon tusks, from an archaeological party on the tundra. Then the aircraft secured geological samples from Peters Lake Camp, a research facility located in a tight, U-shaped valley in the Brooks Mountains. The high point of the trials came when the P2V dropped a rescue package near the icebreaker USS *Burton Island*. Retrieved by the ship's boat, the package was brought on deck, the balloon inflated, and the cargo picked up without incident.

The Navy was pleased with the test of Skyhook, which seemed ready for use in rescue work in isolated locations. As an article in the October 1960 issue of *Naval Research Review* noted, Fulton deserved great credit for perfecting the innovative pickup method. "Through his ingenuity and courage," the article concluded, "many technical and operational obstacles were overcome to make the present SKYHOOK system development safe, practical, and operationally acceptable."

Lieutenant LeSchack, who had become aware of the tests during his tour in ONR, now had the means to embark upon Project COLDFEET.

The Fulton Skyhook pickup gear mounted on the B-17 at Intermountain Aviation's operational base at Marana Air Park, north of Tucson, Arizona, 1962. *(C. W. Seigrist)*

The Skyhook team, Lt. (jg) Leonard LeSchack, Capt. Daniel L. Walter (USA), and Maj. James F. Smith at Resolute Royal Canadian Air Force Base on Cornwallis Island, at the outset of Project COLDFEET, April 1962.

A gathering of Intermountain personnel at Marana: Carson Gerken, Leo Turk, Connie Seigrist, Gar Thorsrud, Douglas Price, Conrad Peterson, John D. Wall. *(John D. Wall)*

The Intermountain Aviation B-17 at Marana following modification to permit entry of retrieved personnel through an opening in tail where tail gunner's position had been. *(John D. Wall)*

Poster left on wall in mess hall when Soviet drifting station North Pole 8 (NP8) was abandoned on March 19, 1962. A handwritten note, signed Chief of Station Romanov, states that anyone visiting the station after the above date should report their visit to the following address: Arctic Institute, Leningrad, USSR.

A Soviet scientist poses near open lead adjacent to NP8 (photo from a negative recovered on NP8).

NP8 as a functioning Soviet drifting station (photo from a negative recovered on NP8).

NP8 after its abandonment by the Soviets.

One of the three antennas located at NP8 in a triangular array. *(U.S. Navy)*

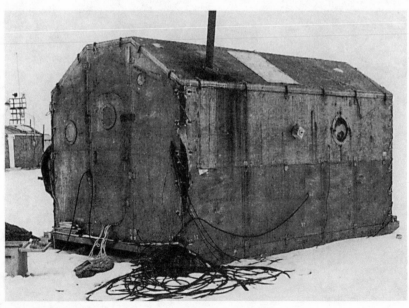

Ionospheric laboratory structure on NP8.

Intermountain B-17, outfitted with Skyhook gear, and C-46 at Barrow, Alaska, May 1962. *(John D. Wall)*

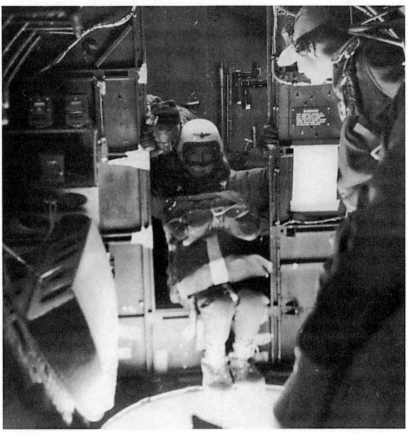

LeSchack prepares to exit B-17 over NP8, May 28, 1962. *(Robert E. Fulton, Jr.)*

LeSchack uncovering heavy duty armored cable, believed used for underwater acoustic research, at NP8. *(U.S. Navy)*

Smith examining a Soviet hydrographic winch, which was more mobile and versatile than its U.S. counterpart. *(U.S. Navy)*

Project COLDFEET mission commander Capt. John Cadwalader on B-17 during return flight from NP8, June 2, 1962. *(Robert E. Fulton, Jr.)*

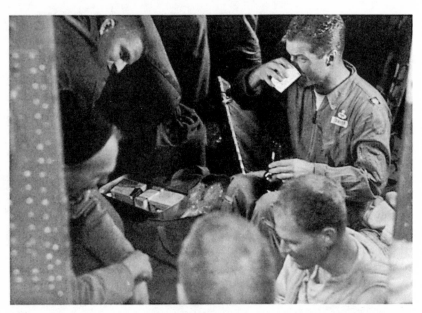

Smith enjoys a drink of "medicinal" Scotch while returning from NP8, June 2, 1962. Also visible in the photograph are LeSchack (lower right),Cadwalader (left), and Walter (upper left). *(Robert E. Fulton, Jr.)*

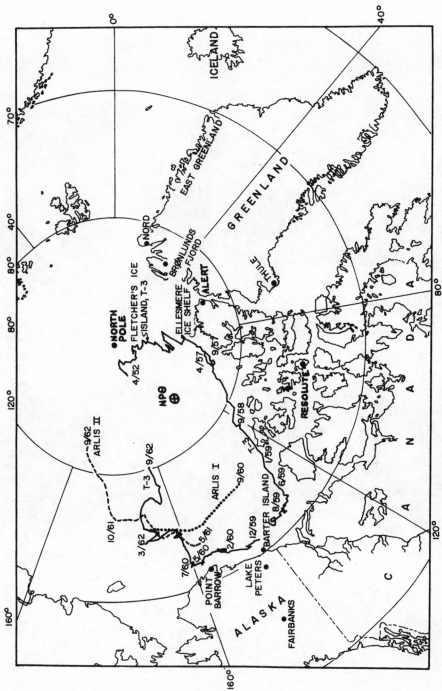

Polar projection map showing the location of significant points and the drift tracks of the T-3, ARLIS I, and ARLIS II stations (1952–1962). (*U.S. Air Force Cambridge Research Laboratory*)

End of the mission, Barrow, Alaska, June 3, 1962: Connie Seigrist, Robert Nicol, Jerrold Daniels, Miles Johnson, Douglas Price, Carson Gerkin, John Wall, Lt. (jg) Richard Olsonoski, Lt. Larry Lowe, Lt. (jg) Fred Maier, William Jordan, Maj. James Smith, Capt. Daniel Walter, Garfield Thorsrud, Capt. John Cadwalader, Lt. (jg) Leonard LeSchack, Max Brewer, John Schindler. *(Robert Zimmer)*

LeSchack (left) and Smith being presented with Legions of Merit, November 1962. *(U.S. Navy)*

6

Resolute

Despite the promise of Fulton's Skyhook aerial retrieval system, Britton remained skeptical about LeSchack's plan to investigate NP9. The subject, however, continued to come up over the next few weeks, with LeSchack growing ever more enthusiastic. Finally, Britton began to show signs of taking the proposal seriously. Who might conduct such an investigation? he asked. LeSchack responded that he would be happy to volunteer for the assignment. After all, he had the experience to know what to look for. He easily could become qualified as a parachutist, then learn how to be picked up by the Skyhook system.

Although LeSchack's interest in volunteering certainly came as no surprise to Britton, the senior scientist realized that a more experienced officer who was both a qualified parachutist and familiar with the Arctic would be essential to the success of the project. As it happened, Britton had someone in mind. Maj. James Smith, commander of drifting stations Alpha and Charlie, seemed ideal for such an assignment. LeSchack, who knew Smith mainly by reputation, quickly agreed.

When approached by Britton, Smith expressed interest in the scheme. He also informed Britton that he had been trained as an intelligence officer and had studied the Russian language. It was obvious that Smith had superb qualifications for the task of investigating an abandoned Soviet drifting station.

LeSchack and Britton next visited ONR's Air Programs Branch, the office funding the development of Skyhook. Capt. Robert Trauger and

Comdr. Benjamin Levitt, the naval aviators who headed the branch, liked the adventurous nature of the plan and pledged their support. Trauger, who was wise in the ways of the Department of Defense, suggested that it would be a good idea to add an Army member to the Navy and Air Force team. After considerable discussion LeSchack and Britton decided to request a medical doctor who was a qualified parachutist. This individual could be useful in the event of a medical emergency. If Smith or LeSchack were injured during the parachute jump onto the drifting station, the doctor could parachute down, deal with the medical problem, then assist with the Skyhook pickup.

The request for a jump-qualified medical officer went to Col. Edward O'Dell, chief surgeon of the 18th Airborne Corps. As it happened, O'Dell had someone in mind who might be interested in an adventure. 1st Lt. Daniel L. Walter, a graduate of the University of Michigan Medical School, had entered active duty in the Army's senior medical student program in August 1958. After completing his internship at the Madigo Army Hospital at Fort Lewis, Washington, he applied for and was accepted to do an obstetrics/gynecology residency at Fitzsimmons Army Hospital in Denver. As all the slots in the program were filled for 1960, he would have to wait a year to join it. With time on his hands, Walter decided to volunteer for airborne duty. It proved a happy choice, as he enjoyed the pride and camaraderie that he found in the 82nd Airborne Division. Following three months of cold-weather training in Alaska, Colonel O'Dell asked Walter to transfer to the chief surgeon's office as preventive medical plans officer for the STRIKE command. When the unusual request came in from Washington, D.C., for a jump-qualified physician, O'Dell called Walter into his office and asked if he would be interested in volunteering for the assignment. Walter, always ready to try something new, readily agreed.[1]

If LeSchack's project were ever to get off the ground, it would need the approval of the Chief of Naval Operations. With Britton's enthusiastic endorsement, LeSchack's proposal won the key support of Rear Adm. Leonidas D. Coates, the Chief of Naval Research. Once the paperwork left ONR, however, it became bogged down in the conservative inertia of naval bureaucracy.

In the administrative battles of late summer 1961, the experience and rank of Capt. John Cadwalader kept LeSchack's project alive. The senior officer in Britton's office, Cadwalader was on his final assignment prior to retirement. An instructor in the English department at the University of Pennsylvania, he had applied for and received a commission in the Naval Reserve in 1940. After a year on the faculty of the Naval Academy, he was ordered to sea in April 1942 on the recently commissioned battleship USS *Washington* (BB-56), flagship of Task Force 39. *Washington* spent four months with the British Home Fleet at Scapa Flow, then proceeded to the South Pacific, arriving in the Solomon Islands during the battle for Guadalcanal. On one memorable night in November 1942, *Washington* engaged and sank the Japanese battleship *Kirishima* in a midnight gun duel. "I had a ringside seat from my battle station on the foremast," Cadwalader recalled.[2]

In the spring of 1943 Cadwalader became gunnery officer on the newly commissioned cruiser-converted light carrier USS *Monterey* (CVL-26). He went on to participate in all the major campaigns of the Pacific war, with the exception of Iwo Jima. Cadwalader's gunners accounted for a number of Japanese aircraft, while *Monterey* escaped unscathed. The ship, however, suffered severe damage in the great typhoon of December 18, 1944, when several aircraft got loose on the hangar deck and started a fire.

Cadwalader, as a "career reservist," saw a variety of assignments in the decade following the end of the war. Between 1955 and 1959 he served with the Naval Support Force, Antarctica, spending the southern summers "down on the ice" and the rest of the year preparing for the next season's operations. In June 1959 Cadwalader, now a captain, was ordered to the Antarctic Project Office in Washington, D.C. This assignment, he noted, was "the only unpleasant duty I had in 22 years." The office had been created as a job for Rear Adm. Richard E. Byrd when the famous explorer's health had failed. It was then kept going "for no good reason" after his death in 1957. "It had become infested by government drones with influential friends," Cadwalader found, "and though there were some good people there, it was all an example of government waste." Although he learned a number of valuable bureaucratic lessons, Cadwalader was delighted to escape to sea on temporary duty as second in command to his old friend, Capt. Edward McDonald, on what proved to be the first successful attempt by two icebreakers to reach the coast of the Bellingshausen Sea in Antarctica.

Returning to Washington, D.C., Cadwalader was loathe to continue working in the Antarctic Project Office. In August 1960 he approached Dr. Britton to see if there might be something he could do at the Arctic Program of ONR. When Britton indicated that he would be happy to have the senior officer on his staff, Cadwalader arranged the transfer.

Although a number of individuals deserve credit for pushing LeSchack's highly unorthodox proposal through the frequently unyielding naval bureaucracy, Cadwalader merits most of the accolades. To have a senior captain behind the scheme lent it a respectability that was necessary to garner the reluctant approval of superior officers in the Pentagon. Finally, on September 22, 1961, the Chief of Naval Operations gave his approval. While this turned out to be only the first in a string of approvals needed to turn the scheme into reality, the plan had progressed far enough to require an official Navy name. LeSchack suggested "Project COLDFEET." In his mind, this was a double entendre, as he thought it possible he might get cold feet in more ways than one in pursuit of the enterprise. In any event, the Navy accepted his suggestion, and COLDFEET became a U.S. Navy mission.[3]

The precious authorization in hand, LeSchack now had to get ready for the mission. He turned to Commander Levitt in the Air Programs Office for assistance. A high-altitude balloonist and aeronautical engineering graduate of LeSchack's alma mater, Rensselaer Polytechnic Institute, Levitt enthusiastically supported COLDFEET. He promptly made arrangements for LeSchack to receive Skyhook training at the Naval Air Test Center (NATC) at Patuxent River, Maryland, where Air Branch funds were being spent for development work on Fulton's aerial retrieval system.

On October 12, 1961, LeSchack drove from Washington, D.C., to NATC Patuxent River, or Pax River as it is known to those stationed there. He met Lt. Comdr. P. Frank Hunter, III, pilot of the P2V being used in the Skyhook tests. Hunter showed LeSchack the Skyhook equipment on the aircraft, then made several pickups of dummy loads while LeSchack watched from the ground. At the end of the demonstration Hunter told LeSchack he would be picked up the next day.

It was warm and clear when LeSchack arrived at 10:00 A.M. for the start of his great adventure. Hunter was already airborne. LeSchack was handed the specially prepared pickup kit and told to get ready. Following the simple directions in the kit, he opened a canvas bag containing a neatly folded polyethylene balloon. He laid the balloon on the ground, then withdrew the pickup coveralls from another bag. The suit was essentially a one-piece flying suit with a fur-lined parka hood and a self-tightening parachute-type harness built in. He zipped it on, then inflated the balloon from two spherical helium bottles included with the kit. The balloon, which looked like a miniature blimp, was attached to one end of a five hundred-foot coiled nylon line. The other end of the line terminated in a self-locking hook that attached to a D-ring on the pickup suit harness. LeSchack hooked up, released the balloon, then sat down on the ground with his back to the wind, his hands clasped gently around his knees, and waited.[4]

Hunter made a test pass at the balloon, flying level at 450 feet. The aircraft then turned and began its final approach. Aiming for the orange marker fifty feet below the balloon, Hunter engaged the line. LeSchack felt a sudden thump—"like a kick in the pants." Then he was airborne. "I saw first the patch of grass on which I had been sitting," he reported, "then the circle of observers now craning their necks to follow my trajectory, and then the entire promontory which was the pick-up zone, jutting out into the Chesapeake Bay."

In less than ten seconds LeSchack became completely stable as he was towed through the air at 125 knots. Facing aft, his legs extended and his arms at his sides, his body formed a reasonably good aerodynamic section. His head, disturbing the airflow around his body, caused a bubble of air to form, making breathing easy.

While this was happening, Hunter's crew transferred the secured pickup line from the sky anchor to the winch in the aft section of the P2V. As LeSchack was being winched on board at the rate of 250 feet per minute, he experimented with several body positions to judge the effects on his flight attitude. Bringing his legs up near his chest, he found that the whole system became unstable as his body started to oscillate. He was quickly able to dampen this unpleasant sensation, however, by reextending his legs. It was damped even more quickly by extending his arms outward in addition to his legs. By extending his arms alone, and using them as ailerons, he could bank and even roll over 180 degrees.

Some five minutes after the initial pickup LeSchack was able to see the aft section of the P2V directly above his position. As he entered the aircraft's slipstream he experienced some buffeting. Pulled on board through an opening in the bottom of the P2V, he soon was drinking coffee with the crew. Following lunch at the Officers' Club with the pilots of the aircraft, an exhilarated but emotionally exhausted LeSchack drove back to Washington, D.C.

Securing parachute training for LeSchack proved a slightly more difficult challenge for Levitt. The only jump-qualified Navy personnel in 1961 were parachute riggers and instructors. A request for parachute training for a line officer in a research billet, even with proper authority, caused headaches for the bureaucracy. Frustrated by the inertia of the normal chain of command, Levitt finally picked up the phone and called his old friend, Comdr. J. E. Little, in charge of the Naval Air Technical Training Unit at Lakehurst Naval Air Station, New Jersey. Lakehurst was one of the locations where riggers packed parachutes used by Navy pilots in emergencies. The time-honored final test for a rigger was to jump with the chute that he had packed. As the old saying went, there were only two grades on the rigger's exam: pass or fail.

Levitt explained the mission to Little, who promptly agreed to provide a special accelerated course for LeSchack. The Bureau of Personnel reluctantly went along and issued the necessary orders. With their usual bureaucratic logic, the bureau specified that LeSchack was not to receive premium jump pay, since parachute jumping was not in the job description for officers in research assignments.

Five days after his Skyhook indoctrination, LeSchack reported to Lakehurst. He immediately was taken under the wing of Chief Parachute Rigger Marvin Kubler, one of the school's senior jump instructors. After showing LeSchack the care with which parachutes were packed, Kubler led him to an outdoor platform, ten feet off the ground, to practice the parachute landing fall. A gymnast in college, LeSchack had remained in good physical condition and had no difficulty in mastering the landing technique, which he practiced all afternoon.

The next morning, October 19, 1961, LeSchack joined some twenty riggers who were about to take their final exam and boarded an R4D. In order to qualify as a Navy parachutist he had to make six free-fall jumps. It seemed to him that the jump masters, who were all enlisted men, took special pleasure in placing him at the head of the jump line, their logic being that it was an officer's duty to lead. On command, LeSchack leaped out of the aircraft. In his excitement he forgot to count the seconds for pulling the ripcord. Better do it now, he thought, not realizing that only a second or two had elapsed since he had exited the plane. The explosive opening of the chute shook him like a rag doll. He had been in the aircraft's slipstream, thus causing the problem. LeSchack vowed never to repeat that mistake.

Minutes after he had safely reached the ground the instructors placed him back on the airplane with the next group of riggers. His second jump went better. Exhausted, he wobbled back to his BOQ room and fell fast asleep. LeSchack made two more jumps on October 24 and his final two on the following day. After his last jump Chief Kubler came up, congratulated him, then detached the jump wings from his uniform and pinned them on the young officer. The gesture deeply touched LeSchack.

The time consumed in winning approval for COLDFEET meant that the mission to the abandoned Soviet drifting station would likely take place in the darkness of Arctic winter. To this end Fulton and his engineer, Theodore Polhemus, had placed strobe lights along the length of the Skyhook line to facilitate a nighttime pickup. On the evening of October 27 LeSchack drove to Pax River to watch a demonstration of the modified line. Hunter made the first two scheduled pickups without difficulty. His next effort, however, did not succeed. Hunter flew into the line incorrectly, tearing loose the balloon without securing the line to the sky anchor. LeSchack, who likely would be at the other end of the line in a remote location, was not impressed.

In addition to modifying the Skyhook line for night operations, it became necessary to test Fulton's equipment for the expected low temperatures of the Arctic winter. Both Smith and LeSchack, familiar with polar conditions, feared that Skyhook's balloon might be a weak link in the system. Smith arranged for the use of the environmental hangar at Eglin AFB in Florida. Normally used to test Air Force aircraft and equipment in a wide range of conditions, the facility easily could reproduce the −40° temperature that Skyhook likely would encounter in the far north.

Smith and LeSchack's fears were proved correct. Tests during the first week of November 1961 revealed that the polyethylene balloons lost their pliability and would crack and tear at low temperatures. LeSchack turned to Commander Levitt for advice. As it happened, Levitt had encountered similar problems in his ballooning work. He referred LeSchack to a company that made balloons out of mylar. Levitt was confident that the mylar balloons would be capable of withstanding extremely low temperatures.

While LeSchack waited for the new balloons, NP9, which had been within six hundred miles of Thule, Greenland, during the summer, was drifting deeper and deeper into the Arctic ice pack. Originally, COLDFEET envisioned the Skyhook-equipped P2V, based at Thule, making both the drop and pickup. It would be backed up by the search-and-rescue capability of the U.S. Air Force. By November, however, NP9 had drifted so far away that the operation was no longer possible with the P2V alone. ONR sought fleet support, requesting the use of an aircraft that would search for NP9 and then drop the COLDFEET investigators on the station. The P2V would be used for the pickup only. No suitable aircraft was available, however. The Air Force informally offered to help but would require a formal request. The Chief of Naval Operations for Air, for reasons never made clear, declined to make the necessary request.

The new mylar balloons were ready for testing in December. LeSchack flew to Eglin AFB on board Lieutenant Commander Hunter's P2V on December 5, where the engineer from the balloon manufacturer was waiting. As final preparations were being made for the next day's cold weather test, the technician in charge of the environmental hangar asked LeSchack if he wanted to move the wind machine inside the hangar. This would permit simulation of the most rigorous Arctic working conditions: extreme cold temperatures with high wind chill. LeSchack thought it would be an excellent idea. But Hunter, who happened to be passing by, chimed in, "Forget it. We don't need it."

LeSchack faced a dilemma. It was his life—and Smith's—that would be at risk, not Hunter's. Also, COLDFEET was an ONR project. But Hunter was the senior officer. With some trepidation LeSchack told the technician to go ahead and put the wind machine in the hangar.

The mylar balloons easily passed their tests the next day. At –40°, with a fifteen-knot wind blowing, the balloons inflated perfectly and held their shape in the wind. The Skyhook equipment was ready to go.

Although Hunter did not make an issue out of LeSchack's countermanding his orders, relations between the two men were far from cordial. "I considered LeSchack a loose cannon," Hunter recalled, "with a new toy that he wanted to play with!!" LeSchack, for his part, grew increasingly concerned about Hunter's commitment to the project, as well as his skill in using Skyhook.[5]

With the new year of 1962, COLDFEET remained stalled. Without a second aircraft it would not be possible to launch the operation. LeSchack, however, remained hopeful. He continued to prepare for the mission he was sure would be launched in the not-too-distant future. Dissatisfied with the standard Navy parachutes, he enlisted Dr. Walter's assistance to obtain T-10 parachutes from Fort Bragg.

Modified by Navy riggers at Lakehurst, they proved superior to the regular parachutes. LeSchack and Walter each made two jumps at Lakehurst on February 25. The modified T-10s produced a gentle rather than explosive opening, and they were easy to steer. Just prior to landing it was possible to turn into the wind and touch down softly. The new parachutes seemed ideal for windy Arctic conditions.

In March 1962 the Soviets announced that Arctic drifting station NP8 had been abandoned. The station had been established on April 27, 1959, at 76°20′ N, 164°40′ W, or some 350 miles northeast of Wrangel Island, under Vyacheslav M. Rogachev, a specialist in polar weather problems. Over the next three years the 4.5-mile ice floe had drifted slowly northward. In April 1960 N. I. Blinov replaced Rogachev after the normal one-year tour of a station commander. The following April I. P. Romanov took over for Blinov. The stability of the ice floe had been a source of concern ever since the winter of 1959–60. Twice, the entire camp had to be relocated due to repeated fractures in the ice runway. Also, the drift of the station into the central polar basin had complicated the problem of keeping the occupants supplied. By early November 1961 aircraft flying to NP8 had to stop to refuel at NP10, which had been established the previous month by the atomic-powered icebreaker *Lenin* at 75°27′ N, 177°10′ E. A series of severe storms in February and early March 1962 finally forced Romanov to order an evacuation. The Soviets departed in haste as pressure ridges threatened to destroy their camp. Due to damage to the ice runway, light aircraft had to be used. Operating from intermediate airstrips, the aircraft safely removed all personnel but brought out little equipment. The evacuation was completed on March 19, 1962, ending 1,055 days of occupation.[6]

The unusually prompt news from Moscow about the fate of NP8 also gave the station's location—83°15′ N, 132°30′ W. Although clearly an older station than NP9, it had endured the churning ice pack nearly a year longer. LeSchack, Cadwalader, and Britton concluded that NP8 likely would display evidence of more recent submarine surveillance work than NP9. Accordingly, they decided to shift the target for COLDFEET.

Just as word came in about the fate of NP8, the Commander in Chief of the Atlantic Fleet agreed to supply a ski-equipped C-130BL from Air Development Squadron Six. The aircraft, which had just returned from the Antarctic, had eighty hours left before it was due for a major overhaul. ONR was welcome to use the remaining time. Project COLDFEET was on!

On April 3 a full-scale dress rehearsal for the proposed operation was held at Lakehurst Naval Air Station. LeSchack and Walter planned to jump from an R4D to simulate the drop on the ice, then Smith and Walter would be picked up by the Skyhook P2V. This was to be their first experience with a Skyhook pickup.

As the R4D approached the designated drop zone (DZ), the jump master released a smoke flare so that he could judge the wind. Unfortunately, the flare started a brush fire at the edge of the DZ, which did not become apparent until after LeSchack and the pickup kits had left the aircraft. As Walter stood ready to go, the jump master grew concerned about the spreading fire and pushed him away from the door at the last second. Walter stumbled backward as his static line deployed fully from his backpack. As the aircraft circled away from the fire, Walter held the fifteen feet of static line bunched up in his hand. When he finally went through the door the static line ran from his backpack under his left arm and into the plane, where it was anchored. "The ensuing shock," Walter recalled, "nearly tore off my left arm (in fact, it ruptured the long head of my biceps muscle)."[7]

After he landed Walter struggled to inflate the pickup balloon and get into his coveralls. "I had a little trouble with the lame arm," he noted, "but I didn't want anybody to know about my stupid mistake." He sent the balloon skyward, then sat and waited for the pickup. He watched the P2V pass overhead, then felt himself being lifted off the ground. Suddenly, when only a few feet into the air, he dropped back to earth. Hunter, although successful in picking up Smith just previously, had hit Walter's line improperly. The balloon broke away, but the line was not caught by the sky anchor.

Walter, still in his Skyhook pickup suit, limped to the base dispensary and sought a shot of morphine for his aching arm. The corpsman on duty, with a look of disdain on his face, informed Walter that he would need a doctor's prescription. Walter promptly whipped out his prescription pad and wrote one. As the surprised corpsman looked on, Walter filled the syringe with morphine and injected himself.

The dress rehearsal only increased LeSchack's apprehension about Hunter. By this time Hunter had concluded that Project COLD-FEET—which he believed should properly be labeled Project TRUST-TO-LUCK—was bound for disaster. "Key to the operation," he pointed out, "was a very old beat-up P2 whose reliability was in sharp question in my mind." Furthermore, the aircraft was not configured to operate in northern latitudes. Hunter also had questions about the personnel involved in the operation. He considered Major Smith "the only person with any brains at all." As he later concluded: "This thing was poorly planned and I wasn't smart enough to lay it on the line to higher ups." Despite Hunter's private reservations, planning for the mission continued.[8]

Due to the location of NP8, the COLDFEET team scrapped their original intention to stage from Thule in favor of the closer Royal Canadian Air Force (RCAF) base at Resolute on Cornwallis Island. While diplomatic arrangements with the Canadian government were being made, the COLDFEET team completed last-minute equipment preparations. In an effort to develop a means of communication without alerting the Soviets, LeSchack worked with Skyhook engineer Polhemus, who also was a talented radio expert, to modify a Collins KWM-1 amateur radio transceiver so that it could illegally operate just outside the amateur band. This would avoid the congestion and interference normally found within the legal band. It was hoped that the search teams would be able to communicate with ARL at Barrow on a frequency unlikely to be monitored by the Soviets.

❄

On April 17, 1962, the COLDFEET expedition assembled at Pax River. Hunter would command the pickup P2V with Lt. Guy Cane as his copilot, while Lt. Comdr. Charles E. Feiock and copilot Capt. Howard Chapin, U.S. Marine Corps, would fly the C-130 from VX-6. In addition to Smith, LeSchack, and Walter, the COLDFEET team included Captain Cadwalader as officer in charge and Skyhook inventor Fulton. Frank Flohil, a civilian project officer from ONR who had monitored the Skyhook development contract, would represent the Air Branch.[9]

At LeSchack's insistence Chief Parachute Rigger Kubler was included in the party. While stationed in Antarctica, LeSchack had seen too many VX-6 and Air Force para-dropped loads tunnel into the ice without their chutes opening. He had been struck by the fact that no single person ever seemed responsible for the losses. LeSchack was determined that a knowledgeable parachute rigger should be part of the COLDFEET team—someone who personally knew LeSchack and

Smith and who would be responsible for the safe delivery of supplies to the men who investigated the Soviet drifting station.

Departing Pax River the two aircraft flew to Ottawa, where they picked up Flight Lts. Howard Carpenter and W. R. Wilson from the RCAF's 408th Reconnaissance Squadron. The two Canadian officers would serve as official observers for the mission to which the government had extended its ready consent. The P2V and C-130 left Ottawa in the afternoon and flew to Fort Churchill on Hudson Bay in northern Manitoba.[10]

The following day a bad storm stalled the expedition at Fort Churchill. The team used the time to relax and shop in the village adjacent to the air base. During the course of this shopping spree Fulton spied a toboggan for sale. He promptly decided that the expedition would find the sled indispensable. Although LeSchack protested that it would be just another piece of equipment he would have to keep track of, Fulton insisted. The toboggan was added to the COLDFEET gear, courtesy of the Skyhook inventor.

On April 19 the two aircraft finally reached Resolute, one thousand miles north of Fort Churchill. It was clear that the COLDFEET expedition had left civilization far behind. As they checked into their quarters at the Resolute Hotel—a prefabricated hut—they passed a sign that summed up the feeling of their host, Squadron Leader "Black Jack" Hall, and the other Canadian airmen who manned the isolated outpost:

WELCOME
Resolute Hotel
Reasonable Rates
Women Free
In the heart of Canada's Northland
Surrounded by miles and miles of
nothing but miles and miles.
The service is poor
The climate is hell
But you've got to stay here
There's no other hotel

Cadwalader had hoped that the Navy Hydrographic Office's monthly ice reconnaissance flights between Thule and Barrow would spot the Soviet drifting station and provide an up-to-date position.

Neither of the two missions flown in April, however, had seen NP8. One mission had encountered poor visibility; the other flight had experienced a major navigational error.

Cadwalader was not overly concerned. Although NP8's last reported position was more than a month old, the hydrographic office's drift predictions prepared by Walter I. Whitmann were generally dependable. Following a weather briefing by the RCAF, the C-130 would set off in search of NP8, carrying the drop party. Hunter's P2V would stand by at Resolute in the event that an immediate pickup became necessary.

The weather could not have been better when the C-130 began to search for NP8 on April 20. Early spring in the Arctic brings many hours of daylight. The ocean remains almost completely frozen over, free of fog, and with only light winds. The visibility was excellent as Commander Feiock passed over Cape Isacksen, three hundred miles north of Resolute, and proceeded to the ice pack. He was confident that he could find the Soviet drifting station.

Flying at 21,000 feet, Feiock reached the reported position of NP8 but saw only the empty ice. He initiated a box-like square search pattern, flying ten-mile legs. Optimism gave way to disappointment as time passed without sight of the Soviet drifting station. After several fruitless hours of searching Feiock gave up and returned to Resolute.

The failure to find NP8 on the first day of searching caused Cadwalader to grow concerned. VX-6 had released the C-130 on the condition that its flight time not exceed eighty hours. This meant that NP8 had to be found before the C-130 ran out of time. After discussing the day's events with Feiock, the two men decided that they must have flown over NP8 without seeing it. The next mission, they agreed, should employ a tighter search pattern, with legs of five miles instead of ten.

The C-130 set out again on Easter Sunday, April 21, 1962. About halfway through the search copilot Chapin spotted a group of dark objects on the ice about ten miles ahead. Excitement ran through the aircraft. Feiock depressurized the C-130 as Smith and LeSchack got ready for their jump. As the aircraft passed over the camp, Smith examined the site, looking for a suitable drop zone. It did not take him long to realize that he was looking at Ice Station Charlie, his old command, not NP8.

Feiock resumed his search. Charlie had been only eighty miles from NP8 during its active life, so the Soviet drifting station had to be close by. Several hours passed without success. After another long day over the pack ice, he had no choice but to head back to Resolute.

Shortly after the C-130 landed, Corp. R. Ron Gordon of the Royal Canadian Mounted Police approached Dr. Walter with a medical emergency. Besides his regular police duties, Gordon also managed the Resolute Inuit Co-op store and in general looked after the health and welfare of the local Inuit population. Abigal Peeoyo, wife of Gordon's best friend in the native village, was having a difficult pregnancy. In the absence of medical personnel Gordon had been assisting her as best he could, ensuring that she received proper rest and took vitamins. Now in her seventh month, she was starting to miscarry. She was bleeding heavily, Gordon informed Walter, and the baby was not in a proper position for delivery.[11]

Walter climbed on board Gordon's Bombardier ski mobile, and the two men set off for the village. Entering Peeoyo's hut, Walter was struck by the presence of blood-saturated cloth everywhere he looked. The woman was lying in bed, obviously in shock. "I put on the only pair of sterile gloves I had in my jump suit," Walter recalled, "and thrust the gloved hand into the vagina. I immediately felt the small hand and forearm extending from the uterine cervix which was tightly closed. I attempted to manipulate the uterus, both from inside and from the front abdominal wall to try to do a breech delivery, but this was impossible. Finally, I found I had twisted off the arm and hand in that procedure."[12]

Walter started an IV with a small bottle of plasma expander that he carried for emergency use, then he and Corporal Gordon placed the woman on the Bombardier. As they hurried toward the base Walter radioed ahead that Mrs. Peeoyo required immediate hospitalization.

The nearest hospital was at Thule, and the RCAF did not have an aircraft available for the flight. When the station commander approached Cadwalader and explained the situation, he immediately agreed to help. Although Feiock and his crew had just returned from a long search mission, they promptly refueled their aircraft and made ready for the five hundred-mile trip to the Greenland base. After collecting two bottles of IV solution from Gordon's storeroom, Walter placed the desperately ill woman on the C-130 and tended to her as they flew eastward. When U.S. Air Force medics met the airplane on arrival at Thule, they took off the IV bottle and replaced it with O negative low-antibody titer blood, which did not require typing and matching. Walter discussed the case with the doctors at the base hospital, then Mrs. Peeoyo underwent surgery to remove the dead fetus and control the bleeding. Walter adjourned to the Officers' Club for a drink while he waited for the surgeon's report. After learning that the woman was in the recovery room and out of danger, he flew back to Resolute on the C-130.

Walter was obviously shaken when he returned to the room at the Resolute Hotel that he shared with Smith and LeSchack. The doctor produced a bottle of bourbon that he had purchased at Thule and proceeded to unwind. "You know," he told Smith and LeSchack, "delivering a healthy baby for a healthy mother is not difficult. About all you need to do is stand by with a catcher's mitt and wait for the baby to drop out. In this case, parts of the stillborn baby came out in my hands." Walter then made a deliberate effort to get seriously drunk, assisted by his roommates.

The efforts of Walter and the C-130 crew had saved a life. Cadwalader had authorized the flight without a second's hesitation. He realized, however, that more of the C-130's precious eighty hours had been used. Also, the tired crew would have to stand down for a day.

While Cadwalader fretted, LeSchack and Walter decided to take advantage of the free day to test Fulton's toboggan on a large hill near the Resolute runway. It was a long walk up the hill, and the cold air removed the alcoholic cobwebs of the previous night. The two men were comfortable with the cold weather and each other. They shared their concern about not finding NP8 and about the possible problems with the P2V pickup. Above all, they worried that the white nylon pickup line might not be discerned against the gray sky. Hunter, they agreed, certainly did not need additional challenges.

Reaching the top of the hill, they climbed on the toboggan and shoved off for the Resolute ice runway far below. Unconcerned about encountering any aircraft, which were few and far between at the isolated base, they careened down the hill. If nothing else, Fulton's purchase provided a welcome escape from the increasing pressures of the mission.

Returning to the base, LeSchack and Walter continued to discuss their apprehension over the poor visibility of the Skyhook pickup line when viewed by the P2V pilots against a background of snow and ice. They hit upon the idea of coloring the line with the red aniline dye used at Resolute to mark the center line of the ice runway. Although the dye was water soluble, they feared that a dye solution might weaken the nylon line. Instead, they decided to coat the line by running it through a barrel of aniline powder, hoping that enough of the powder would attach itself to the line to give it a distinctive red hue.

LeSchack and Walter, facing each other, undertook the long and tedious task of pulling three 500-foot lines through the dye. Before they were finished the dye was everywhere—in their faces, eyes, hair, and all over their clothing. Sneezing and coughing, it suddenly occurred to LeSchack that the dye might be poisonous. Walter said that he did not know, although the possibility certainly existed. Returning to their quarters, they immediately showered. Walter then sent a radio inquiry to the Poison Control Center in the United States asking about the chemical properties of the dye. With growing apprehension they awaited a reply. Finally, it came through: The dye was harmless. LeSchack and Walter heaved a great sigh of relief.

The seemingly endless search flights were taking their toll on the entire crew. LeSchack especially was growing concerned that it was at his instigation that so many men and so much costly equipment were being brought to bear on an exercise many people thought bizarre. Also, the heretofore good weather was beginning to deteriorate, the P2V was experiencing all sorts of mechanical difficulties, and COLDFEET was rapidly using up the available hours allotted by VX-6 on their C-130.

The search flights resumed the next morning, April 23. LeSchack was despondent and distracted as he struggled to push his rebelling body from the warm crew's quarters to the flight line for yet another tedious search. He was, as was his unfortunate habit, somewhat late, and the rest of the crew already was aboard the C-130. As he trudged across the runway to the open side door of the aircraft, Chief Kubler and the C-130 crew chief jumped out of the plane and rolled a red carpet out onto the ice runway. As the surprised LeSchack walked on it to reach the door, the two chiefs came to attention and piped (actually, whistled) the tardy LeSchack aboard.

To say that LeSchack was embarrassed would be an understatement! In the seagoing Navy, piping aboard is a time-honored tradition reserved for captains and admirals, and the red carpet is reserved for VIPs only. The only person rating such treatment, Captain Cadwalader, was already aboard and looking askance at the now-entering red-faced lieutenant (j.g.). The charade, probably instigated by Chief Kubler, had its desired effect: LeSchack and the entire crew were catapulted out of their doldrums—for at least a while.

NP8, however, remained to be located. Over the next three days, Charlie was sighted twice, but there was no sign of the Soviet ice station. "With the ease at which Charlie was spotted at considerable distances," Cadwalader noted, "it did not seem possible that NP8 could have been in the search area and not be found." With time running out on the C-130, and with the weather beginning to deteriorate with the onset of warmer temperatures, Cadwalader faced the inevitable and called off the operation[13]

On April 26, prior to the departure of the COLDFEET expedition from Resolute, Cadwalader ordered a dress rehearsal of the failed mission. Less a necessary training exercise than a gesture of farewell for COLDFEET, Cadwalader obviously hoped to raise the morale of his bitterly disappointed men.

As the C-130 flew over the Resolute airstrip, Smith and Walter jumped out of the rear cargo hatch. Chief Kubler, the most experienced parachutist, went out the cargo door with red, white, and blue smoke flares attached to his boots. The RCAF observers enjoyed the show, especially the sight of Kubler pirouetting through the frigid sky with his steerable chute.

Commander Hunter then demonstrated Skyhook, using a dummy load. On his first pass he hit the line improperly. The balloon broke loose, but the load remained on the ground. He made a successful pickup on his second pass. Smith, who was on the P2V, decided to test the effect of being towed through the −22° Arctic air behind the aircraft. After suiting up, his pickup line was wrapped around the capstan on the P2V's winch. The winch operator then paid out the line as Smith dropped through the aircraft's bomb bay. For several minutes he was towed behind the aircraft at a speed of 125 knots. Smith suffered no ill effects from the ride. It was apparent that with proper clothing there was no dangerous cooling of the body during the length of time needed for a pickup. Not that it mattered: COLDFEET seemed kaput.

"All hands concerned were still completely convinced of the practicality of COLDFEET's methods and objectives," Cadwalader observed, "but after this unsuccessful venture following nearly a year's efforts to get started, it seemed unlikely that another attempt could get much support. It was certain the Navy aircraft would not be available for another try; the P2V which had the only pickup capability in the Navy had proved a clunker, and its crew, though willing, had other commitments. It had been made clear likewise by those in charge of fleet aircraft that COLDFEET had been very lucky to get what support it had, and could not expect any more."[14]

Perhaps it was just as well that the C-130 had failed to find NP8. If Smith and LeSchack had parachuted onto the Soviet drifting station, they may have been in for a long stay. Commander Hunter had little confidence in his aircraft. Also, the P2V's gyro compass, essential for navigation in the Arctic, was "old and unreliable." Hunter "hated the idea of two Americans down on a Russian ice floe and my P2V a hard down and no repair parts."[15]

LeSchack, for his part, distrusted Hunter. While disappointed that all his efforts seemed in vain, he was relieved that the lives of the team and the success of the mission did not have to depend on the P2V. LeSchack had observed too many of Hunter's "bungled pickup attempts." LeSchack concluded: "With a minimum of three consecutive pickups from the ice under arduous Arctic conditions required for COLDFEET to be success-ful, what were the chances for this to happen with Hunter piloting?"

In any event, it no longer seemed to matter. The COLDFEET team left Resolute on April 27 and flew to Pax River. "No one was in a particularly good mood," LeSchack recalled. He collected his car, which he had left at the station, then he and Cadwalader drove along the back roads of Maryland to Washington, D.C. The atmosphere during the drive was glum. COLDFEET seemed finished.

✳

Shortly after returning from the frustrating search for NP8, LeSchack received a telephone call from Walter Whitmann, chief forecaster for the Navy Hydrographic Office. A Navy patrol plane, Whitmann said, had spotted the elusive Soviet drifting station! LeSchack immediately contacted Britton and pressed for a new expedition to the far north.

Although sympathetic, Britton knew that both the P2V and Marine Corps support aircraft would not be available for the mission. Moreover, ONR had run out of funds for COLDFEET. As it happened, however, the Defense Intelligence Agency (DIA) had begun to show signs of interest in the project. Within a few days the DIA agreed to pro-vide $30,000 for a new attempt to find the Soviet ice station.

Although ONR now had the necessary money, they still lacked the means to accomplish the operation. It was Skyhook inventor Fulton who came up with a possible solution to the problem. Why not, he suggested, use the funds to charter a Skyhook-equipped B-17 and a C-46 support air-craft from Intermountain Aviation, a company secretly owned by the CIA? Fulton had worked closely with Intermountain and felt certain that they were capable of doing the job. Negotiations quickly went forward with the company. Within days COLDFEET was again in business.

7

Intermountain Aviation

Intermountain Aviation would prove an inspired choice to conduct Project COLDFEET. Secretly owned by the CIA, the company specialized in developing and testing aerial delivery techniques. Its president, Garfield M. Thorsrud, was an experienced aviation professional and manager of intelligence operations, while chief pilot Connie M. Seigrist had performed with great skill and courage during a variety of CIA covert paramilitary adventures.[1]

The paths of Thorsrud and Seigrist had crossed during Operation HAIK (pronounced "hike"), a CIA effort to support dissident groups in Indonesia that were opposed to President Sukarno. Early in 1957 festering economic and political disputes led military commanders on Sumatra and the Celebes to rebel against the central government on Java. When the rebel leaders approached the United States for assistance, they received a warm reception in Washington, D.C. President Dwight D. Eisenhower and Secretary of State John Foster Dulles had become concerned about President Sukarno's leftist leanings and feared he would lead Indonesia into the Communist camp. In November 1957 Eisenhower approved a special political action program to support the rebel movement on Sumatra and the Celebes. Following the presidential directive, CIA director Allen M. Dulles placed Albert C. Ulmer, Jr., in charge of Operation HAIK, with a budget of $7 million. The money would be used to provide military assistance to the dissidents, including air support.[2]

Thorsrud became part of Operation HAIK early in 1958. Born in the United States of Norwegian parents, he had been a smoke jumper for the U.S. Forest Service during the summers of 1946–51 while attending the University of Montana. Recruited by the CIA following graduation, he was sent to Taiwan to work as a jumpmaster on a classified project. This covert operation used aircraft flown by personnel of Civil Air Transport (CAT), the first of the CIA's secretly owned airlines, to insert Chinese Nationalist agents on the mainland to foment rebellion against the Communist government. Thorsrud spent several months on what proved to be an abortive scheme. Dropped deep into China, the agents were ultimately captured by the Communist authorities. Thorsrud resigned from the CIA at the end of the Korean War and went through pilot training with the U.S. Air Force. In 1957 he was flying jet fighters for the Montana Air National Guard and preparing for a career as an airline pilot when he was again contacted by the CIA. Offered an attractive position in the agency's Air Branch, Thorsrud accepted.[3]

Having worked closely with CAT, Thorsrud was given the task of coordinating airdrops to the rebels on Sumatra. A CAT C-46 and a CIA-owned DC-4 picked up .50-caliber machine guns, bazookas, 75-mm recoilless rifles, small arms, and ammunition at the CIA's supply base on Okinawa, then flew to Songkhla in southern Thailand. With Thorsrud on board one of the transports to supervise the drop, the two aircraft departed after dark and flew a southerly course to Sumatra. Using the lighthouse near the port city of Padang as a checkpoint, the CAT pilots dropped their cargo on an adjacent airfield. The DC-4 dropped in central Sumatra at Pekanbaru.

The Sukarno government responded with air attacks on the rebel positions, followed by a paratroop assault on the east coast and an amphibious landing near Padang. The dissidents fled to the hills in the interior of the island after only token resistance. At a meeting of the National Security Council on April 24, 1958, CIA director Dulles reported that the rebel movement on Sumatra had "practically collapsed" during the past week. "There seemed to be no willingness to fight on the part of the dissident forces on the island," Dulles observed, "and the dissident leaders had been unable to provide their soldiers with any idea of why they were fighting." It was, Dulles concluded, "a very strange war."[4]

Prospects for resistance on the Celebes, where Cols. Alex Kawilarang and Joop Warouw provided the kind of effective leadership that was so lacking on Sumatra, seemed more promising. Also, the CIA supplied aerial support for the rebels. In March the CIA had established a rebel Air Force at Menado. Initially, two Filipino pilots had been recruited to fly P-51s. Also, a Polish crew that had been trained by the CIA for penetration missions in Europe (but never used) was brought in to man a B-26. CAT mechanics serviced and maintained the aircraft while CAT C-46s shuttled supplies from Clark Air Base in the Philippines.

The project got off to a tragic start. On their first mission the two Polish crew members were killed when their B-26 crashed following a night takeoff from Menado. At this point, the CIA turned to Robert E. Rousselot, CAT's director of operations, to provide volunteer pilots to fly the B-26s. Within a short time two individuals were ready to conduct offensive operations in support of the rebels. William H. Beale, Jr., a retired U.S. Air Force lieutenant colonel, had flown B-26s during the Korean War. Rousselot considered him "a military regimented type, responsive to direction, and a good pilot." The other aviator, Allen L. Pope, also had flown B-26s in Korea. He had joined CAT as a copilot in 1954 and flown supply missions in Indochina to the doomed French position at Dien Bien Phu. "He had venom in his blood," Rousselot recalled. "That's what it takes for this."[5]

Beale and Pope launched attacks on the government's air bases, destroying fuel depots and aircraft. They also bombed commercial shipping in the area, closing the sea lanes to Java. The Sukarno government protested to Washington in the sharpest possible terms. In response, the State Department told the embassy in Jakarta to convey the following to the Indonesian government: "U.S. has no control over bombing by rebels or adventurers whom rebels may have hired. As regrettable as these bombings are, there is nothing we can do to stop them."[6]

Connie Seigrist, a CAT pilot who flew the airline's PBY-5A, joined the rebel Air Force in mid-April. His task was to conduct reconnaissance missions around the Celebes, look for sea traffic that could threaten the safety of the base and identify targets for the B-26s. When strike missions took place Seigrist's PBY acted as search-and-rescue protection for the B-26 pilots.

Seigrist enjoyed his work. An Oklahoma native, he had flown C-46s for the Army Air Forces in the Pacific during World War II. After the war he joined with several ex-servicemen to start an airline in the Philippines, using surplus PBYs. In 1948 Dutch authorities arrested Seigrist for flying arms to the nationalist rebels in Indonesia fighting against colonial rule and sentenced him to a year in prison. Upon release, he joined CAT, which was expanding its operations following the outbreak of war in Korea. Seigrist initially flew C-46s that shuttled between Japan and Korea, carrying supplies to hard-pressed United Nations forces fighting on the peninsula and carrying wounded soldiers back to Japan. Later he was assigned to CAT's PBY and worked mainly with CIA officers who were supporting Chinese Nationalist positions on islands off the coast of mainland China.[7]

Although the rebel Air Forces controlled the skies over the Celebes, CIA officials were concerned about the possibility of an air attack from the government base on the island of Flores, six hundred miles south of Menado, and wanted to conduct a preemptive strike. As the B-26s lacked the range to reach Flores, they hoped to use Seigrist's PBY for the task. Although the PBY had been equipped to drop bombs during World War II, a quick inspection revealed that the bomb shackles had been removed from the wings of the aircraft. Undaunted, Seigrist and his associates loaded four 250-pound fragmentation bombs on board the aircraft through the waist gunner's blister. They then devised a platform to roll the bombs out of the aircraft.

On May 10, 1958, Seigrist took off to bomb a small nearby atoll. Securing one bomb to the platform and installing an arming unit, Seigrist approached the atoll at an altitude of eighty feet, then gave the signal to roll the bomb out of the blister. It hit the target exactly on center! On the next three runs, however, the bombs tumbled instead of streamlining, and the arming mechanism failed to activate. Deciding that the first bomb had been "a lucky hit" and unable to come up with a solution for the tumbling problem, they dropped the project.

Two days later Seigrist participated in a successful attack by Beale against a corvette that had been supplied to the Indonesian Navy by the Soviet Union. As Seigrist circled away from the strike area at three thousand feet, Beale dropped a bomb down the stack of the corvette, sinking it in shallow water near the shoreline on an island two hundred miles southwest of Menado.

The next morning, May 13, Seigrist was awakened shortly after dawn by two loud explosions. He knew at once that rockets had been fired at the airfield. He ran out the back door of his quarters, located across a road at the south end of the runway, and jumped into a slit trench that was used as a latrine. Seconds later a P-51 put two rockets through the roof of his quarters. The aircraft then pulled up and began a strafing pass in line with the slit trench. Seigrist jumped out and sought shelter behind some nearby trees. As a second P-51 attacked the aircraft on the field, destroying the PBY and damaging a P-51, three B-25s bombed the runway. It was all over in five minutes. Following the attack, the odoriferous Seigrist approached Rousselot and asked to be assigned to B-26s. "I was tired of being shot at," Seigrist recalled. Rousselot agreed to the request. That same evening, Seigrist boarded a CAT C-46 and flew to Clark Air Base.

Seigrist spent three days at Clark, training on B-26s under a U.S. Air Force captain who had been detailed to the CIA. It was an intensive course, with flight instruction, gunnery work, and dive and skip bombing practice. Although Seigrist had never before flown a B-26, he quickly adapted to the aircraft. "I found the B-26 to be a dream to fly and very easy and accurate to shoot or bomb from," he noted. "I was happy for the simple reason I could now shoot back."

On May 17 Seigrist obtained a B-26 that had been released from overhaul by the U.S. Air Force and flew it to Menado, arriving shortly after midnight. Ground crews immediately began loading the aircraft with fuel, four 500-pound bombs, and .50-caliber machine gun ammunition in preparation for a strike against Ambon Island, 360 miles southeast of Menado. Two aircraft would be involved in the mission. Seigrist was designated Bluebird Two; Pope had the call sign Bluebird One.

Mission plans called for Seigrist to carry a radio operator, who would communicate with the search-and-rescue PBY, if needed. As the individual was unfamiliar with the B-26, Seigrist gave him a quick briefing prior to takeoff. Above all, Seigrist cautioned, do not touch the red-colored emergency bomb salvo switch. Shortly after Seigrist strapped himself in, the aircraft literally jumped off the ground. Looking out, he saw maintenance personnel scattering in all directions. The radio operator had released two thousand pounds of bombs! Fortunately, the bombs did not have a chance to arm because they fell so short a distance. The radio operator thereupon climbed out of the airplane and refused to return. With time growing short, Seigrist decided to leave without him—and the bombs. Seigrist would have to rely upon his machine guns.

Arriving over Ambon, Seigrist flew to his target, an airfield on the eastern side of the island. "I was instructed to destroy any aircraft parked around the airfield," he recalled, "not to shoot into buildings, and to proceed to assist Bluebird One after hitting my target, providing

I had fuel enough remaining with sufficient ammunition to be of assistance to him." Seigrist found two B-25s and two P-51s on the field, probably the same aircraft that had been used for the attack on Menado. He strafed them all, opposed by only a single machine gunner.

While Seigrist was making his strafing runs, he received a call from Pope asking him how the attack was progressing. Seigrist replied that he was almost finished. Pope suggested that he join him, as he had "some very interesting targets." Seigrist completed his attack, then turned westward to rendezvous with Pope. He called Bluebird One over the radio but received no reply. Approaching the port of Ambon, Seigrist saw an Indonesian P-51 coming in from the right side. He turned his aircraft toward the attacker just as the P-51 pilot fired two rockets. As the rockets whizzed by, Seigrist opened fire with his .50-caliber machine guns. Pieces flew off the P-51 as it passed overhead. Low on fuel, Seigrist headed for Menado. He again called Pope on the radio, but there was only silence.

Landing at Menado, Seigrist felt the aircraft pull hard to the left. As he stepped on the right brake, the B-26 began to shake violently. The aircraft rolled off the runway, and the nose wheel collapsed. It turned out that the left tire of the B-26 had been shot out, probably during Seigrist's attack on the airfield. He had been fortunate to escape without greater damage.

Pope had not been as lucky. A few hours after he arrived back in Menado, Seigrist learned that Bluebird One had been shot down during an attack on an Indonesian naval convoy. Pope had managed to bail out of the crippled aircraft—a difficult feat in a B-26—but had broken his leg during the process. He was now in Indonesian hands.

Pope's capture spelled the end for the CIA's Indonesian adventure. The Dulles brothers agreed that Operation HAIK had failed. Ulmer, who had been ordered to shut everything down, cabled the necessary instructions to Clark Field. "This is the most difficult message I have ever sent," Ulmer wired. "Highest national interest," however, dictated that CIA support of the dissidents be ended. Those at Menado who had worked hard to build up the confidence of the rebels took the news hard. One of the CIA officers, Rousselot remembered, broke down and cried when he received the order to disengage.[8]

On May 21 four B-26s, two P-51s, and a PBY left Menado for the Philippines. CAT personnel were evacuated at the same time, leaving behind a hostel with two large rocket holes in the roof, the charred shell of the PBY that had been destroyed during the earlier attack on the aircraft, and Seigrist's crippled B-26. Menado fell on June 26, 1958, marking the end of effective resistance to the central government.

❋

Thorsrud and Seigrist next came together two years later for what proved to be a far greater paramilitary project—an attempt to overthrow the government of Fidel Castro on the island of Cuba. Seigrist first learned that something new was in the wind in August 1960 when he was given recurrent B-26 gunnery training at the Chinese Air Force range, west of Taipei. Shortly thereafter Rousselot assigned Seigrist and Beale to ferry a C-46 to the United States. They left Taipei on September 3, arriving in Oakland three days later. They then received instructions to proceed to San Antonio. Met by a CIA officer upon arrival, Seigrist and Beale were given their final destination: San Jose, Guatemala.

The two men flew to San Jose on September 9, 1960. A week later they ferried the C-46 to a newly constructed base at Retalhuleu, sixty miles northwest of San Jose. Seigrist was told not to keep a flight log on his activities. Also, he was to use the name "Seig" Simpson while he was working on "a special project."

Over the next three weeks two additional C-46s arrived from Taiwan, together with two C-54s from Florida. Also, two dual-controlled B-26s, belonging to the District of Columbia Air National Guard, appeared. Fifty-seven Cuban trainees soon followed. Beale ("Billy Bell") and Seigrist took charge of instructing the Cubans on the transports, while Maj. Gen. George R. ("Reid") Doster, commander of the Alabama Air National Guard, worked with the B-26 pilots. An eighty-member contingent of Guardsmen serviced and maintained the aircraft.

The training program got off to a shaky start. Beale's first student, Manual Gonzales, was an experienced C-46 pilot who had worked for a Cuban airline. To Beale's horror, however, he flew like he had never before seen the airplane. Early in training Gonzales nearly tore off the transport's landing gear while attempting to set down at Retalhuleu. The aircraft had to be taken out of service for extensive repairs, while the fifty-year-old Gonzales was hospitalized with a herniated diaphram, suffered while wrestling with the heavy controls of the C-46.

The first airdrop mission took place in late September. According to one report the C-54 on this flight was hit by antiaircraft fire as it parachuted arms and ammunition to guerrillas in the Escambray

Mountains near Trinidad in central Cuba. With one engine out the aircraft limped back toward Retalhuleu but was forced to land in Mexico, close to the border with Guatemala. Mexican authorities promptly seized the aircraft and refused to return it.

Seigrist heard a different version of events. Cuban friends told him that no antiaircraft fire had been encountered during the drop. The crew had placed the aircraft on autopilot for the long return flight and then fell asleep. Awakened by the sun they realized they were lost as the notoriously unreliable autopilot had drifted off the preset heading. The crew ran out of fuel while attempting to orient themselves and landed on a grassy plateau.

The troubles at Retalhuleu continued. Shortly after the C-54 incident, Jose Perez-Menendez was practicing airdrops in a C-46 when his wingtip hit the top of a mountain near the training base. He managed to make a forced landing without injuries to the crew, but the aircraft suffered extensive damage.

With three aircraft out of service or lost, relations between the Americans and Cubans deteriorated. "We were tremendously disappointed" at the loss of the aircraft, recalled Eduardo Ferrer, commander of a transport detachment, "but worse still, the Americans were beginning to doubt our ability to carry out further missions."[9]

Supply drops resumed on November 6, 1960. Ferrer flew as navigator on a C-46 that was assigned to drop arms and ammunition to guerrillas in the Escambray Mountains. The flight would involve a round trip of 1,680 miles. Mountains over thirteen thousand feet had to be crossed in Guatemala, and Ferrer had to rely on celestial navigation (LORAN later was added). The C-46 took off at 6:30 P.M. Arriving over Trinidad at midnight the crew began to search the mountains for the ground signal: the letter L, illuminated by seven flashlights. After two passes they received a signal from the ground, but it was not the correct one. They decided to drop anyway, and 11,500 pounds of cargo tumbled into the night.

The mission proved typical of what would follow. There were sixty-six additional drops between November and March 1961. Flights took place during the full moon cycle. Some C-46s flew directly between Retalhuleu and Cuba; others staged through Puerto Barrios on the Gulf of Mexico, 225 miles closer to the island. Only seven of the sixty-six flights were judged successful. Most of the time no ground signal was obtained, and supplies were parachuted blindly into the mountains.

The problem centered on a lack of direct communications between the guerrillas in Cuba and the supply base in Costa Rica.[10]

Although hit occasionally by small arms fire during their drops, no transports were lost. On one mission an aircraft had its landing gear shot out, but the pilot managed to return to Retalhuleu and land with only minor damage to the C-46. It was quickly repaired and returned to service.

While the transports were flying their drop missions, plans for the invasion of Cuba were changing. Initially, the CIA had envisioned the infiltration of a few hundred men into Cuba who would join the guerrilla forces in the mountains. By January 1961, however, this scheme had greatly expanded. A larger force was to be landed near Trinidad. It would establish a provisional government and pave the way for U.S. intervention. The invasion would be preceded by a series of airstrikes that would eliminate Castro's Air Force.

On March 11, 1961, Richard M. Bissell, Jr., the CIA's deputy director for plans (in charge of covert operations), presented the Trinidad scheme to President John F. Kennedy and his National Security Council. Registering concern about the scope of the enterprise, Kennedy directed Bissell to come up with a new plan for a less conspicuous and less obvious U.S. involvement.[11]

Four days later Bissell showed Kennedy the modified plan. A landing now would be made at the more remote Bay of Pigs. U.S. sponsorship would be held to a minimum. Kennedy approved the change but remained uneasy about the extent of U.S. "visibility." In the days ahead he continued to press for a less powerful and less conspicuous air strike. The original plan, which had been approved by the Joint Chiefs of Staff, called for two all-out air strikes by the sixteen B-26s of the invasion force, to take place on the day before the landing. On April 12, however, Bissell responded to adminstration pressure and substituted a single strike by eight B-26s, flown by "defecting" Cubans, that would take place two days before the invasion. If necessary, a second strike could be launched on the morning of D-Day.[12]

In March 1961, unaware of the debates taking place in Washington, D.C., the anti-Castro Air Force had moved from Retalhuleu to Puerto Cabeza ("Happy Valley") in Nicaragua to prepare for the invasion of Cuba. Thorsrud came down from Washington to command the base, with Seigrist as head of transport operations. General Doster continued to be in charge of the B-26s, while Douglas R.

Price, a CAT pilot who had joined the training team at Retalhuleu, assisted Seigrist.

On April 12, 1961, Seigrist recalls, a briefing on the invasion plan took place. A high-level delegation from Washington, D.C., arrived at Happy Valley in a Lockheed Constellation. They briefed Thorsrud and other senior members of the staff on the aerial requirements that would precede and then support a landing by anti-Castro Cubans at the Bay of Pigs. After the group departed Thorsrud and Lt. Col. George Gaines, a U.S. Air Force officer detailed to duty with the CIA's Air Branch, called together Seigrist and other operational personnel and told them about the plans. Doster's B-26s were to attack Cuban airfields on Saturday, April 15. The aircraft then would stand down on Sunday before returning to action on April 17.

"I do recall vividly," Seigrist later wrote, that "I objected to the Plan." The invasion had a chance to succeed, he believed, only if air superiority over the beaches could be maintained. The lengthy pause would enable Castro to mobilize his forces to oppose the landing. It seemed a foolish scheme, and potentially disastrous. Gaines informed Seigrist that the plan had been developed by "brilliant people" who knew what they were doing. Everyone was expected to abide by these orders.[13]

On Saturday morning, April 15, nine B-26s departed Happy Valley (CIA code name JTIDE) shortly before dawn. One aircraft, with fake battle damage and Cuban Air Force markings, headed for Miami to establish the cover story for the air attack. The pilot would claim to be part of a group of B-26 airmen who had defected and turned against Castro. The other eight B-26s, newly modified with eight .50-caliber machine guns and carrying eight 5-inch rockets under the wings in addition to 250- and 500-pound bombs, attacked the three main Cuban Air Force bases at Campo Libertad (Havana), San Antonio de los Banos (25 miles southwest of Havana), and Santiago de Cuba (on the eastern end of the island).

Approaching their targets at low level, the B-26s achieved complete surprise. One aircraft was shot down over Havana; one was hit by anti-aircraft fire but managed to land safely at Key West Naval Air Station; and a third landed at a British field on the Cayman Islands. Five aircraft returned safely to Happy Valley. The mission had inflicted severe damage on Castro's Air Force, leaving it with only two T-33 jet trainers, two or three British-manufactured Sea Fury fighters, and two B-26s.

In accordance with the air plan for the invasion, the rebel air force stood down on Sunday, April 16, 1961. On Cuba, Castro's security forces began arresting the first of some 250,000 people suspected of opposing the government. At the same time, he mobilized his military forces while awaiting the expected invasion.

Meanwhile, U-2 reconnaissance photographs revealed that Castro still had a number of operational aircraft. Thorsrud recommended to Washington, D.C., that six B-26s be launched for a sunset strike against the Cuban airfields. His superiors refused his request. Indeed, as the CIA's cover story about the defecting B-26s began to unravel, officials in Washington were resolving to stop all additional air strikes. By the end of the day, Secretary of State Rusk and National Security Adviser McGeorge Bundy had secured President Kennedy's agreement to cancel the air strikes against Cuban airfields lest they further damage what was rapidly becoming a rather tattered cover story.[14]

Learning of the presidential decision, Bissell and deputy CIA director Charles P. Cabell protested to Secretary of State Rusk on Sunday evening. Although Rusk agreed that the B-26s could be used over the invasion beaches, he remained opposed to strikes against Castro's bases. He offered Bissell and Cabell the opportunity to make their case directly to Kennedy but they declined, considering the effort pointless. Returning to CIA headquarters, Bissell directed that a message be sent to Happy Valley cancelling the morning strikes against Cuban airfields. As one historian has observed, "Bissell's appalled operations staff rightly considered this decision a disaster. . . ."[15]

By the time the cancellation order reached Happy Valley, the B-26 pilots had been briefed for the strike against the Cuban airfields and were ready to depart. They were quickly rebriefed for close air support missions. Thorsrud, who found the cancellation order "totally unbelievable," concluded that any hope of success for the operation had been lost.[16]

D-Day, April 17, saw a series of air and sea battles over the invasion beaches at the Bay of Pigs. Cuban Air Force Sea Furies sank two ships of the assault force and forced the others to withdraw. The T-33s proved terribly effective against the B-26s, shooting down four rebel aircraft. Another B-26 crashed in Nicaragua while returning to Happy Valley, killing the crew. Although Castro lost a Sea Fury and B-26 to antiaircraft fire, the two T-33s remained operational.[17]

Realizing that the invasion would certainly fail without air superiority, CIA officials at Happy Valley again sought permission to strike Cuban airfields. Kennedy relented. Three B-26s departed Happy Valley at 8:00 P.M. for a nighttime mission. Two returned due to engine trouble; the third could not find its target. A second mission by two B-26s also failed when the pilots could not identify their targets. Manuel Villafana, Cuban rebel air commander, thereupon ordered the B-26s to stand down on Tuesday, as he feared the loss of additional aircraft to the T-33s.

When reports reached Happy Valley on Tuesday that the troops on the beach were coming upon intense pressure, Seigrist went to Thorsrud and asked permission to lead a flight of B-26s in support of the ground troops. Price also volunteered for the mission. Thorsrud eventually received authorization for the flight, provided that Cuban-crewed B-26s accompanied the two Americans. Four Cuban crews agreed to fly with Seigrist and Price.

The six B-26s took off from Happy Valley on the afternoon of April 18, arriving over the Bay of Pigs an hour before sunset. Seigrist—radio call sign Lobo One—carried eight 225-pound fragmentation bombs and eight rockets; other aircraft were armed with napalm. Gus Villoldo, Cuban security chief at Happy Valley, rode with Seigrist as an observer. As he neared the coast, Seigrist spotted a line of tanks and trucks heading along one of the two access roads that passed through the Zapata Swamp from the interior to the invasion beaches. Setting his bomb release mechanism to release his eight bombs at four second intervals, Seigrist lined up on the lead tank and dove to the attack. He released his bombs on target and proceeded down the column with his machine guns firing. Seigrist then made a 270-degree turn and attacked with his rockets, hitting several tanks. He continued around and fired his remaining rockets into the last three trucks, hauling artillery pieces, at the end of the column. Out of ammunition, he watched as the other B-26s proceeded to destroy the convoy. Later reports revealed that this attack had been the most costly battle of the invasion for Castro's forces. The B-26s had destroyed thirty vehicles and inflicted some nine hundred casualties on the Cuban militia.

Pulling off the target, Price found that fragments from his own bombs had damaged his elevator trim tabs. The aircraft tended to nose down, and it took constant heavy pressure on the controls to keep it level. To relieve the strain on his arms Price took off his seat belt and buckled it around the yoke. When he reached Happy Valley he unfastened the belt and landed without difficulty.[18]

It could have been much worse. All the B-26s had been hit by small arms fire, but none suffered significant damage. Also, Seigrist learned, two T-33s had appeared in the area less than a minute after the B-26s had departed.

Encouraged by the day's events, CIA officials scheduled a series of B-26 missions over the Bay of Pigs for Wednesday. The day got off to a good start when two B-26s successfully attacked a Cuban column shortly after dawn on April 19. A second two-ship strike force, crewed by Alabama Air National Guard pilots who had been instructing the Cuban airmen, appeared over the beach shortly thereafter. Although the aircraft were supposed to receive air cover from a nearby U.S. Navy carrier, an apparent confusion in timing prevented the scheduled rendezvous. The deadly T-33s were waiting. Both B-26s were shot down, killing the four Americans on board.

Seigrist and Price formed the third mission in what was planned as continuous air cover over the Bay of Pigs. In accordance with instructions from Thorsrud, Seigrist attempted to contact the aircraft carrier USS *Essex* as he approached Cuba. He had been told, as had the Alabamans, that the carrier would send up jet fighters as protection against the T-33s while the B-26s supported the ground troops. The carrier, however, did not answer his calls. Unknown to Seigrist, President Kennedy had decided against additional American involvement. Seigrist continued toward the beach. Just before he arrived overhead he was contacted by the ground and told to leave the area immediately.

The battle on the beach continued into the afternoon but Castro's forces clearly had the upper hand. The end came before sundown. At 5:00 P.M. Brig. Comdr. Jose de San Roman sent his final message: "I have ordered all equipment destroyed. We have nothing left to fight with. The enemy tanks are overrunning our position. Good-bye, my friends." "There was nothing left to say or do," Seigrist wrote. "There was no way to back up and start again. We had lost—period."[19]

❋

Seigrist and Price remained at Happy Valley following the Bay of Pigs disaster, acting as caretakers for the property on the airfield. They flew C-46s filled with undistributed propaganda leaflets, which they dumped into the Gulf of Mexico. They loaded tanks of unused napalm on B-26s and dropped them on some exposed rocks off shore. At the end of July Seigrist and Price were ordered to Washington, D.C. Thorsrud met them upon arrival and informed them that they were now employees of a new company called Intermountain Aviation. Based initially in Phoenix, Intermountain had been established as a "proprietary" by the CIA. Overtly a private commercial enterprise that specialized in aerial delivery techniques and worked under contract for the U.S. Forest Service and other agencies, Intermountain in fact would be secretly owned by the CIA and responsive to the directions of the agency's Air Branch. Thorsrud would be in charge of the company, and Seigrist would be chief pilot.

Thorsrud sent Seigrist and Price to California in August to pick up Intermountain's first aircraft. Arriving in Burbank, they called at Lockheed Aircraft's famous "Skunk Works," home of the U-2, SR-71 Blackbird, and other secret projects. Their aircraft turned out to be less esoteric than most of Lockheed's products. On August 18 they collected a B-17G with registration N809Z. Neither Seigrist nor Price had even flown the World War II Flying Fortress, but after one landing and takeoff each, the check pilot released the aircraft to them. "It was easy to handle," Seigrist recalled.

When the aircraft reached Phoenix, Thorsrud informed Seigrist that the B-17 would be used to test a new Skyhook aerial recovery system that was being developed by Robert Fulton. The tests would take place at Intermountain's new operational base at Marana Air Park, north of Tucson. If it proved satisfactory, Thorsrud said, Skyhook might well be used to extract Al Pope from his Indonesian prison.

The CIA already had worked on a scheme to free Pope, who was under a death sentence in Djakarta. In February 1961 Fulton had gone to Okinawa where he trained Air America pilots on the Skyhook system using a Navy P2V. The mission never took place, in part because the pilot who was to be used in the operation—Woodward Forte—had been killed during an arms drop mission in Laos. As Seigrist and Price began intensive training for the possible rescue, the Kennedy administration continued its efforts to obtain Pope's release through diplomatic channels. If it appeared, however, that the Indonesian government intended to carry out the death sentence, a Skyhook mission might well be authorized.

John D. Wall, Intermountain's vice president, directed the building of a replica of Pope's prison in a remote corner of the Marana complex. "We had various sources of dependable information," Seigrist notes, "on the size of the building and his guard's schedule." The Navy supplied four mannequins that would substitute for Pope during training exercises.

The first problem with the proposed rescue scheme arose during a practice pickup of one of the mannequins. According to information received from the CIA, a balloon, line, and hydrogen pellets would be smuggled into the Indonesian prison. Because of the confined area, Pope would have to be lifted over a fourteen-foot wall during the initial phase of his Skyhook ascent. On the first trial at Marana, the mannequin slammed into the wall with such force that its arm was torn off.[20]

Another serious problem arose as the mannequin was being winched on board the B-17. As it came within fifty feet of the aircraft, the hitherto quiet ride became violent as the figure lost streamlining. Nearing the entry point that had been cut into the belly of the B-17, the head of the mannequin hit the bottom of the aircraft with a resounding thump. It was clear that a human head could not withstand such an impact.

There was little question that the four-engine B-17 created severe turbulence underneath the aircraft that was not present when a twin-engine P2V was used. Various experiments were conducted to get better data on the extent of the difficulties. One of these flights began in a routine manner but nearly ended in disaster. Seigrist made the pickup without difficulty. Again, as the mannequin neared the aircraft it began to oscillate wildly. This time, however, the mannequin proceeded to yo-yo back and forth on the flexible nylon pickup line. Finally, it wrapped itself around the horizontal stabilizer. "Immediately we started a roll to our left," Seigrist recalled. He jammed his foot on the right rudder pedal but could not budge it. "With reflex action I chopped both right side engines before we rolled over into the ground." Seigrist applied full power to the left engines. Helped by the propeller drag on the right engines, he managed to bring the wings level. As the aircraft began to sink slowly toward the ground, Seigrist found that by slighty reducing power on the left outboard engine, he could make a wide, level turn to port. "I continued my turn to the left," he noted, "making about a 10-mile pattern around the airfield until I was able to line up with one of the runways." He landed at the end of the runway just as he ran out of altitude. Thanks to Seigrist's superb airmanship, the B-17 and crew were saved from what might well have been a calamity.

A solution to the problem came with a modification of the entry point for the mannequin. Instead of using the hole in the belly of the aircraft, a new entry was made by constructing an opening in the area that originally had been used by the rear turret gunner of the B-17.

Tests revealed that the mannequin could now be brought on board without the oscillation problems that had been caused when it entered the disturbed airstream underneath the aircraft.

Strong surface winds also caused difficulty for the Skyhook system. "We found 30 knots was marginal for a safe pick-up," Seigrist reported. Above this, the mannequin would not ascend vertically but would be dragged along the ground. Rain also created problems. It covered the balloon and saturated the braided lift line, making the line too heavy for the balloon to keep taut.

The four mannequins suffered during the test program. Two were completely destroyed, while the other two ended up being held together with tape and parachute shroud line. The wooden prison replica had to be constantly rebuilt as the mannequins slammed into the fourteen-foot wall. Nonetheless, by the early months of 1962 Seigrist was confident that it would be possible to rescue Pope "without a scratch."

As it happened, the rescue operation was unnecessary. In February 1962 Attorney General Robert Kennedy received assurances from President Sukarno that Pope would be set free. Five months later he was quietly released from his Indonesian prison. Returning to the United States, Pope found employment with the CIA's Southern Air Transport.[21]

The skill gained by Intermountain's Skyhook crew, which included not only the pilots but the personnel who operated the nose trigger, winch, and other equipment necessary for a successful pickup, would not go for naught. In May 1962 word was received at Marana that a new project was about to be undertaken—one called COLDFEET.

8

NP8

On May 15, 1962, five days after LeSchack received word about the discovery of NP8's location, Intermountain Aviation president Thorsrud informed chief pilot Seigrist that the company had been selected to conduct the Project COLDFEET operation.[1] The news, Seigrist recalled, came as "a tremendous shot of adrenaline to all of us associated with the Skyhook program."

Before Intermountain could be used for COLDFEET, however, LeSchack had to negotiate a contract between the company and ONR. The negotiations, as far as LeSchack was concerned, amounted to "a wonderful farce." He knew how much money ONR was prepared to spend, and it was less than Intermountain needed to do the job. He also was aware that the company, while ostensibly a private concern, was in fact owned by the CIA. And Thorsrud wanted to do the mission as badly as LeSchack wanted it done. In the end, an agreement was reached for an amount of money that clearly would be overrun. LeSchack figured that if the operation succeeded, he would have no trouble securing the additional funds. On the other hand, if it failed, he probably would not be around to worry about it.

Having solved one problem, another difficulty quickly reared its head. All previous live pickups by the Fulton aerial retrieval system had been made by military aircraft and had involved military personnel. The Federal Aviation Agency (FAA) considered Intermountain's B-17 to be in a special category that restricted its operations. These restrictions,

LeSchack learned in a frantic phone call from Thorsrud, would have to be lifted before the aircraft could proceed to Barrow. LeSchack prepared a letter from ONR that Thorsrud then hand-carried to the chief of the FAA's Flight Standards division. The FAA promptly granted approval for the B-17 to conduct "cold weather testing" from Barrow. Thorsrud, however, worried throughout the ensuing operation that the FAA might precipitously withdraw the permission.

As the B-17 would have to be in place at Barrow no later than May 26, preparations for the mission began at once. On May 18 Seigrist made a practice pickup of a static load to test all elements of the Skyhook system. The horns were then removed from the B-17 and placed on board the support aircraft, together with balloons, lines, radio, and other gear. Five days later Seigrist tested the long-range bomb bay fuel tanks that had been installed in the B-17 to ensure that the lines and valves were operating properly. At the same time he checked out the Kerfoot directional gyro system that had been placed on board to assist with polar navigation.[2]

As no one connected with Intermountain had any experience flying in the far north, Thorsrud sought the assistance of an experienced navigator. Through the contacts of B-17 copilot Price, who had once worked for Pan American Airways, Intermountain obtained the services of William R. Jordan. An experienced pilot, Jordon also was a licensed navigator. During the 1950s he had served as Pan Am's chief navigator and FAA-designated flight examiner, authorized to issue flight navigator licenses. The early 1960s brought the additional duty of checking out new crews on grid navigation for Pan Am's polar route to Europe.

Jordan recalls receiving a late-night phone call inquiring if he would be available for a mission "to test some Arctic rescue gear for the Navy." The plan, he was told, called for a departure from Thule, Greenland, for a flight of three hundred miles to the northwest. "What kind of aircraft would be involved?" Jordan asked. "A B-17," came the reply. Jordan demurred. The idea of flying over polar ice fields in a World War II bomber held little appeal for him. Not to worry, he was told; the B-17 had been completely rebuilt and was like a new airplane. When Jordan continued to hesitate, he was informed that the job would pay $100 a day, plus expenses. Also, Pan Am would continue his base pay while he was away. Jordan was persuaded. "I'll go!" he said.[3]

On Wednesday, May 23, the Intermountain C-46 picked up additional Skyhook equipment at Fulton's factory in Newtown, Connecticut, then collected the COLDFEET team in Washington, D.C., and flew to Marana. LeSchack found the experience rather exotic, arriving at a remote desert airfield late at night and meeting with a colorful group of individuals who obviously were engaged in deeply secret activities. Smith was less impressed. Apprehensive about Intermountain's lack of Arctic experience, he was reassured when he learned that a skilled polar navigator had been added to the mission.

The next day the B-17, flown by Douglas Price and Robert Zimmer, proceeded to San Francisco and picked up Fulton and Jordan. While en route to Fairbanks, Fulton approached Jordan and told him that the story about testing naval survival gear was not true. They were not going to Thule. Instead, they would be flying to Barrow to search for an abandoned Soviet ice station. Jordan replied that he would not miss this trip for the world. "I didn't say it to Bob," Jordan remembered, "but it did go through my mind that now, maybe I could pay back a little something for the great education I had received first in naval flight training and then at the University of California under the G.I. bill."

While the B-17 was flying up the West Coast, the C-46, which had been delayed at Marana with hydraulic problems, headed to Fairbanks via Great Falls, Montana, and Edmonton, Alberta. Both aircraft reached the Alaskan city shortly before midnight. The COLDFEET team then transferred to the B-17 and flew immediately to Barrow, with the C-46 to follow the next afternoon.

Operations from Barrow, home of ONR's Arctic Research Laboratory, got underway on Saturday, May 26. Cadwalader had asked the commander of the Alaska Sea Frontier to provide a P2V from Patrol Squadron One (VP-1) to assist in the search for NP8. The aircraft, flown by Lt. Larry T. Lowe, was waiting at Barrow when the B-17 arrived. On Saturday morning the P2V departed for the predicted position of the Soviet drifting station, carrying Cadwalader and Robert Fischer, ARL's chief pilot.

Cadwalader's decision to seek VP-1's help would prove crucial to the success of COLDFEET. Lieutenant Lowe had deployed to Kodiak Naval Air Station on his second tour to the Alaskan post in mid-March 1962. He had great faith in his aircraft, a P2V-7S. This final production model of the highly successful Lockheed Neptune series was powered by two Wright R-3350 engines that featured water injection and power recovery turbines, plus two underwing Westinghouse J-34-WE-36 jet engines. The jets ordinarily were used only on takeoff or when one of the piston engines failed.[4]

Lowe's aircraft had excellent range, with four fuel tanks in the wings, two tip tanks, and one bomb bay tank. The 4,170 gallons of fuel translated into an endurance of 15 hours and 30 minutes. As it turned out, Lowe would need it all.

Lowe had equal confidence in his crew. Lt. Dale B. Petty was second pilot, while Lt. (j.g) Frederick J. Maier acted as third pilot and navigator. In addition to the three officers, the aircraft carried eight enlisted personnel. In April 1962 Lowe's crew had won the squadron's "Crew of the Month" award. Assigned to a specific aircraft, the crew would stand down when their P2V underwent maintenance. This system, Lowe observed, worked well: "You knew the capacity of both."

Prior to leaving for Barrow, Lowe had been given an additional navigator. While Lowe's crew had never flown over pack ice, the crew of his BOQ suitemate, James Barnes, recently had operated from Barrow on a project to drop explosives over leads in the pack ice for underwater acoustic propagation tests. Barnes volunteered his navigator, Lt. (j.g.) Richard L. Olsonowski, for the search mission. Olsonowski and Maier, who was the squadron's navigation officer, spent several hours reviewing a textbook on polar navigation, brushing up on the grid navigational techniques that would be used over the pack ice.

Lowe and his crew gave a good deal of thought to the requirements of the search mission. The APS-20 radar on the P2V was useful only near the coastline; over the pack ice the screen showed only clutter. Also, the drift meter worked over water but not over ice. As the magnetic compass was unreliable this close to the magnetic North Pole, reliance would have to be placed on the aircraft's two gyro compasses and celestial navigation.

Lowe decided to bend the regulations on reserve fuel. Usually, bad weather required that a pilot have sufficient fuel to reach his destination, shoot an instrument approach, then proceed to an alternate airport and arrive with a 10 percent reserve. This would not be possible when flying out of Barrow, as there was no alternate airport. Lowe would time his departure from the search area based on the predicted flying time to Barrow on one engine. While other pilots might have used a greater safety margin, Lowe had enough confidence in his airplane and crew to cut short the usual requirements.

Lowe's takeoff from Barrow was anything but routine. At a maximum gross weight of eighty thousand pounds, the P2V needed most of the four thousand-foot pierced-steel-planking (PSP) runway to become airborne. At least the weather was good as Lowe headed for the predicted position of NP8, some 750 miles distant. He remained at a low altitude while flying over the pack ice, employing a maximum-range power setting on his engines. Navigator Maier used a periscope sextant to take constant sun lines, while Olsonowski consulted navigational tables and plotted the lines on a grid map. Although the navigators could accurately place the aircraft somewhere along the sun line, there was no way to obtain a cross bearing and fix the P2V's position on the line. It was the best that could be done, however, given the limitations of Arctic navigation in the days before LORAN and OMEGA radio positioning systems covered the Arctic, and well before Global Positioning System satellites were in place.

The hours passed without incident as the aircraft droned northward over the polar ice field. Only one problem arose for the navigators. Cadwalader and Fischer kept pressing into the tiny navigational compartment to check the aircraft's position. Olsonowski hesitated before raising the issue with a four-striper. Finally, he had to tell Cadwalader that his presence was interfering with the navigational work. The senior officer took the admonishment with good grace and left Maier and Olsonowski to their task.[5]

Arriving in the area where NP8 had been reported, Lowe climbed to a higher altitude and set up a square search pattern. Using a power setting that would give maximum endurance, he flew the expanding square legs of the pattern in good visibility as the crew of the P2V searched the horizon. Lowe's crew, trained for antisubmarine warfare and ship identification, was expert at the task. The P2V provided excellent visibility from the cockpit, nose dome, and windows on each side of the fuselage and in the tail. Also, the crew rotated their positions frequently, a technique that kept them alert.

After some four and a half fruitless hours in the search area, Lowe decided that the time had come to return to Barrow. As he was making his last circuit prior to departure, the crew spotted the elusive Soviet drifting station. The navigators fixed the position of NP8 as best they could, then Lowe headed south. The P2V missed its estimated time of arrival at Barrow by twenty minutes, crossing the coastline well east of the field. Lowe followed the coast until he reached the airfield, then landed after a flight of fourteen hours and forty-two minutes.

That evening Cadwalader called a meeting of the B-17 and P2V crews. He showed the assembled group photographs of Soviet pre-fabricated buildings used in the Arctic and of American quonset huts, emphasizing the differences. Remembering the mission from Resolute, Cadwalader wanted to make sure that Smith and LeSchack were placed on the correct target! Cadwalader then displayed the position of NP8 and its estimated speed and direction of drift.

At 9:50 A.M. the next morning the B-17 took off in search of NP8. The aircraft carried a heavy load of fuel and passengers. In addition to the normal wing tanks, the B-17 featured long-range tanks in the outer wing panels and a huge tank in the bomb bay. Six 55-gallon drums of fuel sat in the main cabin; the fuel would be pumped by hand into the large tank as it became exhausted, then the drums would be dropped overboard.

The aircraft's Skyhook crew consisted of jumpmaster Wall, assistant jumpmaster Miles L. Johnson, winch operator Jerrold B. Daniels, nose-trigger operator Randolph Scott, and tail-position operator Robert H. Nicol. In addition to the COLDFEET team of Smith, LeSchack, and Walter, the B-17 also carried Thorsrud, Fulton, and Cadwalader.

Like Lowe, pilots Seigrist and Price had to use most of Barrow's PSP runway to get into the air. As the aircraft lined up prior to takeoff, Jordan set his gyro to the runway heading. The weather remained excellent as the B-17 flew northward. While most of the crew and passengers settled down for the long, cold, noisy flight to NP8, Jordan worked on his navigational task. His first sun line showed that the initial setting of the gyro was a few degrees in error. He reset the compass and told the pilots to turn to the proper heading. Jordan continued to take sun lines at twenty-minute intervals as the aircraft proceeded over the pack ice.[6]

At 2:00 P.M. the B-17 reached the predicted position of NP8, according to Jordan's calculations. But the crew saw only a field of ice that stretched to the horizon in all directions. "It was the most desolate, inhospitable looking, and uninviting place I had ever seen," Seigrist recalled, "or ever would want to live in much less fly in as a steady diet." He promptly initiated a square search pattern, as had Lowe. After completing several legs of the pattern the pilots announced that they had the ice station in sight! As the aircraft headed for the location, Smith and LeSchack, with their adrenalin pumping, began last-minute preparations for their parachute drop. Arriving overhead, however, the ice station turned out to be a flattened pyramid of fuel drums. Cadwalader believed they were looking at a piece that had broken off NP8. The ice station could not be far away.

The search continued. Although the B-17 located Ice Station Charlie, there was no sign of NP8. Finally, after nearly five hours in the search area, Seigrist was forced to head for Barrow.

As the B-17 droned southward, Cadwalader asked Jordan for an estimated time of arrival. The navigator later confessed that he was "a little stressed" by the request. He was over seven hundred miles from Barrow in a relatively slow airplane. He knew that the slower the airspeed and the greater the distance, the more likely small errors would occur. "I quickly reviewed my outbound ground speed calculations and wind drifts," he noted, "and put it all in my E6B navigation computer [basically, a circular slide-rule] and came up with an ETA [estimated time of arrival] for Captain Cadwalader." Seigrist touched down at Barrow in the constant Arctic daylight at 11:30 P.M.—within one and a half minutes of Jordan's estimate.

Cadwalader faced a dilemma. Both Jordan and the navigators of the P2V were convinced that their navigation had been accurate. Jordan believed the Navy had given him the wrong position; Maier and Olsonowski were positive that they had properly placed NP8 and that the problem lay with Jordan. Cadwalader was impressed with the accuracy of Jordan's ETA for Barrow. The P2V, on the other hand, had missed its ETA by twenty minutes, suggesting that NP8 lay north of its plotted position.

In the end Cadwalader decided on a plan of action that would involve both aircraft. The P2V, with ARL pilot Fischer on board, would leave Barrow two hours before the B-17 and attempt to locate NP8. The B-17, following behind with the COLDFEET team, would conduct its own search. If the P2V succeeded in finding the Soviet ice station, it would contact the B-17 and direct it to the area by radio.

Lowe left Barrow at 9:00 A.M. on May 28. Following the same procedure they had used earlier, Maier and Olsonowski directed the aircraft toward the spot where they believed the drifting station could be found. Lowe arrived in the search area at 2:00 P.M. in deteriorating weather conditions. With restricted visibility, he had to set up a tight square search pattern as he hunted for the target.

Meanwhile, the B-17 had departed from Barrow at 10:50 A.M.

Directed by Jordan, the aircraft reached its search area at 4:00 P.M. Seigrist also began to fly a square search pattern as all eyes scanned the barren ice pack below.

At 5:00 P.M., following three hours of searching, the P2V located NP8 at 83° N, 130° W. Lowe immediately sent the agreed upon radio signal to Seigrist: "The magnetic survey has been completed!" The B-17 lay some forty-two miles distant. Lowe took an Ultra High Frequency (UHF) radio bearing on transmissions from the aircraft and gave Seigrist the proper heading to fly to reach the target.

Word that the elusive ice station had at last been located energized the COLDFEET team. Smith, LeSchack, and Walter again checked their main and reserve parachutes, then reexamined their survival and survey equipment. They paid special attention to the parachutes on the Skyhook retrieval containers, upon which their survival depended. Smith, as usual, betrayed little emotion, with only the slightest hint of a smile of anticipation around his eyes. The ebullient LeSchack, however, could hardly contain his emotions as the project he had set in motion so many months ago at last neared its denouement.

Jumpmasters Wall and Johnson gathered their wind drift markers and proceeded to their assigned stations—Wall in the bombardier's window in the nose, Johnson at the "Joe hole" that had replaced the wartime belly turret. Fulton darted forward and aft, jumping over drop bundles, as he prepared to photograph the action.

Arriving over the drifting station, Seigrist began to circle at three hundred feet to inspect the camp. He observed a group of buildings, an abandoned tractor, and an ice runway. "A long ridge of pressure ice had formed and ran across the mid section of the runway," he noted, "making it inactive for large aircraft." The Soviets obviously had had to abandon the station in haste before the runway became unusable. Logistical support of the camp, Seigrist recognized, had been "totally dependent on the runway length being capable of accommodating large aircraft" (see Figure 4).

Smith carefully examined the site to ensure that they were looking at NP8 and not Drifting Station Charlie. After Smith confirmed the identity of the camp and made sure there was no sign of life—man or bear—Seigrist climbed to 1,200 feet while Johnson opened the Joe hole. Upon Wall's command from the nose, Johnson dropped a smoke grenade. When it failed to ignite, he threw out a second marker. Although it, too, failed, Wall and Johnson had supervised so many jumps for the U.S. Forest Service that they were confident they could place Smith and LeSchack anywhere they wanted to go on the ice below.

After Smith pointed out a drop zone near the station, Seigrist—who had made hundreds of airdrops for CAT/Air America—set up his approach. He had agreed with Price that as a former Army Air Forces

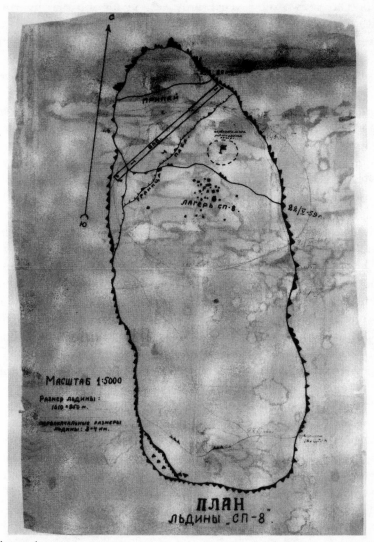

Figure 4
Russian map of NP8. Note changing dimensions as floe disintegrates.

pilot he would fly the B-17 for Smith's drop, while ex-Navy flyer Price would take the controls for LeSchack's exit.

As Smith positioned himself at the Joe hole, sitting on a step aft of the radio compartment, LeSchack leaned over and shouted a final reminder to ignite a smoke flare as soon as he landed. Smith nodded in acknowledgment. Moments later Johnson began the countdown to jump. Three. Two. One. Then he gave a gentle shove as he eased Smith through the hole and into the cold Arctic air at 5:50 P.M.

As Smith descended toward the snow-covered pack ice, he found himself drifting toward the station's radio antenna. With thoughts of possible impalement passing through his mind, the experienced jumper pushed down hard on both of his parachute toggles in an effort to increase his forward speed. The technique worked. Smith avoided the radio mast and made a soft landing in one and a half feet of snow. He set off a smoke flare, then radioed Wall to make his next pass fifty yards to the right.[7]

Meanwhile, LeSchack positioned himself over the Joe hole. Johnson double-checked his static line, which was hooked into a bulkhead D-ring behind him. As LeSchack was putting on his helmet, Cadwalader leaned over and shouted above the roaring engine, "Good luck, Leonard. I envy you."

Thoughts of apprehension and elation passed through LeSchack's mind as Johnson began the countdown. Finally, Johnson shouted "Jump!" in his ear. LeSchack breathed a quick prayer, then eased himself out of the Joe hole at 5:57 P.M. Remembering his training, LeSchack kept his feet together, held the kit beneath his reserve chute with his left arm, and tightly grasped the ripcord of the reserve chute in his right hand. Seconds later he felt a jerk, looked up, and with immense relief saw his canopy fully deployed.

LeSchack experienced a sense of near euphoria as he floated down—a feeling of freely floating that only parachutists know, combined with the realization that the culmination of all his planning, aggravation, badgering of senior officers, and personal commitment was at hand. Looking downward, he saw the green smoke of Smith's flare. He tugged gently on one of his toggles to alter the direction of his descent. As he neared the landing spot, he pulled both toggles as Smith shouted encouragement and instructions. The ice approached faster and faster as LeSchack got closer to Smith's position. Finally, he wheeled the chute into the wind and touched down perfectly. It was the softest landing LeSchack had ever made on his tenth—and what would prove to be his last—jump.

With the two men safely on the ice and no need for Dr. Walter's assistance, Seigrist commenced a series of eight cargo drops. Between 6:02 and 6:22 P.M., equipment rained down from the B-17, all on target. Smith promptly retrieved the Forest Service beacon and turned it on. Designed for short-range use (lest the Soviets pick up the signal), it could be heard clearly within five miles of the station. After final assurances from Smith and LeSchack that all was well, Seigrist left the area at 6:45 P.M. for the long flight back to Barrow.

As the B-17 disappeared over the southern horizon, Smith and LeSchack experienced a sudden sense of isolation and exhaustion. They stood together in the center of the camp for what seemed a long time, then turned their attention to the task at hand. They first conducted a hut-by-hut examination of the station to identify the best location to set up housekeeping. After about an hour they selected what appeared to be the senior scientist's cabin. There were two double-decker beds on either side of the hut, a work table at the end opposite the entrance, and, near the door, a wood-coal stove and small table.

They next opened all their drop bundles and arranged the contents outside the hut so they could begin their investigation the next day. After bringing in the food supplies, Smith lit a small sterno stove and began cooking a couple of cans of stew for dinner. To Smith's delight LeSchack produced a flask of Canadian Club he had managed to stash—with some difficulty—among the medical supplies, two Leica-M3 cameras, notebooks, and .45-caliber magnum in his jump kit. The two promptly prepared a drink familiar to all those who have worked on ice: C.C. and snow.

Although Smith and LeSchack found blankets and mattresses in the camp, the bedding was so smelly and grimy that they opted for their own sleeping bags. For added comfort they inflated their air mattresses, which they placed on top of the Russian mattresses. After finishing off LeSchack's pint of whiskey, they crawled into their sleeping bags to get some rest. Exhausted, both mentally and physically, they quickly fell into a deep sleep.

After they awoke in the morning, they fired up the sterno stove, made coffee, and discussed their day's activities. After making a preliminary survey of the camp, they would identify an order of priority for detailed study. Using a photogrammetrically prepared map of the station, they would divide their investigation into four geographical areas. They then would work independently, comparing their findings at the end of the day.

After Smith departed for his designated search area, LeSchack set up their radio equipment. In accordance with arrangements made with Cadwalader, both NP8 and Barrow would monitor the designated band twice daily but would not transmit unless there was something urgent to report. NP8 would transmit twelve hours prior to the scheduled pickup on the third day. Using the toboggan Fulton had insisted that he acquire for the previous operation from Resolute, LeSchack moved the case of heavy batteries to the hut that the Soviets had used for their radio station. All that remained were switches, control panels, one high-frequency transmitter, an antenna coupler, and a huge pile of electronic-parts debris on the floor.

LeSchack's radio, which had been wrapped in both sleeping bags for the paradrop, was ready for immediate hookup. Although prepared to string his own antenna, LeSchack hoped to save himself the work by using the existing arrays. After looking carefully at the Soviet antennas, he selected one that had the best orientation for communicating with Barrow. Not surprisingly, it was the least-sophisticated antenna; the more directive arrays were pointed toward the Soviet Union. He hooked up his transceiver to the storage batteries and turned on the set. It worked without any problems. He then tuned the receiver to the twenty-meter band and picked up Russian-language broadcasts. The transmitter also seemed to load up properly when attached to the antenna. He believed that if propagation conditions were right, contact could be made with Barrow.

While LeSchack worked on the radio, Smith investigated the abandoned camp. In general he found the Russian facilities to be "crude." The shelters were doubled-walled plywood. Unlike the Jamesway huts on Ice Station Charlie, they were not mounted on skids. This would make them more difficult to move when pedestaling took place during the summer months.

Several of the huts were rather crudely holed for wiring for instrument leads, almost as if hatchets or hammers had been used. Electrical systems could only be described as "haphazard"; some huts were not wired at all. The equipment left behind by the Soviets was World War II vintage. An abandoned D-4-sized tractor was in sad shape and likely prewar.

The Soviets had used coal for heating. The smoke not only would produce a great deal of contamination, but also would settle down and create problems during the summer when anything dark on the ice accelerates melting. The Soviets seemed to put effort into their equipment only when absolutely necessary.

Later in the day Smith and LeSchack came together to inspect the kitchen and mess hall. "What a horror!" LeSchack observed. "Food was still on the stove, frozen in greasy skillets. There was dried blood all over, and animal carcasses, including dog carcasses, were laying around in an adjacent shed." The mess hall had a seating capacity of about fifteen. No doubt the station's complement was fed in two shifts.

In one corner of the mess hall Smith and LeSchack found a dozen 16-mm motion picture films, indicating that the hut also served as a social center. Tacked to the walls were political posters that exhorted citizens to work hard for the Communist party. Scribbled across one of the posters was a note from the station commander giving the date of abandonment and asking anyone finding the message to contact the Soviet Arctic and Antarctic Institute in Leningrad. Smith folded up the poster and stuffed it into the pocket of his coveralls.

The two men continued their investigation in favorable weather. The temperature stood at 15°, with ten knots of wind. The sky was overcast, and a light but steady snow came down. After some twelve hours of activity the men came back together to share an evening meal and compare notes. Smith had some scientific items that he asked LeSchack to identify, while LeSchack had material in Russian that he wanted Smith to translate. After a C-ration meal they climbed into their cold sleeping bags for a second night's sleep in the high Arctic.

They split up again the next morning, this time making a detailed examination of each hut, sifting carefully through the debris, collecting important artifacts, photographing instruments, and in general seeking information that might be useful to intelligence analysts. In one of the huts that had been used as a photographic darkroom LeSchack found a strip of 35-mm negatives in the negative carrier of an enlarger. They turned out to be photographs of the camp staff. LeSchack was particularly amused by one showing a burly scientist in a bathing suit smiling for the camera as he sat on the ice next to a lead.

Smith also discovered several personal mementos of the previous occupants. The radio hut, for example, contained a pad of messages from family members to the camp's staff. One was from a mother admonishing her son to wear plenty of warm clothes when he stepped outside. Both Smith and LeSchack found a number of pinup girls attached to the walls of the huts—they were all pictures of ballerinas.

The major thrust of LeSchack's efforts was to determine how advanced an oceanography program the Soviets were conducting, and to find any clues about the state of Soviet acoustical surveillance. He took photographs showing generators that were cushioned on rubber tires. The Soviets obviously were trying to muffle the noise on the station, something that would be done in association with acoustical surveillance work.

The two investigators met again at the end of the day to discuss their findings. Pleased with their progress, they turned in for the night, confident that they could complete their work before the scheduled arrival of the B-17 the next day.

When LeSchack awoke on the third day, May 31, he turned on his transmitter and began sending a weather report to Barrow. Using his own amateur radio call sign (W4RVN), he couched the message in jargon that ham operators invariably use. Transmitting just outside the twenty-meter amateur radio band, where there would be no interference from ham operators, LeSchack figured that should the message be picked up by unintended listeners, the worst anyone would think was that he had accidentally drifted out of the assigned amateur band. After sending at the agreed upon time and hearing no response, LeSchack reluctantly concluded that propagation conditions were not adequate to establish communication with Barrow. As it turned out, he was only partially correct. A fragmentary and garbled weather report had reached ARL.

✳

While Smith and LeSchack were conducting their investigation of NP8, preparations for their pickup were being made at Barrow. Under Fulton's scrutiny, Intermountain mechanics Leo Turk and Carson Gerken installed the Skyhook horns on the B-17 and rigged the deflection lines. On May 30 Seigrist and Price checked out the equipment by making a practice pickup of a static load in front of ARL. The next morning Cadwalader heard enough of LeSchack's weather report to judge that conditions at NP8 would permit a pickup.

The B-17 left Barrow at 9:35 A.M. on May 31. Navigator Jordan directed Seigrist toward the predicted position of NP8, shooting a series of sun lines as the aircraft flew northward over the pack ice. Reaching the target area at 2:40 P.M., Seigrist began his usual square search. The weather, contrary to expectations, was terrible. With a ceiling of only five hundred feet, Seigrist had to fly tight patterns. The restricted visibility of one to three miles further hampered the search.

Seigrist flew the search pattern for over four hours as the crew of the B-17 scanned the bleak ice field for signs of the Soviet drifting station. They saw nothing. Seigrist, listening for the UHF beacon at NP8, heard nothing. Finally, at 7:00 P.M., fuel considerations forced an end to the search.

On the Soviet drift station, Smith and LeSchack, according to their plan for their Skyhook retrieval and their collection of Soviet artifacts, had chosen a pickup zone outside of the camp area. The original plan had been to leave their findings for the last of the three pickups, allowing a measure of safety so that in case one of the pickup kits was inoperable, the last kit would be switched to personnel pickup. However, it became clear with the increasing surface wind that there would be no safe way of keeping two balloons aloft in the same area at the same time. It also became clear that it would take two men to launch an inert load.

Smith and LeSchack had to carefully choose what would be sent skyward. The combined weight and size of their findings would have to approximate the weight of an adult male (150 pounds) and be configured so that the pickup container would be aeronautically stable in flight and able to fit through the tail entrance of the B-17. They decided to use a duffle bag that originally had served as a drop container. Then they carefully packed the selected material into the bag, ensuring that a pear-shaped configuration would be produced.

Smith and LeSchack took the duffle bag via sled to an area close to the abandoned tractor. Next they prepared a pile of debris, including old rubber tires, which they planned to ignite as the pickup time approached. At 3:00 P.M. they turned on the U.S. Forest Service radio beacon and lit the pile. The expected pillar of black smoke quickly dissipated in the wind. In any event, it likely could not be seen against the gray, overcast sky. After waiting several hours for the arrival of the B-17, the disappointed men gave up and returned to their hut.

✳

Cadwalader's confidence in Jordan's navigational skills had diminished during the earlier search for NP8. Although he had released the Navy P2V following the successful insertion of Smith and LeSchack, he had reserved the option of recalling the aircraft if necessary. Before departing Barrow on May 31 for the pickup at NP8, he had arranged with ARL director Max Brewer to recall the P2V upon receipt of a radio message from the B-17. As Seigrist flew southward, Cadwalader sent the prearranged signal to Brewer: The P2V should return to Barrow.

Lieutenant Lowe and several of his crew were attending a movie at their home base of Kodiak Naval Air Station on the evening of May 31 when they were called to Operations and ordered to fly to Barrow. A run-up check of the P2V, however, revealed problems with the engines. The trouble turned out to be the propellers, which had been pitted by rocks thrown up when reversing pitch on Barrow's PSP runway. Both propellers would have to be changed. Although reluctant to give up his own aircraft, Lowe had no choice but to use a substitute.

Lowe's troubles continued as he headed toward Barrow. En route, the substitute P2V developed engine and compass problems. He arrived at Barrow after midnight with an aircraft that could not be used for the search until repaired with parts that had to be flown in from Kodiak.

Meanwhile, on NP8, LeSchack and Smith were behaving with a surprising lack of concern despite not being retrieved on the appointed day. They began to prepare for a long siege. They had the makings for all the potable water they needed and sufficient C-rations for a month, and when these ran out, they could start on the frozen carcasses in the Soviet food storage locker. While the latter did not appeal to their "bourgeois" tastes, they knew they could remain there with enough food for at least a year. When they returned to their hut, Smith announced that it was time to "clean house," whereupon he found a broom and began sweeping. They did indeed clear out the hut they now called home, tossing unnecessary furniture and debris left by the previous tenants out into the snow. The coal and wood stove, which they had not bothered to light during the first three days, was now cleaned out, refueled with the ample coal supplies left on the station, and fired up. They rearranged the tapestries hanging from the walls to their liking, and within a few hours had transformed the hut into more livable quarters.

✳

That evening, with the stove providing a pleasant warmth, Smith and LeSchack removed several layers of clothing, melted enough snow to take sponge baths, and attempted to transform a C-ration meal into more gourmet fare. They had completed, according to their previous plan, the significant part of their investigation at this point. Since it was now clear they would have additional time, they relaxed and discussed future plans for work on the station. They had an opportunity to evaluate what they had accomplished and what the ramifications of their findings were. Clearly they had made a worthwhile intelligence find. The fact that they might never return to report it never entered their minds. They felt secure that ultimately they would be picked up, but, recognizing that Captain Cadwalader was undoubtedly "going through hell" at the moment, they wondered just how and when the pickup would be accomplished. After a long discussion of the implications of their investigation and of the general plan for the following day's research until the pickup aircraft arrived, they banked the stove fire and retired to their sleeping bags, knowing they would sleep well while Cadwalader would not.

The following morning they awoke early, and LeSchack went to the radio shack to find out if he could hear any transmissions from Barrow. He and Smith, after some discussion, and knowing that the crew at Barrow would be continually looking for them, decided it would not be wise to transmit again for fear of giving away their activities. In retrospect, this was a bad decision, because the crew at Barrow actually could hear them, and a transmission at the time would have relieved Cadwalader tremendously. Upon hearing nothing, from Barrow, however, Smith and LeSchack resumed their investigative activities and began a much closer examination of each hut.

✳

Cadwalader, having heard nothing from Smith and LeSchack since the initial partial weather report, was anxious to reach the two men. Rather than wait for the P2V to be repaired, he arranged for Lieutenant Maier to join the B-17 crew for another try at locating the Soviet drift station.

Seigrist lifted off the PSP runway at Barrow at 1:40 P.M. on June 1. With Maier shooting the sun and Jordan plotting the positions, the aircraft once again headed northward. Reaching the predicted position of NP8 at 6:30 P.M., Seigrist began his square search in weather that had improved since the previous day. The ceiling had risen from one thousand to three thousand feet, and the visibility was ten to twelve miles, occasionally reduced to one mile. After fifteen minutes observers on the B-17 spotted the ubiquitous Ice Station Charlie. As the range and bearing from Charlie to NP8 was known, Cadwalader grew optimistic about the prospects of locating Smith and LeSchack. "Success seemed assured," he reported.[8]

Seigrist, using the gyro compass, took up a heading for NP8. Arriving at the location, he saw nothing. Again, he began a square search. Four fruitless hours later he abandoned the search, climbed up through the overcast, and headed for Barrow. As Maier and Jordan once again shot sun lines in the Arctic midnight, their calculations revealed that the gyro compass had precessed 30 degrees. With an error of this magnitude, the chances of flying an accurate course from Charlie to NP8 had been nil.

At about 7:00 P.M. down on the ice, Smith and LeSchack thought, as they had the previous day, that they heard the drone of engines, but it may have been wishful thinking. In any event, they saw no aircraft, so they continued their work until the evening radio schedule. Once again they listened without transmitting, then retired to the hut for dinner, an evaluation of the day's activities, and finally sleep.

On the morning of June 2 they awakened, monitored the Barrow frequency, had breakfast, and continued to refine their intelligence gathering. They took more notes and photographs and recovered more artifacts. They rearranged their "booty" bag to include new finds and excluded items they now believed to be less important.

❋

The tired B-17 crew reached Barrow at 4:00 A.M. on Saturday, June 2. The aircraft had flown twenty-eight hours and thirty minutes during the previous two days, and Cadwalader was growing concerned about the condition of both the aircraft and the pilots. Adding to his worries was the continued lack of communication with Smith and LeSchack.

Cadwalader recognized the chances were excellent that LeSchack and Smith, with their extensive polar survival experience, were safe, having plenty of food and much to keep them completely occupied; consequently, Cadwalader was not overly concerned about them. The specter of facing the Washington admirals, however, who had warned strongly against the scheme and who now might be forced to lose face by requesting that the Air Force Air Rescue Service be brought in to help find the men, was both real and imminent. Messages, of course, had gone out from Barrow detailing COLDFEET's progress; Phases I and II were complete, and Phase III was continuing . . . and continuing. It would be only a matter of hours before the Washington brass recognized that Phase III was going on considerably longer than planned, and they would react strongly and unfavorably. Cadwalader wanted to avoid this at all cost; accordingly, he was anxious that the next mission be successful so that he would not have to delay reporting on a completed Phase IV. Clearly, further delays would trigger a larger, publicized search.

While the B-17 had been looking for NP8 on June 1, Lieutenant Barnes arrived from Kodiak with Lowe's aircraft. He had not carried additional navigators as he did not expect his crew to be used for the search. Cadwalader, however, was drawing up contingency plans to meet the growing emergency. He made tentative arrangements to have a third P2V brought in from Kodiak, together with enough navigators so that there would be two on each aircraft. The three P2Vs would conduct staggered searches on subsequent days, "allowing the B-17, which was showing signs of wear, to stand down until the site was located."[9]

Before putting this plan into action, Cadwalader decided to make one more effort to find NP8 with the assets on hand. He wanted to duplicate the successful search of May 28. Lowe's P2V would leave two hours before the B-17. Both aircraft would search for the Soviet drifting station. If the P2V managed to locate it, Lowe would again direct Seigrist to the target by UHF radio bearings.

✳

The search for the stranded investigators was renewed on Saturday, June 2. In accordance with Cadwalader's plan, the P2V took off at 10:00 A.M., six hours after the B-17 had returned to Barrow following its failed attempt to locate the Soviet drifting station. The tired crew of the Skyhook aircraft was scheduled to depart again at noon, allowing time for only a brief rest. A problem with the deflection lines, however, caused a delay while Fulton worked on the rigging. As a result, it was not until 1:25 P.M. that the B-17 lifted off the Barrow runway.

As he headed northward, Lowe found the weather conditions far less favorable than they had been on his previous searches. He had to fly above a solid layer of clouds at ten thousand feet in order for Maier and Olsonowski to see the sun. Using this altitude meant higher fuel consumption. Arriving over the predicted point, Lowe let down to five hundred feet, remaining in and out of clouds. The visibility was no more than a half mile. It did not matter, however; he had only begun to fly the first leg of the square search when he picked up the short-range UHF beacon on NP8. Maier and Olsonowski, in an impressive display of navigational skill, had brought the P2V almost on top of the drifting station. Lowe contacted a delighted Smith on the radio, made sure that the two men were well and ready for pickup, then waited for the arrival of the B-17.

As time passed without hearing anything from the B-17, Lowe began to get concerned about his fuel reserves. The need to fly at a high altitude from Barrow had burned more gasoline than previously, reducing his loiter time in the search area. Lowe finally established radio contact with the tardy B-17, but it became questionable whether or not he could remain on station long enough to direct Seigrist to NP8. Although the B-17 received a strong signal from the P2V, it took thirty minutes for the Skyhook aircraft to reach the ice station, which it had missed by seventy-five miles. Finally, seven minutes *after* Lowe's absolute deadline for departure, the B-17 flew into sight. "I stayed a bit longer than the time needed to reach Barrow on one engine," Lowe recalled, "figuring it would be OK if [an] engine failed a few minutes after I departed the area." Lowe's decision spelled the difference between success and failure. As Cadwalader reported: "It was lucky that he waited, as the visibility was no more than a mile and the ceiling 500 feet, and without [Lowe's] aid, the B-17 would probably never have arrived."

❋

LeSchack had been hauling his toboggan from one hut to another when he first heard the welcome sound of aircraft engines. He looked up and saw the unmistakable shape of a P2V in the distance. In his excitement he jumped up and down and waved his arms. He then yelled for Smith, who was working inside one of the buildings. Smith retrieved the UHF survival radio from inside his parka and quickly established voice contact with "Backdoor Four." Lowe said that the B-17 was on its way but would not arrive for another two hours.

Smith and LeSchack returned to their hut for what they hoped would be their last C-ration meal. As they made final preparations for departing NP8, Smith kept in touch with the P2V. The news was not good. Lowe was short on fuel, and the B-17 had not yet made radio contact. The P2V had throttled down to minimum speed in an effort to conserve every possible drop of precious gasoline. From the ice, the patrol aircraft was moving so slowly that it looked as if it was about to fall out of the sky.

Smith and LeSchack moved to the pickup location, carrying their special Skyhook overalls, the pockets of which were now packed with their notes and exposed film. They wanted to at least ensure the safe return of these items if for some reason the pickup of the dead-weight cargo was unsuccessful. After many anxious minutes of watching the P2V circle slowly overhead, Lowe finally announced that he had established radio contact with the Skyhook aircraft and that it was en route to the station.

Smith and LeSchack strained their eyes through the gray overcast sky for sight of the B-17. The wind was picking up, and blowing snow had begun to decrease visibility. At last, to the immense relief of the two men, the B-17, resplendent with its nose yoke, appeared on the horizon. Lowe wished the COLDFEET team luck, then announced that he was returning to Barrow.

Establishing UHF radio communications with Seigrist, Smith asked him to drop the spare Skyhook package so that 150 pounds of cargo could be lifted off the station. He also wanted an additional cylinder of helium, as he feared that the cold might have caused shrinkage of the gas in the cylinders they had with them. At 6:20 P.M. the B-17 dropped the requested items.

Smith and LeSchack inflated all three balloons and tethered them to the abandoned tractor. With the wind rising, it proved difficult to manage the helium-filled balloons, which required the efforts of both men. At the same time, the blowing snow threatened to cause white-out conditions, alarming the COLDFEET team. "It was beginning to get a bit sweaty," Smith observed.

As Seigrist set up his approach, Smith and LeSchack struggled to ready the booty bag for the pickup. The wind over the ice had reached fifteen knots, as measured by the Soviet pocket anemometer that LeSchack had found in the meteorology hut. As the balloon reached the end of its tether, it drifted downwind. The pickup line lay over a considerable distance from the vertical in the strong wind. Smith and LeSchack struggled to keep the duffle bag from sailing down the ice.

After the line was fully extended for several seconds, the two men felt a sharp jolt, followed by a sudden release of tension. They realized that a safety system, designed by Fulton to prevent the balloon from breaking loose if a pilot struck the lift line but failed to engage it, had activated. The top portion of the lift line consisted of a special braid, called a slip or monkey knot, that compressed 175 feet of line into 35 feet. The braid was secured with a piece of eighty-pound test line. If the pickup plane's wing struck the line, the shock would cause the monkey knot to unfasten, releasing the extra 140 feet and allowing it to pass around the wing tip without breaking the balloon. This would give the pilot a second chance to make the pickup. The wind over NP8, however, was so strong that it caused the monkey knot to unravel, releasing the 140 feet of line. It took ten seconds for the balloon to travel to its new apex; the pull on the line then returned with increased force.

As Seigrist approached the ice station, he knew that the pickup would be far from routine. He later described the scene:

> The buildings passed under my right wing on my final flight path to the line. Instantly upon loss of sight of the buildings the horizon definition disappeared into the grey ice crystal-dominated atmosphere. I was instantly in a situation that could be imagined as flying in a void. I could see the line ahead with no problem but realized I was on the borderline of up or down or left or right vertigo although with the line going straight up ahead I had wings-level information. As soon as contact was made on the line I immediately went from visual to flying by instruments to avoid vertigo.

The sky anchor locked onto the line, which was pulled on board and attached to the winch. As the cargo neared the B-17, tail position operator Nicol discovered that its contents had shifted during retrieval, causing the bag to assume a shape that could not be pulled through the tail opening. Calling for assistance, he began to unload the bag while it remained hanging just outside the tail. After the removal of several items, he was able to drag it into the aircraft.

With the cargo safely aboard, Seigrist and Price traded seats for the retrieval of LeSchack. As previously agreed, Seigrist would fly the B-17 during Smith's drop and retrieval, while Price would handle LeSchack. "Now the moment of truth had arrived," Seigrist emphasized. "After all the months of practice, Doug and I were to make our first live pickup under conditions we had never experienced or could even have imagined."

On the ice below, LeSchack, fastened into his harness and holding the inflated balloon as close to the surface as possible in order to maintain control in the ever-increasing wind, trudged to the pickup zone near the tractor. The area was reasonably clear, with the nearest obstacle of consequence being the pressure ridge, three hundred yards away, that had destroyed NP8's runway.

After moving some one hundred yards from Smith and the tractor, LeSchack decided he had found a safe spot and released his balloon. Turning slowly toward Smith, LeSchack threw a salute at his senior colleague, then plopped down on the ice and assumed the standard pickup position.

LeSchack looked upward. Seeing the balloon about to extend the pickup line to its full length, he pulled his balaclava helmet (stitched to resemble a modern ski mask) over his face so that only his eyes were visible. This would protect his face from the 125 knots of icy wind he would encounter while being pulled behind the aircraft. He then waited. In a matter of seconds the pickup line reached its full height. At that point, to LeSchack's horror, he became almost weightless!

With the strong wind at the balloon's altitude exerting an upward pull nearly equal to LeSchack's 185 pounds, he began to bounce across the surface toward the pressure ridge. Frantically, he tried to grab hold of a piece of ice to halt his progress. If he could not stop, he faced the prospect of being severely battered by the jagged blocks of ice that comprised the pressure ridge and having his pickup line entangled. Adding to his woes, LeSchack's face mask had twisted on his head during his struggle, leaving him sightless.

LeSchack suppressed an urge to panic. The thought came to him that his pickup line would react in similar fashion to the line on the booty bag. The wind stress would release the monkey knot, allowing the line to extend an additional 140 feet. LeSchack tried desperately to arrest his progress across the ice as he waited for the eighty-pound test line to break. Seconds later he felt the jerk. His weightlessness immediately disappeared. He had about ten seconds before the balloon would reach its new elevation and he once again would be dragged toward the pressure ridge.

LeSchack applied his full weight to the surface and with a strength born of desperation dug small holes in the ice with his mittened hands. By the time the balloon had reached the end of its tether, he was able to lay prone on the ice and maintain his fragile handhold to prevent further sliding. As he waited anxiously for the pickup, he began to wonder about the likely effects of his highly unorthodox and possibly dangerous lift-off position.

Price, following Seigrist's advice, had oriented his approach on ground markers as he flew toward the station. Nearing the nylon line, he lost peripheral sight of the buildings that had been providing a useful horizon. Slightly disoriented, he contacted the nylon line below the mylar marker. Nose-trigger operator Scott watched as the line slid down the horns and locked into the sky anchor. As it streamed along the underside of the fuselage, assistant jumpmaster Johnson reached down through the Joe hole and placed a clamp on it. He then signaled Scott to release the line. After tail position operator Nicol secured it, Johnson released the clamp. The line was then attached to the winch, and Daniels began to pull it on board.

LeSchack felt the normal jerk when he was lifted off the ice. As he began to streamline behind the B-17, his unusual pickup position caused problems. The pickup line harness had tightened with the connection in front of his face instead of behind his head, as it was supposed to do. This meant LeSchack was being towed through the air at 125 knots with his face into the wind. He found it nearly impossible to breathe. Recalling the aerobatics experiment he had conducted during his first pickup at Pax River, LeSchack stretched out his arms. Using them as ailerons, he forced himself into a 180-degree roll so that his back was to the wind, enabling him to catch his breath. The technique worked, but it required all his remaining strength to keep his arms extended. If he relaxed for a moment, his body would roll back to the more stable face-into-the-wind position.

Finally, six and a half minutes after he lifted off the ice, the disoriented and breathless LeSchack was hauled into the B-17. He looked exhausted, Wall recalled. A quick examination by Dr. Walter, however, showed no obvious ill effects from the adventure. With LeSchack safely on board, attention now shifted to Smith.

Keenly aware of LeSchack's problems, Smith released his balloon from his position next to the tractor. Although he had hoped to hold onto the machine, he soon lost his grip in the strong wind. Like LeSchack, Smith also began to drag across the ice toward the looming pressure ridge. He had traveled some seventy-five yards before he managed to hook his heels onto an irregularity on the ice. Also, like LeSchack, Smith lost his vision as the hood of his pickup coveralls covered his eyes. "Then," Smith recalled, "I was flying." Unknown to Smith, he nearly missed the ride of his life.[10]

Following LeSchack's pickup, Price again traded seats with Seigrist. With the weather continuing to deteriorate, Seigrist made a tighter approach to the ice station, hoping to engage the line before vertigo became a problem. As soon as the buildings disappeared beneath the wings of the B-17, Seigrist felt the urge to turn right to catch the line, despite the fact that he had been lined up and stable up to this point. "I forced myself not to turn right," he noted, "trying to overcome any vertigo."

Seigrist caught sight of the mylar marker some two hundred yards ahead. The marker was a bit off to his left, but there was no time to correct the approach. The line made contact with the outer portion of the left horn. "It just hung there," Seigrist recalled, "what for me was an eternity." Finally, the line slowly slid down the horn and locked into the sky anchor. Listening over the radio, Seigrist heard Smith break into song on his UHF radio as he was being towed through the air. At 8:18 P.M. the tired but elated senior investigator was winched on board.

With Smith and LeSchack and their precious cargo safely off the ice, the B-17 headed back for Barrow. As the aircraft departed NP8, Thorsrud opened his ever-present briefcase and drew out its only contents, a bottle of Vat-69 scotch. Paper cups appeared, and the COLDFEET team toasted their success. The last thing Smith and LeSchack heard before falling into an exhausted sleep was the gruff voice of an obviously relieved Cadwalader, famed for his acerbic sense of humor, admonishing them for drinking and disorderly conduct "on board a military aircraft."

It was 2:15 A.M. on June 3 when the B-17 touched down at Barrow. Brewer and his assistant, John Schindler, had arranged a celebration for the tired adventurers. After posing on the ramp for a photograph with the P2V crew, everyone adjourned to the library of ARL. Large tables were filled with food and booze. Smith and LeSchack passed around Russian cigarettes from the drift station. "They tasted terrible," Lowe recalled. Smith presented Cadwalader with the poster signed by the Soviet station commander that he had retrieved from the wall of the station's mess hall. Congratulations and laughter filled the air. A difficult and dangerous mission had been accomplished without accident or injury.

9

Conclusion

While an operational triumph, Project COLDFEET also achieved the primary purpose of uncovering information about the activities on Soviet drifting stations. As noted in a once classified intelligence assessment that appeared in *ONI* [Office of Naval Intelligence] *Review* in November 1962, COLDFEET provided ONI with "first hand observations of the nature, extent, and sophistication of the Soviet Arctic research program." LeSchack and Smith had taken extensive notes and over three hundred photographs while on NP8. They brought back eighty-three documents and twenty-one pieces of equipment. "From their observations and the physical items retrieved," the ONI appraisal pointed out, "emerges a rather clear picture of life and activity aboard NP8 when it was manned by the Soviets."[1]

The Soviet programs in oceanography and meteorology especially impressed the intelligence analysts. Both were "well developed and apparently conducted with a high degree of efficiency." Most of the equipment used by the Soviet scientists was in serial production; in many cases it was "superior in quality to comparable U.S. equipment." The weather program, which included surface observations and upper air soundings, seemed "extremely complete" and in most respects "superior to U.S. drift station meteorological programs."

Inconclusive evidence suggested that the Soviets were engaged in acoustical research on NP8. Although LeSchack and Smith found no trace of hydrophones, four notebooks recovered from the station contained information and diagrams of acoustical significance. The two investigators also observed a large number of batteries scattered on the ice. In addition, they noted that a diesel generator had been mounted on rubber tires to reduce vibration and sound output. Clearly, NP8 was capable of the kind of "silent running" necessary for acoustical experiments.

The analysts were less impressed with the living conditions on the Soviet drifting station. Sanitation seemed "non-existent." All of the literature retrieved by LeSchack and Smith consisted of "typical propaganda." A movie found on the station, the analysts observed, told the story of how a Russian girl fell in love with her tractor; it surely would have been deemed entertaining "only by an avid Communist." Nonetheless, the analysts concluded, "In spite of the austere, unsanitary, and politically pressured conditions under which the Soviet scientists lived, all evidence indicates that they were engaged in a highly developed, successful, and extremely useful program of science."

ONI considered COLDFEET an impressive intelligence success. "The U.S. intelligence community," it observed, "now has a tremendously more accurate and positive mass of data upon which to base its evaluation of Soviet activities on Arctic drift stations. Much speculation has been confirmed as fact; and some has been shown to have been unfounded. Only from firsthand observation by qualified observers could such an unusual and concrete intelligence result have been obtained."

✻

COLDFEET also saw the first operational use of Fulton's Skyhook aerial retrieval system. It had performed superbly under extremely challenging circumstances. As Rear Admiral Coates, Chief of Naval Research, wrote to Intermountain Aviation's Thorsrud: "The recovery [of LeSchack and Smith], which as a result of long and successful prior experience would have been a routine matter under ordinary conditions, was conducted under stronger winds and lower visibility than had previously been attempted; nonetheless through the exceptional skill of the pilots and the coordination and efficiency of the crew, all pick-ups were made without a hitch, and in the best time (6.5 minutes) yet achieved."[2]

The following year ONR again turned to Intermountain for its Skyhook expertise. On July 9, 1963, Jerome A. Hirschman, a thirty-nine-year-old geophysicist from the University of Wisconsin, became ill while working on ARLIS II. Experiencing a rapid pulse and lung congestion, Hirschman was given oral antibiotics and confined to bed. The runway at ARLIS II had been closed due to melting since June 23, and the station was too deep inside the ice pack to be reached by icebreaker. Also, radio communications with Barrow had been erratic due to atmospheric conditions. As Hirschman could not be evacuated, Max Brewer at ARL decided to send a doctor with the scheduled airdrop flight on July 11 so that he could discuss the scientist's condition with station personnel while the aircraft circled overhead. The doctor concluded that Hirschman likely had pneumonia, and, as it seemed he was improving, decided that no further action would need to be taken.[3]

Two days later, however, Hirschman took a turn for the worse. When he requested evacuation, Brewer arranged through ONR to charter Intermountain's B-17 to make a Skyhook pickup. By the time the aircraft reached Fairbanks on July 15, Hirschman's condition had again improved. The scientist spoke to Brewer on the radio and asked that the aircraft be released. The doctor at Barrow agreed. As all signs pointed toward recovery, the physician noted, "his request should be honored, particularly since aerial pick-up can be a disconcerting experience." After holding the B-17 at Fairbanks for thirty-six hours, Brewer released it to return to Marana.

During the evening of July 26 Hirschman suffered a serious relapse, slipping into and out of a coma. With ARLIS II in the midst of a communications blackout, it was not possible to report the news to Barrow until the next day. Hirschman, who had regained consciousness and seemed to be improving, asked to be evacuated at the earliest possible moment. In the midst of the radio contact, Hirschman collapsed while eating a bowl of peaches and died.

His death, it was later learned, had been due to a heart attack. The problem had been caused by a malignant tumor that had metastasized into the carinal and peritracheal lymph nodes and pericardium. Brewer ordered his body preserved by freezing while awaiting word from the family. Although he preferred to return the body when the runway reopened, Hirschman's mother wanted it brought out immediately for burial in Wisconsin. Brewer responded to the request by asking ONR to send the Intermountain B-17 back to Barrow.

The Skyhook-equipped aircraft reached ARL on August 9. The B-17's crew, mainly veterans of COLDFEET, consisted of pilots Price and

Zimmer, navigator Jordan, and Skyhook operators Wall, Daniels, Johnson, Nicol, and John Samsel. The flight would be a challenge for the Intermountain crew. ARLIS II was located over one thousand miles from Barrow and less than one hundred miles from the North Pole. The weather at the station had been poor, with overcast skies and ice fog.

On August 11, with improving weather, Wall flew to ARLIS II aboard a Wien Alaska Airlines DC-4 on a scheduled airdrop. Included in the cargo were 850 pounds of Skyhook equipment. The airdrop went off without incident. As the station personnel prepared Hirschman's body for pickup, the B-17 left Barrow for the long flight northward. By the time the aircraft reached ARLIS II, however, a low ceiling and fog had once again developed in the area. Unable to see either the balloon or the cable, Price returned to Barrow.

Two days later, with reports from ARLIS II of improving conditions, the B-17 tried again. As the aircraft headed northward Price and Zimmer encountered a series of cloud layers that gradually increased in height. They kept climbing into the clear so that navigator Jordan could shoot his sun lines. Also, the B-17 lacked de-icing equipment, except for propeller alcohol, and the pilots feared that the clouds would be laden with ice. The aircraft continued to climb until it reached eighteen thousand feet, forcing the crew to resort to oxygen masks. It proved impossible, however, to avoid the clouds, and the pilots soon found themselves flying by instruments.

A short time after the B-17 entered the clouds Jordan noticed that ice was starting to build up on the Skyhook deflection lines. Within minutes the entire aircraft began to shake. Then the left wing suddenly dipped, followed by the nose. As the aircraft plummeted toward the ice pack, Jordan, convinced that the B-17 had suffered a structural failure, struggled to get into his Arctic jacket and boots. Donning his parachute harness, he found it difficult to snap the buckles due to the thickness of the jacket. "When I finally got everything into place," he recalled, "I clipped my boots into the harness and was ready to bail out."[4]

By the time Jordan was ready to exit the aircraft, Price had managed to bring the wings level, slowing the rate of descent from two thousand to five hundred feet per minute. Jordan climbed up from his position in the nose, stuck his head through the hatch into the cockpit above, and yelled, "What are we going to do? Fly over to T-3 and bail out?" One of the crew shouted back, "That's not the worst idea I've heard in the last fifteen minutes."

Price then explained that he intended to continue his descent in the hope that he would find some clear air below the clouds. Both pilots anxiously watched the radio altimeter as the aircraft lost altitude. At four hundred feet above the ice pack the B-17 broke out into the clear. To everyone's great relief the ice gradually sublimated off the aircraft until it disappeared.

As the B-17 continued toward its objective, Jordan caught glimpses of the sun and was able to align the gyro compass. Price soon picked up the radio beacon on ARLIS II—now located at 88°26′ N, 165° E—and began to home in on the station. Arriving overhead at 10:36 P.M. local time, he found that the fog had returned; however, it lay on the surface of the ice only to a depth of three hundred feet. As the Skyhook pickup line extended to five hundred feet, Price told the station personnel to release the balloon near the radio beacon antenna. Although he could not see the station, he could see the balloon rise through the fog. He successfully engaged the line on his first pass, and the B-17 crew brought Hirschman's frozen body on board.

The operation, later reports revealed, had been an impressive sight from the ice. The personnel on ARLIS II could not see the aircraft. Hirschman's body lay in a clear area near the station, with the Skyhook balloon invisible in the overcast. They watched as the body slowly lifted off the ice and ascended vertically into the clouds until it disappeared from view. The only thing missing from the eerie tableau was the sound of heavenly music![5]

Fulton's Skyhook received a good deal of publicity over the next few years. The high point came in 1965, when Hollywood hired Intermountain's B-17 to perform a pickup for the end of the James Bond movie, *Thunderball*. Zimmer flew the aircraft for the movie scene, retrieving dummies that substituted for Sean Connery and his leading lady.[6]

Skyhook became less visible following *Thunderball*, when it entered the inventory of special operations. Fulton's invention likely found employment in a number of specialized clandestine missions over the years, although its subsequent use by the CIA and the military services remains shrouded in secrecy. The Air Force retains a Skyhook capability, using C-130s with an improved system capable of making multiple pickups in a single pass.

❋

The success of COLDFEET was due to a fortuitous combination of individuals and circumstances. From the beginning, LeSchack's bold proposal had received the essential support of his superiors in ONR, especially Dr. Britton. It gained the approval of a somewhat skeptical naval hierarchy beyond ONR in large part due to the efforts of Captain Cadwalader. The experienced naval officer then assumed responsibility for supervising the operation, bringing to it a seasoned judgment that contributed significantly to the final outcome.

Fulton's Skyhook provided the necessary means to accomplish the objective. The product of years of trial and error by the determined inventor, the aerial retrieval system became available at just the right time to be employed for use in COLDFEET. The selection of Inter-mountain Aviation to operate Skyhook proved a key element in the success of the plan. The skill of pilots Seigrist and Price, combined with the efficiency of the pickup crew on the B-17, permitted the use of Skyhook at the outer edge of its operating limits. In less competent—and less determined—hands the triumph of COLDFEET might well have turned into disaster.

Lieutenant Lowe and the crew of his P2V also happened to be the right people in the right place at the right time. Without their presence at crucial junctures, investigators LeSchack and Smith might have faced a very long stay on the Soviet drifting station.

Major Smith and Lieutenant LeSchack received well-deserved Legions of Merit for their roles in COLDFEET. Smith brought to the operation experience, maturity, and calm judgment. An ideal partner for the ebullient LeSchack, Smith radiated a confidence that encouraged everyone around him—even during the times he did not feel it.

Finally, COLDFEET began, continued, and succeeded because of Leonard LeSchack. "Let us give credit where same is due," Britton observed. "The whole idea of COLDFEET was Leonard's," he emphasized, "and after all these years of classified facts, I would like him to enjoy the full credit he deserves."[7] LeSchack conceived of the project, undertook it with excitement and enthusiasm, and saw it through to a successful conclusion despite the many disappointments and frustrations encountered along the way.

Thanks to the efforts of a select group of talented and determined people, the United States successfully accomplished one of the most daring intelligence operations of the Cold War in the far north—Project COLDFEET.

Appendix A

Geographical Coordinates

Drifting stations can be located on a map by geographical coordinates. Lines or parallels of latitude begin at the equator (0°) and extend horizontally for 90 degrees to the North and South Poles. The North Pole, therefore, would be 90° N. Distance from the North Pole can easily be determined by remembering that one degree of latitude always equals 60 nautical miles. A degree of latitude can be divided into 60 minutes, with one minute of latitude equaling one nautical mile. Thus, when Storkerson established his base at 73°30′ N, he was 990 miles from the North Pole. When the Soviets abandoned NP8 at 83°15′ N, the station was 405 miles from the North Pole.

Lines of longitude extend vertically from the North Pole to the South Pole. Longitude is measured east and west from the meridian of Greenwich (0°), also known as the Prime Meridian, which extends from the North Pole, passes south of Spitzbergen, crosses the Greenwich Observatory in southern England, and proceeds southward to the South Pole. On the opposite side of the earth, the 180° line of longitude, also known as the International Date Line, proceeds from the North Pole, through Wrangel Island, then continues to the South Pole. In general, the 180 degrees of longitude east of the Prime Meridian encompass Scandinavia and the Soviet Union in the far north; the 180 degrees of longitude west of the Prime Meridian include Alaska, Canada, and Greenland.

To find the exact location of a drifting station on a map, one need only locate the point where the lines of longitude and latitude intersect. In the case of Storkerson's station—at 73°30′ N, 148°32′ W— this would occur at a point north of Prudhoe Bay, Alaska (148°32′ W), 990 miles from the North Pole (73°30′ N).

Appendix B

Soviet Drifting Station, 1937–April 1962

Station	Station leader	Established	Coordinates	Abandoned	Coordinates	Length of drift (days)	Distance covered straight line (km)	(Total km)
NP1	I. D. Papanin	21 May 1937	89°25' N 78°40' W	19 Feb 1938	70°40' N 19°16' W	274	2,200	2,850
NP2	M. M. Somov	2 Apr 1950	76°03' N 166°36' W	11 Apr 1951	81°44' N 163°48' W	374	640	2,600
NP3	A. F. Treshnikov	9 Apr 1954	85°58' N 178°00' W	20 Apr 1955	86°44' N 24°00' W	376	825	1,863
NP4	E. I. Tolstikov	8 Apr 1954	75°48' N 178°25' W	19 Apr 1957	85°52' N 0°00'	1,108	2,111	6,969
	P. A. Gordienko (17 Apr 1955)							
	A. G. Dralkin (18 Apr 1956)							
NP5	N. A. Volkov	21 Apr 1955	82°10' N 156°51' E	8 Oct 1956	84°18' N 63°20' E	536	1,080	3,629
	A. L. Sokolov (20 Apr 1956)							
NP6	K. A. Cychev	19 Apr 1956	74°24' N 177°04' W	14 Sep 1959	82°06' N 3°56' E	1,245	2,913	8,650

	V. M. Driatskii (19 Apr 1957)							
	S. T. Serlapov (8 Apr 1958)							
	V. S. Antonov (12 Apr 1959)							
NP7	V. A. Vedernikov	23 Apr 1957	82°06' N 164°11' W	11 Apr 1959	85°14' N 33°03' W	721	1,240	3,520
	N. A. Belov (11 Apr 1958)							
NP8	V. M. Rogachev	27 Apr 1959	76°11' N 164°24' W	19 Mar 1962	83°15' N 132°30' W	1,057	1,964	6,090
	N. I. Blinov (3 Apr 1960)							
	I. P. Romanov (15 Apr 1961)							
NP9	V. A. Shamont'ev	28 Apr 1960	77°23' N 163°00' E	28 Mar 1961	86°30' N 176°00' W	335	1,340	2,660
NP10	N. A. Kornilov	17 Oct 1961	75°27' N 177°10' E	14 Nov 1961	76°55' N 161°00' E	198	470	850

SOURCE: P. A. Gordenko, "Scientific Observations From, and The Nature of Drift of the 'North Pole' Stations," in N.A. Ostenso, ed., *Problems of the Arctic and Antarctic: Collection of Articles No. 11* (Leningrad: Arctic and Antarctic Research Institute, 1962). Translated by J. H. Slep, J. B. Filmonov, and A. Malahoff (Arctic Institute of North America, 1966), 6–4.

Appendix C

Catalog of Items Recovered in Project Coldfeet
May 1962

I.

This catalog describes the items recovered in [Project] Cold Feet. The catalog is divided into two major subcategories: Documents and Hardware. Each document is assigned an [Project] Cold Feet Catalog Number herein, and the documents are further subdivided into the following groups: Charts; Electronic/Electrical; Political; Oceanographic/Bathymetric/Meteorological; Aviation; Medical and Personal.

II.
Documents

A. Charts

1. "*Blank Chart of the Northern Polar Basin.*" Centered on the Geographic North Pole. "North Pole Number 8" and "Number 10" drift stations marked on chart. Land and sea areas displayed from 60° N. Polyconic projection. Scale: 1:7,500,000. Prepared by Kartofabrika Gosgeolizdat. (Map Plant of the State Geological Publishing House). Undated.

2. "*Northern Arctic Ocean*" chart. Scale 1:5,000,000. Published by the Arctic-Antarctic Scientific Research Institute of the Administration of Northern Sea Route. 1959. No marks placed on chart. Polyconic projection with True North Pole offset to right and upper portion of chart. Land and sea areas from about 70° N to 90° N.

3. "*Aircraft Chart of the Central Polar Basin.*" Chart 1 of a four-part polyconic series with the True North Pole lying in this chart of the series.

Scale: 1:3,000,000. Prepared in 1958 with 1960 magnetic overlay. Prepared by engineers of the Aeronavigational Group of PA GUSML MMF USSR. Editor: Chief Navigator P. A. Akkuratov, V. L.; Printed by the Rizhaskoi Cartographic Plant, GUCK. Land and sea areas depicted. No markings. Five-color chart.

4. *Chart No. 2 of four-part series mentioned above.* Two "North Pole Number 8" positions marked on chart plus "North Pole Number 10" area-type position.

5. *Chart No. 3 of four-part series.* No positions or markings.

6. *Chart No. 4 of four-part series.* No positions marked.

7. *Blank Chart of the Arctic.* A polyconic chart. Sheet no. 10 in a series. No land masses depicted. Covers following area: 144° W to 150° E and 87°30′ N to 80°30′ N. A detailed track is displayed in an area centered at 83° N, 175° E. No scale stated.

8. *Blank Chart of the Arctic.* No scale stated. Polyconic projection with the True North Pole placed at the top border of the chart and offset to right of center. Area 83° N to North Pole and 180° of longitude. No markings. No land masses displayed. Sheet no. 9 in a series.

9. *Arctic Ocean* chart. Scale: 1:5,000,000 (1 cm = 50 km). Reference to cutting the 75° N latitude line in a polyconic projection. Sheet no. 2 in a series. Land and sea areas depicted in area 62° N to 85° N and 130° E eastward to 110° W. Dated 1959. Printed 1960. Compiled by the Arctic-Antarctic Scientific Research Institute. Editor: K. V. Sidorov. No markings on chart.

10. *Untitled Chart.* Scale: 1:1,000,000. Reference to parallel 82° N. Polar "stereographic" projection. Land masses of Komsomolets Island and October Revolution Island at extreme left of a chart covering 80° N to 85° N, 076° E eastward to 150° E. No indication of series layout or of compiler-publisher.

B. Electronic/Electrical

11. *Technical Manual for Radio Station Type 1-RSB-70,* 229 pages. Waterlogged but legible. Divided into four major sections: Descriptions (five chapters); Installation and Checkout (two chapters); Operation (four chapters); and list of illustrations (50 illustrations). The text states that the "radio is designed for installation aboard long-range aircraft for distant communications" and, with auxiliary elements, may be used in the medium-wave bands for navigation. Water damage obscures date and authorship of the text. A separate schematic diagram is supplied.

12. *Four photo-reproduced pages of an electronic part list* listing such items as quartz crystals, tubes, fuses, and switches. These are items in "Box 31P-110."

13. *Partially used clerical notebook.* Electrical entries on about 28 pages. Entries not exploited fully. Data on weights of electrical conductors, tubes, extracts from schematic and tube diagrams, a device ("Efir" with

S. P.-7) diagrammed schematically, a switch diagram for "Efir S. P.-6," impulse measurement. A 19.1 megacycle device, etc. Entry dated February 23, 1960; another dated May 27 and 29, 1960. A 3KC oscillator Oct, XTAL-controlled.

14. *Carton tag* for a conductor or cable. Refers to a diagram 5.15.070. Length of conductor 300 mm ± 10 mm; lot: 5 U; quantity: 50.

15. *Data sheet* for an electronic tube type GU-29.

16. Technical description and operating instruction for the *AC/DC converter PO-550F and PO-550AF*. Three copies are registered and dated in 1956. Published by the Ministry of Electrotechnical Production, USSR. The units convert DC to AC and employ a noise filter. The two models vary in that the PO-550F is designed for 100 VDC to 125 VAC and 10.8 amps DC to 9.4 amps AC of 50-cycle AC current. The PO-550AAF converts 200 VDC to 125 VAC and 5.4 amps to 9.4 amps of 50-cycle current. Both rotate at 3,000 RPM ± 180. Date of publication not given. (16 pages each.)

17. *Description and instructions for a Wavemeter of Medium-Accuracy Types VST-1 and VST-2*. (20 pages plus six photographic illustrations). The meters are for use in measuring signal frequencies in the 150–375 megacycle band for both continuous and impulse signals. VST-1 covers 150 to 240 megacycles; VST-2 covers from 237 to 375 megacycles. Temperature range is +10°C to +30°C. Sensitivity for unmodulated signals is one millivolt and for pulses 0.1 millivolt. Power supply is 50-, 400-, or 800-cycle current at 110, 127, or 220 VAC. Either meter weighs 22 kilograms.

18. Two carton covers for magnetic tapes of 1,000-m length each. One is Type 2 and produced by the Kharkov Soviet Factory No. 3. The tape was produced January 1960. The remaining carton is also Type 2 and was produced by Factory No. 3 in Shostka.

19. *Notebook of E. Deimidov* (16 pages of electronic notes, including description of the RP-2 radar, a device for balloon tracking, an antenna drive system, the PRB-15, and other data.)

20. One personal notebook with electronic data, including calculations for sonic measurements and devices. (In exploitation by the Chief of Naval Operations [OP-922F2].)

C. Political

21. *Mimeographed Leningrad City Election District No. 14 campaign sheet* advancing the candidacy of Dimitri Dimitrivich Shostakovich, the famous composer, recipient of the 1958 Lenin Prize and a belated (1961) Party member.

22. *Election poster* asking the voter to vote for candidates to the Supreme Soviet, USSR. "Everybody Vote." Painted by A. Antonchenko. One of 400,000 printed under Order No. 504. Price: 10 kopeks.

23. Brochure, *"The Visit of N. S. Khrushchev to the USA,"* 45 pages. Author: Sh. Sanakoev. Published by the "Znanuye" ("Knowledge") Publishing House, Moscow, 1959. A somewhat prejudiced account of the trip.
24. *Large election poster* featuring A. F. Borisov for deputy to the Supreme Soviet, USSR. Brief biographical sketch included. Borisov was a 57-year-old stage and screen actor. A nonparty candidate endorsed by the Party. Printed February 20, 1962, under Order No. 289.

D. Oceanographic/Bathymetric/Meteorological

25. Two *large wall-type notices* from the Polar Insitute at Murmansk to their "highly-regarded comrades" requesting that the expedition members note and report fish habits and forward the data to the Bottom Fish Laboratory PINRO in Murmansk.
26. *Journal for Working up Deep Water Temperature Data.* No entries. About 30 identical pages with 30 columns per page, each column entry headed by its descriptive heading. Publish date October 11, 1958.
27. *An "attestation" slip No. 224* given on April 22, 1935, for a device with a lens travel of 35 mm and a focusing range of 380 mm. Slip given by Analysis Lab OTK of "Geophysica" Factory, Moscow.
28. *A note of about 30 identical pages for entering water temperature and bottom data.* No entries. Published under the auspices of the Arctic Scientific Research Institute of the Northern Sea Route Organization. Two pages of instructions precede pages for entering observations of layer number, lower boundary of layer, water color, etc.
29. *A one-page Table of Contents* providing references to writers' articles describing technical meteorological functions.
30. *Journal for Recording Magnetic Observations.* No entries made. About 75 pages of identical columned sheets. All entries to be made in "strict chronological order." Columns provide places for logging "variom and termograph," temperatures, current strength, battery voltage, date/time, levels, and readings on scales D, N, Z, and T. Publish date October 6, 1958, by the Arctic Scientific Research Institute of the Northern Sea Route Organization.
31. *Two completed radiosonde recordings* in strip-chart form with entries, initials, and observations.
32. *Instructions of Grading (Leveling) and Water-Level Measurements at Polar Stations of Glavsevmorput.* By Glavsevmorput, Moscow, 1944. 41 pages with several diagrams.
33. *Astronomical Observations Journal.* About 100 pages of identical columned sheets. Two pages of entries. Journal No. M-38 produced by the Arctic-Antarctic Scientific Research Institute in 1960.
34. *Psychrometric Tables.* Published by the Hydrometeorological Publishing House, Leningrad, 1952. Contains "rules for measuring humidity" on 2 pages plus 252 pages of tables. Notes inside the tables state a "collective

of four aerologists" were assigned to the expedition to "research the lower level of the atmosphere via radiosondes." Daily "at 0300 and 1500 Moscow time a thousand man army, all over the world, send up radiosondes to aid in measuring temperature, humidity and winds."

35. *One page of Sun Attitude Tables.*

36. *Receipt for frame for "Deep Water Temperature Measuring Devices."* Dated June 1957. Produced by GUGMC in concurrence with the Council of Ministers USSR Factory "Gudrometpriborov" ("Hydrometeorological Devices") in Leningrad. Guaranteed one year.

37. *Two graph charts with entries.* Y axis in meters/second; X axis in turns/second. Calibration tables on the reverse side.

38. *Two "Vertical Sounding of the Atmosphere"* forms published in August 1959. Columns for entering day, time, "characteristic," and calibrated altitudes.

39. *Ionosphere data graph form* published by Kartfabrika VMF. Spaces for entering station, date/time, and meridian. Squares 1 to 16 placed vertically, each subdivided in fifths, and squares 00 to 09 and 10 to 24 placed horizontally, each square divided in fifths.

40. *Instruction Book for Working up Data Obtained via Radiosonde RZ-049.* A photo-reproduced copy of a 1959 Gidrometeorologicheski Publishing House book. Moscow, 1957. Attached tables and one page of handwritten observations. 26 pages plus tables.

41. *Five code books* for preparing meteorological telegrams. Code books KN-01, KN-03 (two copies), and KN-04 (two copies). Instructions for use contained within. Each about 15 pages and published by Hydrometeo-publishing Leningrad, 1960, for the Main Hydrometeorological Service.

42. *Journal for entering observations using the M-2 Variometer.* About 60 pages. No entries. Published by the Arctic Institute of Glavsevmorput. Undated.

43. *Five wind-cloud logs.* No entries. Printed December 1957. Very comprehensive data required to complete the forms.

44. *Chronometer logbook.* About 25 pages. Published for use by expeditions by the Arctic Scientific Research Institute, January 1961. No entries.

45. *Packet of radiograms from Moscow to "North Pole Eight—'Chess'."* Mostly coded. Possibly weather. Some partly plain text. One entirely plain text from "Mama Nina" to her son.

46. *Logbook for recording anemometer* (?) observations. 10 pages. No date. No entries.

47. *"Criteria and Notes on Recording Wind Data."* Published by the Main Hydrometeorological Service, Moscow, 1960. 28 pages with illustrations. Detailed and well written.

48. *"Work Journal No. 2 on Astronomical Drift—North Pole Number 8, 1956."* Six of about 30 pages have entries or headings.

49. *Instructions for Making Temperature Observations.* Published by the Arctic Scientific Research Institute for Glavsevmorput, Moscow, 1944. Complied by K. A. Gomoyunov. 81 pages. Illustrations and descriptions of water-temperature equipment.
50. *"Instructions for Conducting Chemical Investigations of Sea Water."* Published by Arctic Scientific Research Institute of Glavsevmorput, Moscow, 1944. 83 pages. Illustrated.
51. *Part III of a series publication.* This part covers "Vertical Sounding of the Atmosphere via Radiosondes" in 129 pages plus tables, etc. Published by the Hydrometeorological Publishing House, Leningrad, 1954, for the Main Directorate of the Hydrometeorological Service. Authorship of each chapter credited to individuals named.
52. *Journal for Recording Deep Water Observations.* Date and publisher not stated. About 38 pages arranged for column entries. 4 pages of entries made.
53. *Brochure describing a general-purpose Komovskii pump* for evacuating air-increasing pressure. 8 pages. Pump produced by Glavuchtekhprom (Administration for Instructional Technical Enterprises). April 1955. Edited by L. I. Fedorov.
54. *Workbook for logging observations* via an Alekseyev Current Recorder.
55. *Description and instructional brochure* for a deep water temperature rack ROT-48. 7 pages.
56. *Radiation meter (Pyranameter) booklet* for use in conjunction with a galvanometer Type G. S. A-1. Made in Tbilsi (Tiflis) by the Hydrometeorological Factory.
57. *Handbook for a device for measuring speed and direction of ocean currents at any depth.*

E. Medical
58. *Booklet listing the contents of a "Blood Transfusion Kit."* Published by "Mednabor," Moscow Factory, for medical kits. 2 pages. 13 different items. Booklet publish date: February 1953.
59. *"Instructions for Use of an Antibiotic."* Two 2-page booklets. Approved by Z. Yermol'ev for the Committee on Antibiotic, May 11, 1959, and printed by the Ministry of Health of the RFSSR on June 15, 1959.

F. Aviation
60. *Aircraft Navigational Log Forms* for piston-engined aircraft. 4 copies. No entries. Made for use on both sides of the form.
61. *Ticket and baggage claim* for Aeroflot flight to Dikson. Four tickets, each serialized and stamped with an Aeroflot seal for April 14. Price: free. Different passenger name entered on each of the four tickets.
62. *Celestial observation logbook.* About 70 pages of scattered entries. No publisher or date evident.

63. *Packet of about 40 aircraft passenger/freight manifest forms* by Aeroflot airline. No entries.
64. *Celestial navigation forms* (Shipboard Type). No data entered. Large number of forms housed in hard-board holder with tie strings and "Blank" penned on the surface.

G. Personal

65. *I. Romanov's July 12, 1961, instructions* to the duty galley man. He is instructed to serve, clean and wash tables, haul water, help with chow, and pass word to the doctor, who must test all dishes.
66. *Four examples of an impressive stamped ID* paper issued to N. T. Morozov and others for a 60-day period by the director of the Arctic-Antarctic Scientific Research Institute based on Order No. 78, good in each instance for the period April 6, 1961, to June 7, 1961.
67. An "ACT" attesting to the distribution of goods in the "meteorology" division. No entries made.
68. Handwritten list of items on the back of a mistyped "ACT" (attestation).
69. Note of January 1961 from deputy director of the Arctic-Antarctic Scientific Research Institute to the chief of North Pole Eight. Two copies of a questionnaire are forwarded via the memo, and guidance is given in technical matters. The deputy director is Gordienko. Chief of the station is N. I. Blinov. All questions on observations are to be referred to PINRO, 6 Kol'skaya Street, Murmansk, via radio or letter; fish and oceanographic matters were to be referred to TTINPO's N. M. Knipovir section.
70. *Brochure on the "Techniques of Safety when Working on the Ice."* Illustrated. 35 pages. Assembly of tents, etc., illustrated. Published by "Sea Transport," Moscow, 1959.
71. *Special personal letter envelopes* with imprint "Drifting Ice Station North Pole Eight." The envelopes bear a publishing date of March 1961. "Galvsevmorput" (Administration Northern Sea Route) also is imprinted.
72. *Large ledgerbook marked "Receipt and Distribution of Supplies and Cigarettes."* 4 pages of entries.
73. *Two large personal notebooks* with very few entries.
74. *Colorful illustrated booklet for operating a "Leningrad" 35-mm camera.* (Camera appears to be modeled on the East German "Contax.") 30 pages in color. Well done. Camera is a "gold medal winner at the Brussel's World Fair in 1958."
75. *Four photos* taken by Soviets, including close-ups of "Colt" biplane and six individuals.
76. *Box of photo print paper,* size 18 x 24 cm and sealed in light-tight paper and an outer box crediting Fotobumag Factory No. 4, Leningrad, with its manufacture. 100 sheets.

77. *Three empty notebooks.*
78. *Book titled "Works of the Drift Station 'North Pole'"*, published by the Galvsevmorput Publishing House, 1940. Provides an account of the 1937–38 expedition's experiences. 335 pages. Photos, drawings, and maps included in the numerous illustrations.
79. *One-year guarantee* "attestation" for a "Leningrad" 35-mm camera. Dated May 13, 1961, for camera serial 016599 with lens no. 5340562. 4 pages.
80. *Watch instruction for the camp guard.* 14 items. Instructions on keeping stoves operative and warning personnel of the approach of polar bears.
81. *Order No. 4 from the chief of the drift station,* which calls attention to improper watch standing, log entries, eating hours, etc. Meal hours are appended.
82. Personal notebook of Fedorov (?) with extensive electronic notes, abstracts, and sketches, with frequent reference to underwater sonic applications. (Under translation by ONI.)
83. *Large ledger-type notebook titled "Our Statements—Outfitting—North Pole Eight."* A long list of equipment and supplies are listed in hand-written form and divided by functional activity such as Aerology, Hydrology, etc. (Under translation by ONI.)

III.
Hardware

1. Twenty-one rolls of movies. Usually newsreel type praising advances in economy, science, transport, etc. Only three viewed by U.S. personnel by June 20, 1962.
2. Radiosonde
3. Two hand-held anemometers.
4. Two packages of "White-Sea Canal" cigarettes. Filter type. Poorly made and taste ghastly.
5. Brass device. Possible geophone suspended on severed two-conductor cable. Each conductor is protected by rubber shield, and the whole is encased in a rubber-like covering over braided shield with an outside cable diameter of about 3/8".
6. A nine fixed-contact ceramic switch with three rotating contacts. One cable is connected to one contact; another cable connects to four side-by-side contacts in a series. The cables have a heavy shielded braid and an inter conductor of about size 16 wire. Associated with the switch are 5 other cables not connected, with both ends of each cable free.
7. One length of galvanized steel cable with an outside diameter of about 1/8".
8. Two 15-amp fuses made in St. Louis, MO, U.S.A.
9. Several 5- and 10-percent resistors of various values.

10. 32 medical items, including various medicines and small items of equipment. (To be exploited by U.S. Navy).
11. One unexposed roll of 35-mm film. Cost: 2 rubles-50 kopeks (about $2.60). Produced by the Dzerzhinskii Promkombinat at No. 36, Vosstaniya St., Leningrad. Undated.
12. Two cathode ray tubes, Type 8L029, with serial designator. Complete with tube diagram sheet providing specifications. Apparently new and unused.
13. One GMI-83 high-power tube.
14. One OTK-15 tube with seven pins and two plate caps.
15. Cable and switch assembly. A jury-rigged arrangement with undetermined function. A cable with six large shielded conductors surrounding a seventh center conductor is encased in a rubber-like covering of about one-inch outside diameter. Five shielded conductors terminate at four switches mounted on a phenolic board and are interconnected there. One cable terminates in a female Amphenol-type connector, and the center conductor is free.
16. A partial device (consisting of two small coils, a resistor, fuse, and three capacitors plus a copper yoke-shaped fitting) has an unfathomable application. Interconnections are made by light hookup wire. Overall size 2.5" x 3.5".
17. A large metal-jacketed transformer can—possibly an I. F. or R. F. transformer with primary and secondary adjustment positions. Pasted to its surface are Nos. 242, 102, and 241.
18. A filament battery, about 8" x 8" in size, has markings stating the following:

Voltage at an external resistance of 2 ohms	New	1.28V
	After 6 months	1.2V
Capacity at continuous use with 2 ohm external load up to 0.8V.	New	525 amp. hrs.
	After 15 months	315 amp. hrs.
Work life with periodic use, external resistance of 2 ohms to a voltage of 0.85V.	New	665 hours
	After 15 months	500 hours

The brand name is "Deviz." Made at the Factory "Kuzbasselement," March 1961, in the city of Leninsk-Kuznetskii. Instructions indicate storage should be in a cool dry place, preferably at temperatures below 0°C. "Thawing restores them to full capacity."

19. A plate battery "Druzhba" ("Friendship") was made on March 13, 1961, at the same plant as the above battery and has the following specifications:

Voltage with external	New	70V
resistance of 1000 ohms.	After 6 months	64V
Capacity continuous at	New	5 amp. hrs.
external resistance of	After 15 months	3.5 amp. hrs.
1000 ohms at up to		
.35V.		
Work life continuous at	New	725 hours
external resistance of	After 15 months	565 hours
7600 ohms and up to		
40V.		

Battery size is slightly larger than the filament battery.

20. A motor generator Type U-600, 27 volts, 32 amps; 6,000 RPM as a motor, and rated at 750/400 volts 0.35/0.75 amps as a generator. Serial number DM 7041621. The motor/generator is fan-cooled, in new (unpacked) condition, fitted with six external leads, and has no manufacturer's data affixed. The dimensions of the cylindrical motor/generator are about 12" x 5" and finished in a black, crackle finish. The overall impression is one of quality. The cardboard carton provides a blurred manufacture date, possibly December 1960.

21. A length of three conductor cables with rubber-like outer covering. Outside diameter about 1/2". Unshielded conductors are about No. 16-size copper in white plastic insulators.

Notes

Introduction

1. Since many of the sea ice terms used in this book may be unfamiliar to a general audience, Leonard LeSchack has prepared a glossary to aid in understanding the polar operational environment.
2. All temperatures are given in degrees Fahrenheit.

Chapter 1: Arctic Drifting Stations

1. For excellent brief surveys of drifting stations, see Cadwalader, "Arctic Drift Stations," 67–75; and Smith, "Drifting Ice Stations," 34–48.
2. Guttridge, *Icebound*; Caswell, *Arctic Frontiers*, 68–82.
3. Nansen, *Farthest North*, 1:14.
4. Ibid., 2:234.
5. Mirsky, *To the Arctic!*, 213.
6. Stefansson, *Friendly Arctic*, 108. See also Hunt, *Biography of Vilhjalmur Stefansson*.
7. Storkerson's account of the expedition, "Drifting in the Beaufort Sea," first appeared in *McLean's Magazine*, March 15 and April 1, 1920; it was reprinted in Stefansson, *Friendly Arctic*, 689–703.
8. Stefansson, *Friendly Arctic*, 702.
9. See Taracouzio, *Soviets in the Arctic*; and Armstrong, *The Northern Sea Route*.
10. Papanin, *Life on an Icefloe*.
11. Von Hardesty, introduction to Baidukov, *Russian Lindbergh*, 3–4.
12. O. J. Schmidt, foreword to Brontman, *On Top of the World*, 12. See also Schmidt, *The Conquest of the Arctic*.

13. Brontman, *On Top of the World,* contains the best account of the preparations for the expedition.
14. Armstrong, *Russians in the Arctic,* 67–79.
15. M. M. Somov, "The Drift of a Scientific Research Station of 1950–1951," trans. by David Kraus of the American Meteorological Society for the Air Force Cambridge Research Center, 1956; copy in the Smith Papers.
16. The account of NP2 is based on the report by station leader Somov, cited in note 15.
17. *Washington Post,* July 6, 1946; Carlson, *Lifelines Through the Arctic,* 191. See also Leviero, "Air War Across the Pole," 10, 61, 63–65.
18. White, *World in Peril,* 11.
19. Ibid., 31–32.
20. Bates and Fuller, *America's Weather Warriors,* 167; *Polar Record* 6 (July 1951): 268.
21. Oron P. South, "The Development of Rescue and Survival Techniques in the North American Arctic," Air University Documentary Research Study, August 1950; copy in the U.S. Air Force Historical Research Agency (USAFHRA).
22. Ibid. On Balchen, see his autobiography, *Come North With Me;* and Knight and Durham, *Hitch Your Wagon.*
23. "History of the 10th Rescue Squadron, Fort Richardson, Alaska, 1 January thru 31 March 1950," USAFHRA; Air Force Manual 86-5, *Ice Airfields,* September 10, 1958, USAFHRA.
24. *Polar Record* 6 (January 1953): 650–51; Diary of Albert Crary, April 18, 1950, in the Crary Papers.
25. Balchen to Byrd, April 3, 1950, in the Balchen Papers, USAFHRA.
26. *Polar Times* 44 (June 1957): 10–11; Rodahl, *North,* 128–30.
27. Crary, Cotell, and Oliver, "Geophysical Studies in the Beaufort Sea," 211–16.
28. Koenig et al., "Arctic Ice Islands," 67–103.
29. Ibid.
30. Joseph O. Fletcher, "Origin and Early Utilization of Aircraft-Supported Drifting Stations," in Sater, ed., *Arctic Drifting Stations,* 6.
31. Fletcher, foreword to Bushnell, ed., *Scientific Studies at Fletcher's Ice Island.*
32. Ibid.
33. Rodahl, *North,* 133.
34. Fletcher, foreword to Bushnell, *Scientific Studies.*
35. The best accounts of Project ICICLE are Rodahl, *North,* and Fletcher, "Three Months on an Arctic Ice Island."
36. Crary to his parents, April 13, 1952, Crary Papers.
37. A. Crary and Norman Goldstein, "Geophysical Studies in the Arctic Ocean," in Bushnell, ed., *Scientific Studies,* 7–30.
38. Crary to his parents, May 3, 1952, Crary Papers; Brontman, *On Top of the World,* 242–43.

39. A. Gordienko, "Scientific Observations from, and the Nature of Drift of the 'North Pole' Stations," and Gordienko and M. Kozlov, "High-Latitude Aerial Expeditions, 1956–1962," both in Ostenso (ed.), *Problems of the Arctic and Antarctic*, pp. b-1 to b-19 and m-1 to m-8.

Chapter 2: Bravo and Alpha

1. The story of the IGY is told by Sullivan, *Assault on the Unknown*.
2. Ibid., 48.
3. Louis O. Quam, "Station Charlie," in Sater, ed., *Arctic Drifting Stations*, 17–21.
4. The account of Alpha under Freeman's command is based on "Project ICE SKATE," *History of the Alaskan Air Command, 1 January–30 June 1958*, USAFHRA; and Freeman, "Project ICE SKATE," September 1, 1957; copy in the Smith Papers.
5. Kenneth L. Hunkins, "Remarks to Major Freeman on the Geophysical Research Program on Drifting Station A," n.d., Smith Papers; "Summer Activities—Drifting Station Alpha," *IGY Bulletin* 39 (December 1958): 1213–15. See also Cabaniss, Hunkins, and Untersteiner, *Drifting Station ALPHA*.
6. Leary interview with Smith, August 6, 1994.
7. Balchen, Ford, and LaFarge, *War Below Zero*.
8. Balchen, *Come North with Me*, 224.
9. Smith to Commander, 11th Air Division, September 28, 1958, Smith Papers.
10. The account of the breakup of Alpha is taken from Smith to Commander, 11th Air Division, November 17, 1958; and the draft of an unpublished article, "Double Scotch, No Ice," written by Smith in 1961; both in the Smith Papers. See also *New York Times*, November 7, 8, 9, and 10, 1958; *Polar Times*, December 1958, 12; and Sullivan, *Assault on the Unknown*, 253–68.

Chapter 3: ONR in the Arctic

1. Harvey M. Sapolsky, *Science and the Navy: The History of the Office of Naval Research*, 27.
2. Ibid., 37.
3. John C. Reed and Andreas G. Ronhovde, *Arctic Laboratory: A History (1947–1966) of the Naval Arctic Research Laboratory at Point Barrow, Alaska*, 35–41; Shelesnyak, "Some Problems of Human Ecology," 405–9.
4. *Arctic Laboratory*, 67, 81–82.
5. Solberg to the Chief of Naval Operations, September 29, 1950, in Office of Naval Research, "Project Skijump: A Report of the Arctic Flight Experiments, February–May 1951," October 1951; copy at the Naval Historical Center.
6. *Polar Record* 6 (January 1953): 650–51.
7. Ward, "Report on SKIJUMP," in ONR, "Project Skijump."

8. Worthington, "Oceanographic Results," 543–51.
9. "German U-Boats in the Arctic," *ONI Review* 6 (June 1951): 235–41; (July 1951): 275–80; (August 1951): 326–31.
10. "The Reminiscences of Dr. Waldo K. Lyon," Oral History Department, U.S. Naval Institute, 1972.
11. Waldo K. Lyon, "The Polar Submarine and Navigation of the Arctic Ocean," November 18, 1948 (reissued May 21, 1959), U.S. Navy Electronics Laboratory Report 88, copy courtesy of Richard J. Boyle; Department of the Navy, *Naval Arctic Operations Handbook,* pt. 1, 281.
12. "Reminiscences of Lyon."
13. Ibid.
14. Ibid.
15. Anderson, *Nautilus 90 North*; Jenks, "Navigating Under the North Pole Icecap," 62–67.
16. Isenberg, *Shield of the Republic,* 410.
17. Calvert, *Surface at the Pole.*
18. Ibid.; "Reminiscences of Lyon"; Steele, *Seadragon Northwest Under the Ice*; Strong, "The Opening of the Arctic Ocean," 58–65.
19. "Reminiscences of Lyon." Lyon received the President's Award for Distinguished Federal Service.
20. Leary interview with Britton, March 16, 1994; Britton to Leary, March 28, 1994.
21. Britton, "Administrative Background of the Developing Program," in Sater, ed., *Arctic Drifting Stations,* 29–35; Reed and Ronhovde, *Arctic Laboratory,* 344.
22. Britton to Leary, March 28, 1994; Max C. Brewer, "New Applications of Old Concepts of Drifting Stations," in Sater, ed., *Arctic Drifting Stations,* 23–28.
23. Britton to Leary, March 28, 1994.
24. Quam, "Station Charlie," 17–21.
25. On the establishment and operation of Charlie, see James Smith, "Summary Report, Drifting Station Charlie," December 15, 1959, in *History of the Alaskan Air Command, July–December 1959,* Supporting Documents, vol. II, USAFHRA.
26. James Smith, "Station Alpha Two, Project ICE SKATE, Commander's Daily Log," April 29, 1959, Smith Papers.
27. Quam, "Station Charlie," 17–21.
28. Ibid.
29. Arthur H. Schroeder, "Station Charlie, Project ICE SKATE, Commander's Daily Log," December 29, 1959; copy in the Smith Papers.
30. Quam, "Station Charlie," 17–21.
31. Ibid.
32. *Polar Times,* June 1960, 8.

33. Britton, "Administrative Background," 29–35.
34. Brewer, "New Applications," 23–28.
35. Robert J. Fischer, "Air Support of Drifting Stations—A Decade of Experience," in Sater, ed., *Arctic Drifting Stations*, 49–78.
36. Brewer, "New Applications," 23–28.
37. Britton, "Administrative Background," 29–35.
38. Fischer, "Air Support," 49–78; John F. Schindler, "The Impact of Ice Islands—The Story of ARLIS II and Fletcher's Ice Island, T-3, Since 1962," in Sater, ed., *Arctic Drifting Stations*, 49–78; Weeks and Maher, *Ice Island.*
39. Gordienko, "Scientific Observations," pp. b-1 to b-19.
40. *Polar Times,* December 1959, 14.
41. Leary interview with Britton, March 16, 1994.

Chapter 4: LeSchack at ONR

1. Sullivan, *Assault on the Unknown,* 4; *Polar Times,* June 1957, 3.
2. *IGY Bulletin* 38 (August 1957): 612–17.
3. Sullivan, *Assault on the Unknown,* 310–12; *Polar Times,* June 1958, 17.
4. One of these mountains, Mt. LeSchack, located at 85°25′ S, 124°00′ W, has been named for Leonard LeSchack.
5. *Polar Times,* December 1958, 24–25.
6. LeSchack, "ARLIS II—New Arctic Drift Station," 12–18.
7. Gordienko, "Scientific Observations," pp. b-1 to b-19; "Soviet Drifting Stations in the Arctic Ocean, 1961–62," *Polar Record* 11 (September 1962): 278–79.

Chapter 5: Fulton's Skyhook

1. Fulton's background is from an interview with Leary, November 9, 1988, and biographical material in the Fulton Papers.
2. On de Florez, see Taylor, "Captain Among the Synthetics," November 11, 1944 and November 18, 1944.
3. Ibid., November 11, 1944, 36.
4. On the airphibian, see Price, "The Automobile Gets Wings," 28–29, 51–52, 54, 56; and Chiles, "The Airborne Auto," 144–46, 148, 150, 152, 154, 156, 158, 169–72.
5. The All-American system is best described in Lewis and Trimble, *Airway to Everywhere.*
6. See Leary, *Perilous Missions.*
7. The early development of Skyhook is detailed in Fulton, "Summary Report on Fulton Skyhook Aerial Recovery System, 1953 thru 1963," January 1964, Fulton Papers.
8. Fulton, draft of report, May 30, 1958, Fulton Papers.
9. The El Centro tests are documents in a series of reports in the Fulton Papers.
10. A copy of this study is in the Fulton Papers.

11. Fulton, "Report of Operational Development Tests of the 'Skyhook's' Air/Sea Rescue System for In-Flight Pickup of Men and Materials with High Performance Aircraft," June 15, 1958, Fulton Papers.
12. Fulton published a publicity brochure, "Skyhook," that contained material on the pickup of Woods.
13. Smith memorandum, "Ice Skate Reports and Recommendations," December 8, 1958, Smith Papers.

Chapter 6: **Resolute**
1. Walter to Leary, July 20, 1995.
2. Cadwalader to Leary, May 5, 1995.
3. ONR to OPNAV (OP-56), September 27, 1961; copy in the LeSchack Papers.
4. LeSchack wrote about his first experience with Skyhook in "Skyhook Retrieval."
5. Hunter to Leary, January 22, 1995.
6. Gordienko, "Scientific Observations," pp. b-1 to b-19; "Soviet Drifting Stations in the Arctic Ocean, 1961–62," 278–79.
7. Walter to Leary, August 2, 1994.
8. Hunter to Leary, January 22, 1995; Leary telephone interview with Hunter, January 19, 1995.
9. The plans for the mission are detailed in Hunter to Director, Service Test Division, Naval Air Test Center, April 16, 1962; copy in the Fulton Papers.
10. Fulton, "Pictorial Report of Operation 'COLD-FEET,'" June 23, 1962, Fulton Papers.
11. Gordon to Leary, October 3, 1994.
12. Walter to Leary, August 2, 1994.
13. Cadwalader, "Project COLDFEET," 344–55.
14. Ibid.
15. Hunter to Leary, January 22, 1995.

Chapter 7: **Intermountain Aviation**
1. On Intermountain, see James Long and Lauren Cowen, "CIA Proprietary Kept Arizona Air Park Humming," *The Oregonian,* August 22, 1988.
2. Prados, *Presidents' Secret Wars,* 128–48; Grose, *Gentleman Spy.*
3. Leary interview with Thorsrud, August 22, 1993.
4. *Foreign Relations, 1958–1960,* 121–22.
5. Leary interview with Rousselot, August 10, 1987.
6. *Foreign Relations, 1958–1960,* 130, 142.
7. Seigrist, unpublished memoirs. The authors are grateful to Captain Seigrist for providing access to this material.
8. Grose, *Gentleman Spy,* 452–54; Leary interview with Rousselot, August 10, 1987.

9. Ferrer, *Operation Puma,* 66.
10. Ibid., 82.
11. Higgins, *Perfect Failure,* 93–94.
12. Ibid., 122–23.
13. Seigrist, unpublished memoirs.
14. Wyden, *Bay of Pigs,* 200–202.
15. Higgins, *Perfect Failure,* 133.
16. Wyden, *Bay of Pigs,* 202.
17. See Mets, *Land-Based Air Power,* 65–88.
18. Leary interview with Price, January 28, 1995.
19. Seigrist, unpublished memoirs.
20. Leary interview with Wall, January 28, 1995.
21. Schlesinger, *Robert Kennedy,* 571–73.

Chapter 8: **NP8**

1. The most accurate account of this phase of Project COLDFEET is given by Cadwalader. See his "Report on COLDFEET TWO," June 6, 1962, copy in the Fulton Papers; and "Project COLDFEET." In addition, John D. Wall kept a detailed record of dates and times. Fulton, "Pictorial Report on Operation 'COLD-FEET'," June 23, 1962, Fulton Papers, provides an excellent photographic record of the operation but contains a number of inaccuracies on dates and events. During a COLDFEET reunion in Las Vegas in January 1995, Leary and LeSchack conducted interviews and held roundtable discussions in an effort to clarify details of the operation. Participants included Max C. Brewer, Maxwell E. Britton, John Cadwalader, Robert E. Fulton, Jr., Carson S. Gerken, Miles Johnson, William R. Jordan, Larry T. Lowe, Robert H. Nicol, Richard L. Olsonoski, Douglas R. Price, Randolph Scott, Connie W. Seigrist, James F. Smith, Leo L. Turk, John D. Wall, and Robert Zimmer.
2. Seigrist, unpublished memoirs.
3. Jordan, "Operation COLD FEET," February 1994. Captain Jordan prepared this document at the request of the authors.
4. Leary interview with Lowe, December 7, 1994.
5. Leary interview with Olsonowski, January 28, 1995.
6. Jordan, "Operation COLD FEET."
7. Leary interview with Smith, August 6, 1994.
8. Cadwalader, "Report on COLDFEET TWO."
9. Ibid.
10. Leary interview with Smith, August 6, 1994.

Chapter 9: **Conclusion**

1. "Project COLDFEET: The Intelligence Results," *ONI Review* 17 (November 1962): 486–93.

2. Coates to Thorsrud, n.d.; copy provided to the authors by Thorsrud.
3. This incident is detailed in Arctic Research Laboratory, "Progress Report For the Month of July 1963" and "Progress Report for the Month of August 1963"; copies courtesy of Thorsrud.
4. Jordan to Leary, September 15, 1995.
5. Leary interview with Fulton, November 9, 1988; Wall to Leary, September 16, 1995.
6. An article on Skyhook, including a diagram of a pickup, appeared in *Time,* December 4, 1964. The Fulton system also was featured in Milton Caniff's "Steve Canyon" cartoon strip on March 12, 1966.
7. Britton to Leary, March 28, 1994.

Glossary of Ice Terms

Arctic Ice Pack: The diverse mantle of floating ice of more than 10 percent concentration that covers the Arctic Ocean and adjacent seas to varying extent year-round.

Brash Ice: Small fragments of floating ice, not more than six feet across; the wreckage of other forms of ice.

Crack: Any fracture or rift in sea ice not sufficiently wide to be described as a lead. It is usually possible to jump across a crack.

Crevasses: Open cracks or fractures in glaciers. They may be several yards wide at the top and two hundred feet deep. They often are bridged with a thin ice or snow cover that conceals their presence. The bridge will collapse under the weight of an adult human or vehicle, making crevasses dangerous.

Drifting Station: A man-made base for conducting scientific research or military operations established on an ice floe or an ice island. These stations literally drift with the pack ice, the movement of which is caused by wind and ocean currents. Drifting stations have been known to move thousands of miles over time. Also called ice stations.

Fast Ice: Sea ice of greatly varying width that remains along the coast, where it is attached to the shore, an ice wall, an ice front, or over shoals, generally in the position where originally formed. Fast ice may extend over two hundred miles from the coast.

Floe: A piece of sea ice other than fast ice, large or small. Light floes are pieces up to ten feet thick. Thicker floes, both level and hummocked, are called "heavy" floes. Floes over 10,000 yards across are "giant"; those between 1,000 and 10,000 yards across are "large"; those between 200 and 1,000 yards across are "medium"; and those between 10 and 200 yards across are "small." Floes less than 10 yards across are called ice cakes.

Iceberg: A large mass of floating or stranded ice. If broken away from a glacier, it is referred to as a glacier berg; if broken away from an ice shelf, it is referred to as a shelf berg.

Ice Canopy: Ice cover from the submariner's point of view. In polar regions, the ice canopy is a complex ocean surface containing many different ice types and open-water features.

Ice Island: A shelf berg that is caught in and surrounded by the pack ice and drifts along with the pack. Because ice islands are much thicker than ice floes, and thus more durable, they generally are more desirable for drifting stations.

Ice Keel: From the submariner's point of view, a downward-projecting ridge on the underside of the ice canopy; the counterpart of a pressure ridge.

Icing: The accumulation of ice on exposed objects; e.g., aircraft, ships, antennae, instruments (anemometers, thermometer screens). The ice may be either dense or clear (transparent), white and opaque, or anything in between. Icing may be produced by the deposition of water vapor as frost (in which case quantities are usually small and of importance only to aircraft), or by the freezing on impact of droplets suspended in the air (e.g., supercooled fogs, cloud droplets, supercooled drizzle and rain, or, in the case of ships, sea spray or breaking waves).

Ice Pack: A large concentration of sea ice, which may include fast ice and which is found in the same region every summer. These concentrations are usually named for the region, such as the "Taymyr Ice Pack."

Ice Shelf: A floating ice sheet of considerable thickness. Ice shelves usually extend very far horizontally and have a level or gently undulating surface. They are nourished by local snow accumulation and often also by the seaward extension of land glaciers. Limited areas may be aground. The initial stage is called bay ice until the surface is more than about six feet above sea level. The seaward edge is termed an ice front. An example is the Ellesmere Ice Shelf, from which ice island T-3 is presumed to have broken off.

IGY: The abbreviation of International Geophysical Year, a great international scientific undertaking during 1957 and 1958 to improve the knowledge and understanding of the changes taking place on earth and in its surrounding water and air. It included studies and investigations in many fields, including airglow and ionospheric physics, the aurora, cosmic rays, Earth's magnetic and gravity fields and its volcanic activity, glaciology, meteorology and nuclear radiation, oceanography, rockets and satellites, and solar activity. The establishment of Drifting Station Alpha was largely a result of the IGY requirement for a scientific station near the North Pole.

Lead: (Pronounced "leed.") A long, narrow passage through pack ice, navigable by a surface vessel and usually large enough to allow a submarine to surface in or through it. If covered with relatively thin ice, a lead my be referred to as an ice skylight.

Melt Pond: A depression on the surface of a floe, shelf berg, or glacier filled with water (melted ice and snow), which in most cases is fresh and drinkable. Also called a puddle.

Pack Ice: Any area of sea ice, other than fast ice, composed of a heterogeneous mixture of ice of varying size and age types. Pack ice is usually in motion and is often referred to as "drift ice." The concentration of pack ice can be of any degree.

Polynya: A Russian word (pronounced "pole-lin-yah") meaning any enclosed sea water area in pack ice, other than a lead, not large enough to be called open water. In summer it may be referred to as a lake; in winter, with a covering of relatively thin ice, it may be called an ice skylight. If a polynya is found in the same region every year (e.g., off the mouths of big rivers), it is called a "recurring polynya." A temporary small clearing in pack ice consisting of small floes and brash ice in continuous local movement is called an "unstable polynya"; an opening flanked by large floes, thus appearing relatively stable, is called a "stable polynya."

Pressure Ice: A general term for sea ice that has been squeezed. If the sea ice has been forced upward, it can be described as hummocked ice or a pressure ridge.

Pressure Ridge: A ridge or wall of hummocked ice where one floe has been pressed against another. Maximum height above sea level in pack ice is about thirty feet. A corresponding ridge may also occur on the underside of the ice canopy and may extend as much as 160 feet below sea level. See also *Ice Keel.*

Rime: A deposit of ice composed of grains more or less separated by trapped air, sometimes adorned with crystalline branches, produced by the rapid freezing of supercooled and very small water droplets. See *Icing.*

Shatter Ice: See *Brash Ice.*

Sea Ice: Any form of ice at sea that has originated from the freezing of sea water.

Shelf Berg: A large mass of floating or stranded ice that has broken away from an ice shelf. The size varies from a few thousand square yards to 250 square miles or more in area. In the Arctic, the thickness varies from about fifty feet to more than two hundred feet. Arctic shelf bergs are characterized by a regularly undulating surface, giving them a ribbed appearance from the air; they are often referred to as ice islands.

Sunspots: Great electrical and magnetic storms (or perhaps areas of calm) on the sun that appear as dark spots because they are not as hot as the surrounding surface. They vary in number but reach a maximum amount about every twenty-two years. They influence auroras in the polar regions, as well as weather and climate, because Earth's average temperature is higher when sunspots are at a minimum. For this reason sunspot activity is thought to be related to variations in glaciers.

Whiteout: Diffusion of daylight by multiple reflection between a snow or ice surface and overcast clouds. Contrasts vanish, and the observer is unable to distinguish the horizon or any snow or ice surface feature.

References

Boyle, R. J. *Ice Glossary.* San Diego, Calif.: U.S. Navy Electronics Laboratory, 1965.

Dyson, James L. *The World of Ice.* New York: Knopf, 1962.

Bibliography

Manuscript Collections

The Papers of Albert P. Crary, Record Group 401, National Archives, Washington, D.C.

The Papers of Robert E. Fulton, Jr., Newtown, Conn.

The Papers of Leonard A. LeSchack, Calgary, Alberta, Canada

The Papers of James F. Smith, Spokane, Wash.

The Records of the United States Air Force, U.S. Air Force Historical Research Agency, Maxwell Air Force Base, Ala.

The Operations Archives of the United States Navy, Naval Historical Center, Washington, D.C.

Books

Anderson, William R. *Nautilus 90 North*. New York: Harper & Row, 1959.

Armstrong, Terence. *The Northern Sea Route: Soviet Exploration of the North East Passage*. Cambridge, Eng.: Scott Polar Research Institute, 1952.

——. *The Russians in the Arctic*. London: Methuen, 1958.

Baidukov, Georgiy. *Russian Lindbergh: The Life of Valery Chkalov*. Washington, D.C.: Smithsonian Institution, 1991.

Balchen, Bernt M. *Come North With Me*. New York: Dutton, 1958.

Balchen, Bernt M., Corey Ford, and Oliver LaFarge. *War Below Zero: The Battle for Greenland*. Boston: Houghton Mifflin, 1944.

Bates, Charles, and John F. Fuller. *America's Weather Warriors, 1814–1985*. College Station: Texas A&M Press, 1986.

Brontman, L. *On Top of the World: The Soviet Expedition to the North Pole 1937*. London: Victor Gollancz, 1938.

183

Bushnell, Vivian, ed. *Scientific Studies at Fletcher's Ice Island, T-3.* Geophysical Research Papers, no. 63, vol. 1. Bedford, Mass.: Air Force Cambridge Research Center, 1959.

Cabaniss, G. H., K. L. Hunkins, and N. Untersteiner. *US-IGY Drifting Station ALPHA Arctic Ocean 1957–1958.* Special Report No. 38. Bedford, Mass.: Air Force Cambridge Research Laboratory, 1965.

Calvert, James. *Surface at the Pole.* New York: McGraw-Hill, 1960; rpt. Annapolis, Md.: Naval Institute Press, 1996.

Carlson, William S. *Lifelines Through the Arctic.* New York: Duell, Sloan and Pearce, 1962.

Caswell, John Edwards. *Arctic Frontiers: United States Exploration in the Far North.* Norman, Okla.: University of Oklahoma Press, 1956.

Ferrer, Edward B. *Operation Puma: The Air Battle of the Bay of Pigs.* Miami, Fla.: International Aviation Consultants, 1982.

Foreign Relations of the United States, 1958–1960. Volume XVII: Indonesia. Washington, D.C.: Government Printing Office, 1994.

Fulton, Robert E., Jr. *One Man Caravan.* New York: Harcourt, Brace, 1937.

Glines, C. V., ed. *Polar Aviation.* New York: Franklin Watts, 1964.

Grierson, John. *Challenge to the Poles.* Hamden, Conn.: Archon Books, 1964.

———. *Sir Hubert Wilkins: Enigma of Exploration.* London: Robert Hale, 1960.

Grose, Peter. *Gentleman Spy: The Life of Allen Dulles.* Boston: Houghton Mifflin, 1994.

Guttridge, Leonard F. *Icebound: The* Jennette *Expedition's Quest for the North Pole.* Annapolis, Md.: Naval Institute Press, 1985.

Hartshorn, J. H., ed. *Proceedings of the First Annual Arctic Planning Session, November 1958.* Bedford, Mass.: Air Force Cambridge Research Center, 1959.

Higgins, Trumbull. *The Perfect Failure: Kennedy, Eisenhower, and the CIA at the Bay of Pigs.* New York: Norton, 1987.

Hunt, William R. *Stef: A Biography of Vilhjalmur Stefansson.* Vancouver: University of British Columbia Press, 1986.

Isenberg, Michael T. *Shield of the Republic.* New York: St. Martin's Press, 1993.

Knight, Clayton, and Robert C. Durham. *Hitch Your Wagon: The Story of Bernt Balchen.* Philadelphia, Pa.: Bell Publishing Company, 1950.

Leary, William M. *Perilous Missions: Civil Air Transport and CIA Covert Operations in Asia.* University: University of Alabama Press, 1984.

Lewis, W. David, and William F. Trimble. *Airway to Everywhere: A History of All American Aviation.* Pittsburgh: University of Pittsburgh Press, 1988.

Love, Robert W., Jr. *History of the U.S. Navy, 1942–1991.* Harrisburg, Pa.: Stackpole, 1992.

Mets, David R. *Land-Based Air Power in Third World Crises.* Maxwell Air Force Base, Ala.: Air University Press, 1986.

Mirsky, Jeannette. *To the Arctic! The Story of Northern Exploration from Earliest Times to the Present.* New York: Knopf, 1948.

Nansen, Fridtjof. *Farthest North.* 2 vols. New York: Harper & Brothers, 1897.

Ostenso, N. A., ed. *Problems of the Arctic and Antarctic: Collection of Articles No. 11.* Translated by J. H. Slep, J. B. Filimonov, and A. Malahoff. Washington, D.C.: Arctic Institute of North America, 1966.

Papanin, Ivan. *Life on an Icefloe.* London: Hutchinson, 1947.

Prados, John. *Presidents' Secret Wars: CIA and Pentagon Covert Operations Since World War II.* New York: Morrow, 1986.

Reed, John C., and Andreas G. Ronhovde. *Arctic Laboratory: A History (1947–1966) of the Naval Arctic Research Laboratory at Point Barrow, Alaska.* Washington, D.C.: Arctic Institute of North America, 1971.

Rodahl, Kaare. *North: The Nature and Drama of the Polar World.* New York: Harper & Brothers, 1953.

Salkovitz, Edward I., ed. *Science, Technology, and the Modern Navy.* Arlington, Va.: Office of Naval Research, 1976.

Sapolsky, Harvey M. *Science and the Navy: The History of the Office of Naval Research.* Princeton, N.J.: Princeton University Press, 1991.

Sater, John E., ed. *Arctic Drifting Stations: A Report on Activities Supported by the Office of Naval Research.* Washington, D.C.: Arctic Institute of North America, 1968.

Schlesinger, Arthur M. *Robert Kennedy and His Times.* Boston: Houghton Mifflin, 1978.

Schmidt, Otto. *The Conquest of the Arctic.* Moscow: Foreign Languages Publishing House, 1939.

Simmons, George. *Target: Arctic.* Philadelphia, Pa.: Chilton Books, 1965.

Stefansson, Vilhjalmur. *Arctic Manual.* New York: Macmillan, 1957.

———. *The Friendly Arctic: The Story of Five Years in Polar Regions.* New York: Macmillan, 1921.

Steele, George P. *Seadragon Northwest Under the Ice.* New York: Dutton, 1962.

Sullivan, Walter. *Assault on the Unknown: The International Geophysical Year.* New York: McGraw-Hill, 1961.

Taracouzio, T. A. *Soviets in the Arctic.* New York: Macmillan, 1938.

U.S. Department of the Navy. *Naval Arctic Operations Handbook.* 2 parts. Washington, D.C.: Department of the Navy, 1949.

Weeks, Tim, and Ramona Maher. *Ice Island: Polar Science and the Arctic Research Laboratory.* New York: John Day, 1965.

White, Ken. *World in Peril: The Origin, Mission, and Scientific Findings of the 46th/72nd Reconnaissance Squadron.* Privately printed, 1992.

Wyden, Peter. *Bay of Pigs.* New York: Simon and Schuster, 1979.

Articles

Allard, Dean C. "To the North Pole!" U.S. Naval Institute *Proceedings* 113 (September 1987): 56–65.

Anastasion, Steven N. "Are the Russians Ahead in Oceanography?" *Undersea Technology* 5 (January 1964): 25–28.

Bentley, C. R., A. P. Crary, N. A. Ostenso, and E. C. Thiel. "Structure of West Antarctica," *Science* 131 (January 15, 1960): 131–36.

Brewer, Max C. "Drifting Stations in the Arctic Ocean," *Proceedings of the Arctic Basin Symposium, October 1962* (Washington, D.C.: Arctic Institute of North America, 1963): 305–7.

Cadwalader, John. "Arctic Drift Stations," U.S. Naval Institute *Proceedings* 89 (April 1963): 67–75.

———. "Project COLDFEET," *ONI Review* 17 (August 1962): 344–55.

Chiles, James R. "The Airborne Auto: Flight of Fancy?" *Smithsonian* 19 (February 1989): 144–46, 148, 150, 152, 154, 156, 158, 160–62.

Cottell, Irene Browne. "United States Research at Drifting Stations in the Arctic Ocean," *Polar Record* 10 (September 1960): 169–74.

Crary, Albert P., R. D. Cotell, and Jack Oliver. "Geophysical Studies in the Beaufort Sea, 1951," *Transactions, American Geophysical Union* 33 (April 1952): 211–16.

Fletcher, Joseph O. "The Arctic Challenge," *Air University Quarterly Review* 6 (Fall 1953): 52–62.

———. "Three Months on an Arctic Ice Island," *National Geographic* 103 (April 1953): 489–504.

"German U-Boats in the Arctic," *ONI Review* 6 (June 1951): 235–41; (July 1951): 275–80; (August 1951): 326–31.

Gordienko, P. A. "The Arctic Ocean," *Scientific American* 204 (May 1961): 88–102.

Jenks, Shepherd M. "Navigating Under the North Pole Icecap," U.S. Naval Institute *Proceedings* 84 (December 1958): 62–67.

Kassell, Bernard M. "Soviet Logistics in the Arctic," U.S. Naval Institute *Proceedings* 85 (February 1959): 88–95.

Koenig, L. S., K. R. Greenaway, Moira Dunbar, and G. Hattersley-Smith. "Arctic Ice Islands," *Arctic* 5 (July 1952): 67–103.

Leary, William M. "Robert Fulton's Skyhook and Operation COLDFEET," *Studies in Intelligence* 38 (1995): 99–109.

LeSchack, Leonard A. "ARLIS II: New Arctic Drift Station," *Naval Research Reviews* (April 1961): 12–18.

———. "Skyhook Retrieval," U.S. Naval Institute *Proceedings* 92 (March 1966): 138–42.

Leviero, Anthony. "Air War Across the Pole," *New York Times Magazine* (December 14, 1947): 10, 61, 63–65.

Lyon, Waldo K. "The Submarine and the Arctic Ocean," *Polar Record* 11 (September 1963): 699–705.

———. "Submarine Combat in the Ice," U.S. Naval Institute *Proceedings* 118 (February 1992): 34–40.

McWethy, R. D. "The Arctic Submarine," U.S. Naval Institute *Proceedings* 78 (September 1952): 955–57.

Price, Wesley. "The Automobile Gets Wings," *Saturday Evening Post* 219 (May 17, 1947): 28–29, 51–52, 54, 56.

Shelesnyak, M. C. "Some Problems of Human Ecology in Polar Regions," *Science* 106 (October 31, 1947): 405–9.

Smith, Charles L. "Drifting Ice Stations," *Air University Review* 17 (September-October 1966): 34–48.

Strong, James T. "The Opening of the Arctic Ocean," U.S. Naval Institute *Proceedings* 87 (November 1961): 58–65.

Taylor, Robert Lewis. "Captain Among the Synthetics," *New Yorker* (November 11, 1944): 34–43; (November 18, 1944): 32–43.

Treshnikov, A. F. "The Soviet Drifting Station SP-3, 1954–55," *Polar Record* 9 (September 1956): 222–29.

Worthington, L. V. "Oceanographic Results of Project Skijump I and Skijump II in the Polar Sea, 1951–1952," *Transactions, American Geophysical Union* 34 (August 1953): 543–51.

Index

189

About the Authors

William M. Leary is E. Merton Coulter professor of history at the University of Georgia in Athens and 1996–1997 Charles A. Lindbergh professor of aerospace history at the National Air and Space Museum in Washington, D.C. A widely published scholar of CIA air operations, he received the CIA's Studies in Intelligence Award in 1995. He holds M.A. and PhD. degrees from Princeton University.

Capt. Leonard A. LeSchack, USNR (Ret.), was a key participant in the conception, planning, and operation of Project COLDFEET. After release from active duty, he pursued with equal vigor parallel careers in the Naval Reserve and his own geophysical research business, which took him to the former Soviet Union, the Caribbean, and to Latin America. He returned to active duty in 1980–1981, serving as the coordinator for the Cuban-Haitian Refugee Center at Fort Allen, Puerto Rico, and then as intelligence officer at the U.S. Naval Station Panama Canal. Upon release from active duty he assisted in establishing the Naval Reserve Intelligence Unit to support Commander U.S. Forces Caribbean in Key West, Florida, and became its first commanding officer in 1983. He now heads an oil exploration company in Calgary, Alberta, Canada. He is the author of numerous papers on polar research and other subjects and has published in the U.S. Naval Institute *Proceedings*.

The **Naval Institute Press** is the book-publishing arm of the U.S. Naval Institute, a private, nonprofit, membership society for sea service professionals and others who share an interest in naval and maritime affairs. Established in 1873 at the U.S. Naval Academy in Annapolis, Maryland, where its offices remain today, the Naval Institute has members worldwide.

Members of the Naval Institute support the education programs of the society and receive the influential monthly magazine *Proceedings* and discounts on fine nautical prints and on ship and aircraft photos. They also have access to the transcripts of the Institute's Oral History Program and get discounted admission to any of the Institute-sponsored seminars offered around the country.

The Naval Institute also publishes *Naval History* magazine. This colorful bimonthly is filled with entertaining and thought-provoking articles, first-person reminiscences, and dramatic art and photography. Members receive a discount on *Naval History* subscriptions.

The Naval Institute's book-publishing program, begun in 1898 with basic guides to naval practices, has broadened its scope in recent years to include books of more general interest. Now the Naval Institute Press publishes about 100 titles each year, ranging from how-to books on boating and navigation to battle histories, biographies, ship and aircraft guides, and novels. Institute members receive discounts of 20 to 50 percent on the Press's nearly 600 books in print.

Full-time students are eligible for special half-price membership rates. Life memberships are also available.

For a free catalog describing Naval Institute Press books currently available, and for further information about subscribing to *Naval History* magazine or about joining the U.S. Naval Institute, please write to:

Membership Department
U.S. Naval Institute
118 Maryland Avenue
Annapolis, MD 21402-5035
Telephone: (800) 233-8764
Fax: (410) 269-7940
Web address: www.usni.org